Presented by the author, 2009.

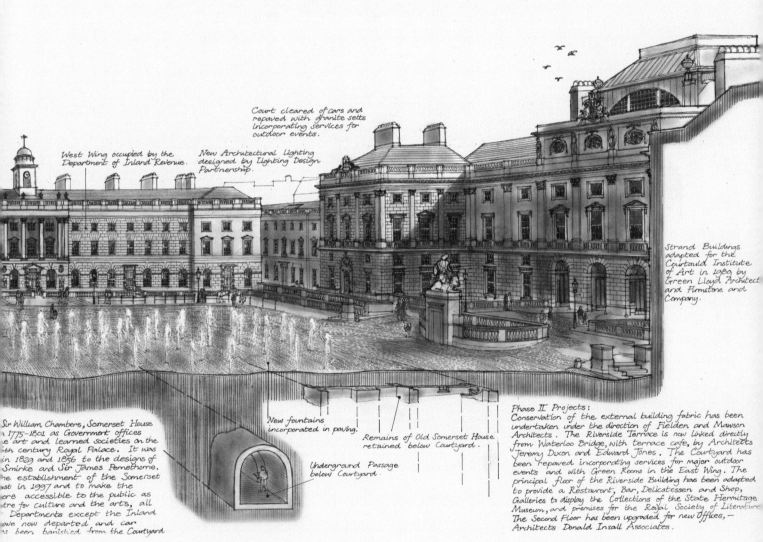

West Wing occupied by the Department of Inland Revenue.

New Architectural Lighting designed by Lighting Design Partnership.

Court cleared of cars and repaved with granite setts incorporating services for outdoor events.

Strand Buildings adapted for the Courtauld Institute of Art in 1989 by Green Lloyd Architect and Firmstone and Company.

New fountains incorporated in paving.

Remains of Old Somerset House retained below Courtyard.

Underground Passage below Courtyard.

Sir William Chambers, Somerset House 1775-1801 as Government offices [for] art and learned societies on the [site of a 16th] century Royal Palace. It was [extended] in 1829 and 1856 to the designs of [Sir Robert] Smirke and Sir James Pennethorne. [With] the establishment of the Somerset [House Tr]ust in 1997 and to make the [building m]ore accessible to the public as [a cen]tre for culture and the arts, all [the] Departments except the Inland [Revenue h]ave now departed and car[s have] been banished from the Courtyard.

Phase II Projects:
Conservation of the external building fabric has been undertaken under the direction of Fielden and Mawson Architects. The Riverside Terrace is now linked directly from Waterloo Bridge, with terrace cafe, by Architects Jeremy Dixon and Edward Jones. The Courtyard has been repaved incorporating services for major outdoor events and with Green Rooms in the East Wing. The principal floor of the Riverside Building has been adapted to provide a Restaurant, Bar, Delicatessen and Shop, Galleries to display the Collections of the State Hermitage Museum, and premises for the Royal Society of Literature. The Second Floor has been upgraded for new Offices, — Architects Donald Insall Associates.

XL. 6. 1ª/4

ÆDES CHRISTI
in Academia Oxoniensi

LIVING
BUILDINGS

Dedication

To my colleagues at Donald Insall Associates,
together with our friends and clients,
contractors and craftsmen – past, present and future.
And to all who love and care for buildings, old and new.

Donald Insall

LIVING BUILDINGS

Architectural Conservation:
Philosophy, Principles and Practice

DONALD INSALL

Donald Insall

images
Publishing

Published in Australia in 2008 by
The Images Publishing Group Pty Ltd
ABN 89 059 734 431
6 Bastow Place, Mulgrave, Victoria 3170, Australia
Tel: +61 3 9561 5544 Fax: +61 3 9561 4860
books@imagespublishing.com
www.imagespublishing.com

National Library of Australia Cataloguing-in-Publication entry:

Author:	Insall, Donald W.
Title:	Living buildings : architectural conservation : philosophy, principles and practice / Donald W. Insall.
Edition:	1st ed.
Publisher:	Mulgrave, Vic. : Images Publishing Group, 2008.
ISBN:	9781864701920 (pbk.)
Notes:	Includes index.
Subjects:	Insall, Donald W.
	Donald Insall Associates.
	Architecture–Conservation and restoration.
Dewey Number:	720.288

Coordinating editor: Robyn Beaver

Designed by The Graphic Image Studio Pty Ltd, Mulgrave, Australia
www.tgis.com.au

Pre-publishing services by Splitting Image Colour Studio Pty Ltd, Australia
Printed by Paramount Printing Company Limited Hong Kong

IMAGES has included on its website a page for special notices in relation to this and our other publications. Please visit www.imagespublishing.com.

Contents

CLARENCE HOUSE

Over the last fifty years, great advances have been made in the art and science of Architectural Conservation. There has been an increasing awareness of the significance and value of our heritage, and of the cultural continuity we enjoy, in the buildings which surround us - from cathedral to church, and from castle to cottage. It is largely these which make up the memorable places of Britain and give us all a sense of belonging, adding meaning to our lives and enabling us to shape our collective future. We are indeed fortunate in having such a heritage; and our response to it may range from simple daily care, through comprehensive repairs, to accurate restoration or, indeed, renewal.

Throughout this period of rapidly evolving change, Donald Insall has been deeply involved, not just as a tireless practitioner, but in mentoring and inspiring others. In the following pages we are given an intriguing account of the philosophy of his pioneering architectural group. Their guiding principle is to seek out and recognize the special needs of each building and place, to be studied and analysed for its own values, qualities and individual worth. In a few instances, as with a revered monument, precise academic preservation is possible, sometimes even involving actual 'restoration'. In others, rather as with a garden, more radical weeding and replanting may be apposite. And in the case of whole historic areas, of whose importance we are today so much more conscious, there are immense opportunities for active and imaginative guidance.

This book examines and sets these questions in their true perspective. If we can all learn from the experience and examples shared here, we may perhaps more closely and wisely understand the living tradition and positive spirit of true Architectural Conservation.

INTRODUCTION

This introductory note was written while on the way to an international conference in Venice about the training of craftsmen, upon whose skills all architecture must ultimately depend. For it is the privilege of the architect to be able to involve himself closely with the actual work of human hands. Building is perhaps the most basic of the crafts, and is often performed under difficult and testing circumstances. It calls for intelligence, for adaptability and resourcefulness through long design and organisation stages, indoors as well as on site and sometimes in the rain, often with a welter of problems to resolve and realise, tidily and well. How can successive generations of architects best be prepared for this exciting and exacting task? And how did we ourselves arrive at the principles and the practices that today are our guide?

Our anniversary

We are currently about to celebrate our team's 50th anniversary. But, one may ask, just when is the exact 'birthday' of an architectural practice, and when precisely was it born? Do we reckon years from the day we first bought a typewriter? Or when, soon after, we appointed a part-time secretary? Or from the times when we were joined by trusted colleagues, some of whom are together still? A life's involvement and concern with buildings does not dawn in a flash; we all attempt more and learn more with every new day.

This book is a response to pressure from many friends to publish a selection of examples of our thinking, to set out something of the principles and approach that have, over five decades, informed and directed our concerns, and to illustrate some of the architectural results. It is also an opportunity to respond to the repeated requests to revise, augment and reprint our 1972 publication, *The Care of Old Buildings Today* – now long out of print, but for the time a somewhat pioneering book. Above all, this anniversary provides us with a welcome opportunity to pause and think – to ask ourselves what we do, and what drives us. So let us attempt to record and share at least the spirit and ideals that have for so long motivated and inspired our team, and continue to do so today.

Training

Everything we do reflects our training; and mine was multiplex. Thanks to wartime, I left school early to join the Royal West of England Academy School of Architecture. During military service in London, I managed a part-time attendance at what was then called 'night school' at Regent Street Polytechnic, returning to Bristol in 1948 as one of a batch of ex-service students. We took our RIBA final exams externally; I can still hear echoing the sepulchral announcement of the adjudicator: '... five more minutes ...'. Life is full of deadlines like that: at least they spur one towards conclusions, and focus the mind.

Architectural training at that time still included a real awareness of history, too often missing today (p. 8). Architecture is above all not only an academic pursuit. Building is a practical expression of its materials and their nature – of bricks and wood, and of concrete (whether mass or membrane). How does a trainee architect achieve any knowledge and feeling of what materials can do? Following our academic student days, a fortunate few of us were exceptionally lucky in finding ourselves imbued with a practical hands-on approach on building sites, as post-war Lethaby Scholars of the SPAB[1]. Together, we handled real materials, felt their decay, aided their renewal, and

---

[1] The Society for the Protection of Ancient Buildings, founded in 1877 by William Morris. The scholarship enables young architects to learn about SPAB principles, and to widen their experience of practice, site and craft activities in caring for old buildings.

Four post-war students during their SPAB Lethaby scholarship; Donald Insall and Peter Locke (at right and left respectively) later jointly pioneered the practice.

began to understand how structures live. The scholarship gave us much of the attitude to buildings upon which, in their own ways, our growing team has since constantly expanded in its many involvements with historic towns, areas and buildings, on an increasingly widening scale.

As Lethaby Scholars, we came to see how each place and structure we may strive to save is alive and constantly changing. For every building is a product not only of its original generator – whether architect or builder, caravanist or monk – but of the continuing effects upon its materials of time and weather, and of generations of successive occupants, each with his own set of values and requirements. Each building carries, and clearly demonstrates, the impact and influence of all its changing and unforeseeable circumstances.

Individuality and character

Another principle has echoed throughout all our subsequent experience of planning, whether for individual buildings and monuments or sometimes for whole towns: what we all most admire and enjoy is each project's unique identity and character. Indeed, we have sometimes proposed as a motto in the guidance of historic places, the simple maxim 'That Every Place may be Truly More Itself'. Over-simplified perhaps but still a worthy precept, where mediocrity and uniformity can otherwise destroy so much that was unique. The message of Christendom during two thousand years has been about the value of every individual human being and of the richness of each person's unique worth. We believe the same is true of places and buildings – each has special qualities to be respected, valued and enjoyed.

The wider perspective

A wider view is equally needed in architecture and town planning, which call for an understanding not only of building techniques but of social resources, and of resolving competitive demands and varied lifestyles in response to the widest environmental issues.

Following my stint as a Lethaby Scholar, I moved on to the Royal Academy Schools, where under 'The Professor' Albert Richardson, and the Master, Marshall Sisson (with whom I lived and worked for some memorable months) I absorbed a little of the current concepts of civic design. Then, for two highly influential years, I joined the School of Planning and Research for Regional Development, the brainchild of E.A.A. Rowse – a remarkable visionary with whom a group of us lived, breakfasted, talked and had our minds almost tangibly expanded. Rowse was a disciple of Patrick Geddes, that now half-forgotten but inspired teacher and environmentalist of the 1920s, and of Lewis Mumford, author of *The Culture of Cities*. He could see, more clearly than any man of his day, the directions and urgencies of world population movement, the forces of hunger and of the natural resources so widely wasted in a world of want. We were all inspired, for the rest of our lives, to see the 'macro' as well as the 'micro' aspects of our work, and to feel something of the force of desperate human need. Perhaps every planner experiences this spirit of calling and of public service. We need to learn to see and focus on not only the detail, but also the greater issues, and to comprehend something of the patterns of human behaviour and idiosyncrasy. Educationalists may note: the microscope and the telescope each has its place in discovery, and in achieving real knowledge.

Rowse aimed to train us in thinking together as what he termed a 'composite mind' – a team of cognate but differing skills. None of us will forget that experience. And it was his great plea always to remember the essential sequence of 'survey before plan' – to know and understand the subject of our care, before we can presume to guide it. Geddes had said just the same. So, in a different way, had William Morris and the SPAB. We in our turn, in following these masters, have felt and tried to express these same principles.

Practice

This was our educational background, and our first inspiration. Entering the real world, our practice and our workload has always had much about it of fortune, of Darwinian natural selection – frequently of broad aim, rather than plan. For if we long sufficiently to follow a given road, it is amazing how often it can appear through the bush. Our main instinct, even if unconscious and unexpressed, has been to save for Britain something of the historic towns and settlements that are so special to the character of this land, yet were then vanishing fast. This has led us in the way of major tasks, and to opportunities quite unexpected until they have arrived.

In the decades of redevelopment following the war, the national public temper, starved of any adequate depth of forethought, was beginning to swing decisively in favour of conserving the best of what we have. Despite the great losses, we all shared a deep human instinct to keep alive what is worthwhile. At endless meetings and gatherings, we pressed our conviction that towns, settlements and buildings, inevitably changing and alive, demanded urgent recognition of their special variety and identity, and an active and positive protection. Now, as then, they are still susceptible to guidance in their daily life and change. In the way that language is so deeply symbolic of feeling, it became our personal mission to press for 'conservation' rather than 'preservation' as a driving principle in environmental care. For we saw the latter as negative, obstructing all change, while the former encapsulates life. Architects and planners can feel it their privilege to 'conserve', to guide, to release that vitality. In this spirit our response

to environment and society must not be limited to negative defence or to rearguard obstruction, but devoted to positive and imaginative forward guidance. This calls first for active recognition, involvement and analysis. Then in planning ahead, we can experience increasingly the power of a knowledge identified with the special spirit of a particular people, a place or a building.

The movement for conservation

When one feels strongly, it becomes a challenge to share ideas. In our case this has involved promoting a lively public interest in buildings and their care. Today among all the pressing claims of preparation for life, an awareness of our environment should surely be a prime aim for every school. In a series of practical studies, published and otherwise, we have tried to develop a method of survey, analysis and organisation (more of which on following pages). In turn, it has been rewarding to work out ways of sharing these findings with students and others of like mind.

So much for the past: what of the future? It would be true to say that we did not consciously plan the direction of our lives – few of us do. But we have been given opportunities, which we have tried to use in the public weal. Over the rapidly passing years, this has been firmly reinforced by an everyday association with the work of quintessentially British bodies such as the earlier Historic Buildings Council and the Ancient Monuments Board, now together subsumed with the RCHM as English Heritage, with which I had the privilege of serving as founder-Commissioner. All these have achieved so much on a remarkably constrained budget, by their own brands of considerate building care, and alongside those of Britain's uniquely remarkable resource – the voluntary Amenity bodies.

Without meaning to, it seems that we have become part of a 'movement', and of a powerful and gathering force for conservation. Meanwhile a professional life within a growing team, all working with a real conviction and a good conscience, is perhaps as much as anyone personally can hope for. We are grateful for our part in such a programme.

As now we land at the incomparable Venice, the Serenissima of centuries, I confess this as perhaps my favourite place on earth, alongside my own birthplace of Britain. When and if Venice goes, she will carry away an irreplaceable human creation, quite ravishing in beauty and variety, expressing a unique human history and spirit. But her abiding lesson is the way in which every place and every building is special, and each has its own unique soul and identity.

Liverpool Town Hall

TEAMWORK IN AN ARCHITECTURAL PRACTICE

Origins and growth

Today our practice is a team of some 40 architects, working together with an equivalent number of supporting staff and branches. We are involved with contracts over a wide area of the country. How did we grow, and what has made us what we are?

The practice began its life in a London flat in Lyall Street, just off Belgrave Square. At first this served as home by night and as office by day. The flat was small and limited, but it was an historic building: one morning we woke up to the sound of hammering, looked out of the window and saw that a blue plaque was being erected to commemorate a previous occupant – no less than Thomas Cubitt, one of London's greatest 19th-century developers.

From that time and for a short while after, the growing responsibilities of every project were mine alone. But this could not last for long, and soon I was joined by trusted friends and allies, both full- and part-time. The practice quickly began to owe its increasingly well-known name to the skills and hard work of this growing team. Family help was equally instrumental; my late father was an angel in handling our accounts, until when he suffered a stroke, my wife bravely took over the administrative tasks, enabling us all to concentrate upon a thriving practical portfolio. As an organisation, we carry still the spirit of an extended family. Today, we are delighted that so many friends from earlier days are together still. In recognition of their valuable contribution, we have added continually to the Associateship the names of an increasing succession of experienced members and colleagues on whose special qualities we so much rely.

At the end of a lease in 1962, and after much searching, our growing team (by then six of us, together with a secretary) found new premises and set up a more formal office at No. 4 Grosvenor Crescent, just off Hyde Park Corner. Here we occupied four upper rooms and an attic penthouse, at the top of some 80 stairs. The feeling was akin to that of isolation by a drawbridge; I occupied the even more remote top room as a (then) bachelor penthouse flat.

Echoes of history; one morning, a Blue Plaque arrived at our practice's first London home.

So in moved our team, by now numbering fourteen, yet rattling like peas in a pod. We had to convert the place around us as we worked; and our own office was itself a building site – a good discipline in helping one to realise the strains and burdens of one's clients. Aided by Arthur, the caretaker from next door, we spent our evenings and weekends in shirtsleeves, feeding skip after skip.

For some years we let the basement floor, the far end of which had apparently served as an almost troglodyte flat for Vincent Harris's chauffeur, but little-by-little this space too became available and came into full use. Gradually, we have taken root in the building, which has suited us admirably, although now becoming quite tightly packed and sometimes overflowing. Our rooms are individual and varied in character; we like to surround ourselves with photographs and drawings of the work we do, so the atmosphere is friendly and congenial. Perhaps we only realise this fully when we have visitors, who immediately comment on how interesting and how very characteristic are our own premises, and are so highly appreciative of what they see.

In 1969 we moved to 19 West Eaton Place, Belgravia.

Four years later in 1966, and by then eight in number, we relocated to two floors of a lovely house in Queen Anne's Gate, occupancy of which we shared as tenants of the National Trust. But the Trust was expanding fast, and soon it needed this space, so we began to look once again. Eventually, our observant cleaner told us of a derelict building she had seen in a courtyard, set intriguingly behind a pair of wrought-iron gates in Belgravia's West Eaton Place. This building had apparently started life as three cottages overlooking a stream, but had later been converted as a house by the architect Oliver Hill. Thereafter it had become the home and more recently the offices of Vincent Harris, RA – the 'competition architect', as he described himself to me when we met. He had by then given the house to the Royal Academy. In 1969, and in a spirit of immense adventure, our family narrowly succeeded in buying it at auction.

Expansion: regional offices

Travelling by train and accompanied then by a motor-scooter, I found it possible to cover most of the country. But at different periods and increasingly since, we have found it convenient to set up local regional offices for a longer or shorter time, to deal with groups of contracts according to their location. The first was in Bristol[1], from which we looked after a great number of jobs in the West and into Wales (see Picton Castle, p. 52). A second regional office was opened in Chester, where from 1974 to 1978 we occupied what had once been the Dean's room in Abbey Square. This offered a valuable local contact-point for our conservation consultancy with the City, and has since reopened nearby as a busy base for all our increasing activities in the Northwest.

[1] Led by our then Associate, the late John Keeling Maggs.

15a A pioneer village survey (1961) at Blanchland, Northumberland.

15b,c Another early town study (1966): Thaxted, in Essex.

We have had no special plan to set up these country branches – they have tended to happen naturally, whether from personal circumstances or from convenience in serving local contracts. Although we find no difficulty today in covering country-wide jobs from London, it is often better still to have regional representation. More recently, and interestingly, several of our experienced younger colleagues have wished to move out of London; happily, in a number of instances it has proved practical to say, 'Yes, do go; but stay with the Practice; and why not set up a local sub-office of your own for us?' This has in turn enabled us to offer more local help regionally, and also provided a ready opportunity for younger architects to spread their wings and to gain direct management experience. So we are happy to have had active regional offices – more recently in Bath, Cambridge, Canterbury, Chester, Conwy and Shrewsbury. Each has been made the concern of a particular director, who maintains daily links and continuity. In turn, with headquarters premises becoming a tighter fit, our administration colleagues now have their own premises nearby, where we also have valuable overflow space for technical members in periods of special work pressure.

Teamwork

We find great strength in working as a team. This has been exemplified in our techniques of group survey, applicable equally to a building complex or to a village or a whole urban settlement. The method is now more common; but in retrospect we realise how our first survey in 1961 (Blanchland village in North-umberland) (15a) was something of a major pioneer.

At the time, this was simply an extension from working solo into working as a group (the 'composite mind', perhaps? p. 10), to cope with the size of the problem. But we immediately found the interaction of different minds with a single concern to be

15a

15b

15c

16a

16c

16b

16d

16a   Lavenham's market place.

16b   Our Lavenham report for West Suffolk (1962).

16c,d Lavenham: before and after removal of overhead wires and services.

much more inspiring and effective. Our method has been to arrive on site with a deliberate minimum of preparation or preconception, staying together at a local inn and concentrating entirely on the task of finding out what it was about the place that made it special.

From the first reconnaissance, we have found we all bring different eyes and concerns to the task; this has made it possible to devote and focus individual skills, bringing a team appreciation to all the multifarious facets of a town. Local people have appreciated that our group was really interested in their place and patterns of relationships have rapidly developed, in which ideas were readily shared and exchanged. We have made a point of talking to anyone known to have individual and sometimes influential views, and of taking endless notes from which some kind of synthesis could then eventually be made. Yet the job has always been one of intense, wide-ranging observation – of opening ourselves

to whatever the place had to say. In particular, the initial 'impact' of any town or building has a special importance. This is something received only once, so we always try to record initial impressions as they come, without the trammels of growing local experience.

In our group methods of data collection, we have developed a system of analysing observations in two main 'axes': subject and location. In this way, a fact or a feeling or opinion from any member of the survey team can find itself within a 'subject' heading, such as traffic or car-parking or the estate market, and at the same time and in parallel, within a geographical 'place' context, along with notes on neighbouring buildings in the same area or street, and together with other members' observations and opinion of exactly the same building. It is always important that no useful initial ideas are lost.

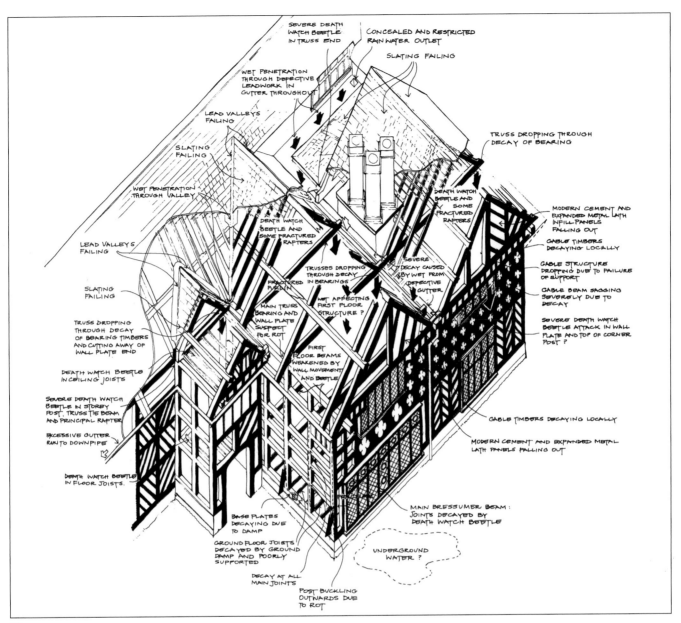

SEVERE DEATH WATCH BEETLE IN TRUSS END

CONCEALED AND RESTRICTED RAIN WATER OUTLET

SLATING FAILING

WET PENETRATION THROUGH DEFECTIVE LEADWORK IN GUTTER THROUGHOUT

LEAD VALLEYS FAILING

SLATING FAILING

WET PENETRATION THROUGH VALLEY

TRUSS DROPPING THROUGH DECAY OF BEARING

LEAD VALLEYS FAILING

DEATH WATCH BEETLE AND SOME FRACTURED RAFTERS

DEATH WATCH BEETLE AND SOME FRACTURED RAFTERS

MODERN CEMENT AND EXPANDED METAL LATH INFILL PANELS FALLING OUT

GABLE TIMBERS DECAYING LOCALLY

SLATING FAILING

TRUSSES DROPPING THROUGH DECAY IN BEARINGS

SEVERE DECAY CAUSED BY WET FROM DEFECTIVE GUTTER

GABLE STRUCTURE DROPPING DUE TO FAILURE OF SUPPORT

FRACTURED PURLIN

WET AFFECTING FIRST FLOOR STRUCTURE ?

GABLE BEAM SAGGING SEVERELY DUE TO DECAY

TRUSS DROPPING THROUGH DECAY OF BEARING TIMBERS AND CUTTING AWAY OF WALL PLATE END

MAIN TRUSS BEARING AND WALL PLATE SUSPECT FOR ROT

FIRST FLOOR BEAMS WEAKENED BY WALL MOVEMENT AND BEETLE

SEVERE DEATH WATCH BEETLE ATTACK IN WALL PLATE AND TOP OF CORNER POST ?

DEATH WATCH BEETLE IN CEILING JOISTS

SEVERE DEATH WATCH BEETLE IN STOREY POST, TRUSS TIE BEAM AND PRINCIPAL RAFTER

EXCESSIVE GUTTER RUN TO DOWNPIPE

GABLE TIMBERS DECAYING LOCALLY

MODERN CEMENT AND EXPANDED METAL LATH PANELS FALLING OUT

DEATH WATCH BEETLE IN FLOOR JOISTS.

BASE PLATES DECAYING DUE TO DAMP

GROUND FLOOR JOISTS DECAYED BY GROUND DAMP AND POORLY SUPPORTED

DECAY AT ALL MAIN JOINTS

POST BUCKLING OUTWARDS DUE TO ROT

MAIN BRESSUMER BEAM: JOINTS DECAYED BY DEATH WATCH BEETLE

UNDERGROUND WATER ?

17a

In later and more developed studies such as that of Chester (p. 195), we have more consciously selected, and allocated to each aspect, those of us with the most relevant special skills. If we have lacked an essential discipline, we have invited someone to join the team, such as a regional planner to set a study area into its right perspective, or a traffic specialist to investigate circulation aspects and solutions.

In the next stage of town survey, that of analysis, the methods our team adopts will include 'brainstorming', conscious or otherwise, or inviting one member to open with observations and ideas, to be widened in discussion, which in turn is tape-recorded and minuted. The subject leader can then produce a draft paper about this particular aspect, to be circulated for further shaping, first in content and subsequently in detail. But it is at the same time equally important to interrelate

17a Defects identified for attention at Speke Hall, Merseyside.

17b Architectural models: this one demonstrates structural timberwork, also at Speke Hall.

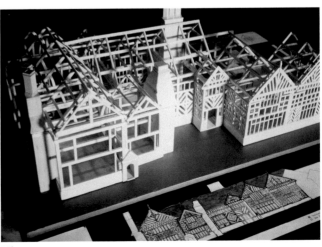

17b

The party take a view of Chester from the ancient walls near the Cathedral. —*Chronicle copyright photo.*

AFTER a two-day tour of Chester last week its official preservationists were impressed—paradoxically—with its liveliness. Mr. Donald Insall, leader of the group, said that it was "a splendid and lovely city" which was, commercially and in every sense "alive."

The group is one appointed by the Ministry of Housing and Local Government to investigate the possibility of a conservation plan for Chester. "We have been commissioned to carry out a survey of the central area comprising the chief historic buildings in Chester with the aim of conservation," was how he put it.

When they had collected their facts and formed their opinions those would be forwarded to the City Surveyor, said Mr. Insall.

His team will cover the whole of the area within the City Walls, plus the area bounded by the line of the inner ring road to its junction with Foregate-street and then along Dee-lane to the south-east angle of the City Walls.

It will not be their task simply to define the buildings and areas which are most characteristic of Chester's historical and architectural legacy. They will also have to suggest ways and means of putting any conservation plan into practice. Their full report must be made by next October.

Chester is one of five cities which are to become the subjects of Crown Surveys. The others are York, Bath, King's Lynn and Chichester.

When the separate reports have been drawn up, Mr. Anthony Walton, technical adviser to Lord Kennet's policy group, will correlate them into a general national policy for historical towns.

18a

18b

18c

specialist aspects, and it is then that we learn the most. A good deal of editing and mutual goodwill are always invaluable at this stage. Since the visual aspect of communication is so vital, illustrations and any good photographs are continually gathered, towards their use in the eventual reports and presentations.

The same team spirit has inspired our more concentrated structural emergency investigations such as that into the failed ceiling of the Lords' Chamber at Westminster Palace (p. 117), and our major part in undertaking the post-fire reconstruction of Windsor Castle (p. 211).

Again, we have adopted the same principles of group work in relation to architectural design and production drawings. From the introduction of any commission at our regular Associates' meetings, we try to assess which member of the team is most in sympathy with, and is available to lead the project. Each job will then be run by one Associate, but with special contributions by colleagues who may be allocated either from the start or as the specific needs of the job begin to reveal themselves. Although in practice a commission has frequently stayed in one or sometimes two pairs of hands, more often the availability of special talents of one kind and another has led to the involvement of additional colleagues. This 'team' approach is highly flexible, and simply expresses our wish to devote the

18a   The survey team in Chester (1960s): a contemporary press cutting.

18b   A church, enlarged: St Peter, Thundersley. Roof-pitch echoed and maintained in a newly added nave (1966).

18c   The interior of Thundersley Church, showing laminated timber roof-trusses.

18d   Stone cleaning; the old Public Record Office (1986).

18d

19a

19b

19c

best skills available for each job. Although no such arrangement is perfect, we think this principle does pay off in terms of giving the best service. One team member for example may be especially observant, another more articulate, or able to research or design; each thus makes his contribution where he most excels. The axonometric drawings in this book are very largely the work of one gifted colleague, the late Ailwyn Best. A number of his and of our other everyday office drawings have been displayed in Summer Exhibitions at the Royal Academy. Even some of our most useful architectural models have been made as a working tool in the office and within the team.

Self-fulfilment for members of an office should be one of its primary aims; whatever brings out the best in each individual may at the same time be the highest form of collective self-service and development. We also enjoy working in association with consultants from allied professions. Our quantity surveyor Allan Tapley joined us as cost consultant; he later established an independent firm[1] whose successors still today join us

in many of our projects. Long experience of working together enables us to trust each other's knowledge and abilities and we maintain ready contact. We value the added skills of such colleagues in forecasting and controlling the vital cost dimension, and in keeping pace with changing financial and tax systems.

Specialist help from those in allied professions is equally valuable in questions of structural engineering. An architect may have been trained to calculate structures mathematically, but it is only the growing and instinctive feeling for materials, informed by experience, that will enable him to know just what they can do, and how they will behave in the actual circumstances of a building. His professional colleague the structural engineer can carry this knowledge still deeper and has, if he is a good engineer, not only theoretical and mathematical skills but a sensitive and intuitive 'feel' for the capacities of structures under load. As with architects, not all engineers are at home with the vagaries of older buildings, and it has been our pleasure to work alongside some brilliant consultants.

19a   New house for a private client (Fordingbridge, Hampshire), (1962).

19b,c   The Mansion House, City of London: interior replanning and refurbishment (1991–1993).

[1] Now part of Rider Levett Bucknall

20a

The best remedies are rarely the most expensive – some memorable financial savings have been achieved by adopting down-to-earth measures based on their long experience.

An expanding workload at home and overseas

The scope and extent of our workload has continually widened, but within the constant theme and principle of identifying, strengthening and complementing the best features of a neighbourhood, a building or a site. The emphasis at first was upon converting and rationalising country houses and estate buildings, mostly for private owners and including the National Trust. This led in turn to associated village and new housing work (for example in Durham, pp. 181–6), and to our designing the occasional single house of special character and quality. Our interest in towns and special areas brought city centre surveys, old building conversions and more new development, especially the design of new buildings for sensitive sites, related to and sometimes incorporating existing work of special value (for example in Winchester, p. 173). The emphasis and range of our coverage has gradually developed to include commissions for larger organisations such as City Livery Companies, banks, universities and schools, for religious bodies and churches and increasingly for local authorities and national organisations, including central government and its many departments.

20b

Some projects have been long, and others more immediate. We were architects to our first major clients at Kedleston (then still in private family ownership) for more than 25 years. Other long-running contracts have included our consultancies for Chester, Cambridge Colleges (notably Trinity College since 1972) and conservation work for the National Trust at Speke Hall, Merseyside. Many of these involve season after season of tightly planned activity. Our varied responsibilities today include a wide range of work, the scope of which can be seen from a pictorial panorama assembled in 1996 by our Chairman, Nicholas Thompson (p. 24).

21a

21c

21b

21a   The National Trust: The Vyne, Hampshire.

21b   Interior redecoration scheme at The Vyne (1960).

21c   City Companies: the redecorated Livery Hall at Goldsmiths' Hall, London.

Meanwhile, a number of opportunities have arisen for service abroad. Here as at home, every job is exciting and new; but some, such as the opportunity to restore the Villa Corner, just outside Venice, have been especially tempting. The owner, Sir Stafford Sands, came to us for advice, but fast work was required. We agreed to go there immediately and to work long hours, if we could stay in a small pensione in Venice. Each day we would take a water-bus to our client's Cadillac at the car park, to be whisked out along the banks of the river Brenta to the Villa, and there be greeted by his great dogs. A young Italian architect meanwhile joined us in London for a while, to learn something of our ways; he went on to direct the job on site.

On another occasion we were invited to provide specialist conservation advice in Nepal. John Sanday, who in the first instance travelled to Nepal as our representative, has since built a highly responsible professional career there, directing exacting work at the Hanuman Dhoka Palace at Kathmandu, and at Angkor Wat, in Cambodia. Other overseas team consultancies have included lecture visits in Europe, India and the Americas, and expeditions to advise on problems of damp in Thai temples, on the restoration and display of major temples in Bangladesh, and on possible grant aid for monuments in Bagan, Myanmar.

Just before the handover of Hong Kong to China, we were offered a major opportunity in Shanghai, to restore the previous headquarters building of the Hong Kong & Shanghai Bank.

22a

22b

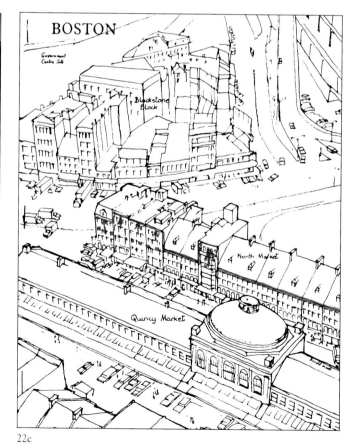

22c

The challenge was both technical, to provide advice on the urgent cleaning of granite stonework, and also administrative, in collaborating with what to us would be an over-manned but enthusiastic local construction team, working under immense pressure from traditional bamboo scaffolding. Again, a short-term branch office was set up in Shanghai for this function. More recently, our advice has been sought in restoring the President's House in Trinidad; other overseas projects will no doubt continue to arise. We maintain constant contact with friends and associates in the USA, and have made useful exchange visits with architects in Russia. Although the great bulk of our work is still in Britain, it is good to be able to take our skills overseas, and to feel ourselves well capable of coping readily with such varied demands.

22a   An overseas project near Venice: the Villa Corner.

22b   Temples in Myanmar (Burma) inspected for the World Monuments Fund.

22c   Boston, USA (1964) – restoration problems since resolved.

23a

23a   Overseas: Shanghai waterfront – a British colonial building, now refurbished for the Pu Dong Bank, in time for Chinese Hong Kong celebrations (1999).

23b   The President's House, Trinidad (1875): today suffering from severe termite damage (2004).

23c   English Heritage: Formal launching party (1984) at No.10 Downing Street.

23b

Teaching and public service

In London, as something of an experiment over nearly a decade, we arranged pioneer courses of lectures for visiting American students, to awaken the interest and stimulate the observational powers of young people from the University of Syracuse. Alas, many of its younger contingent perished when returning from holidays, in the tragic air disaster of 1988 at Lockerbie. This course is now flourishing and has more than quadrupled, with its own effective London staff and headquarters.

It still feels important to spread the word and we have enjoyed an increasing number of teaching and lecture appointments here and abroad. These have included my own annual visits for more than 25 years as Visiting Professor to the specialist Conservation Course at the Catholic University of Leuven, and from time to time at the International Centre for Conservation in Rome. Home and overseas lecture engagements are too numerous to mention individually, but have included travels to widely separated commitments in, for

example, Argentina, Canada, India and Singapore. International consultancy services have included a detailed and published study for the Council of Europe on 'Historic Buildings: Action to Maintain the Expertise for their Care and Repair' and numerous consultancies for the European Commission. We have also regularly attended and lectured at symposia for the International Congress on Monuments and Sites, for the Association for Preservation Technology International, for Europa Nostra and for numerous organisations in the Americas and elsewhere overseas.

Associated with these wider interests, and with the growing work of English Heritage, has been our experience in promoting systems of grant aid. These have included the Getty Grants Programme (now Getty Conservation Institute, USA), whose Advisory Committee I also served as a founder-member.

23c

24a   Souvenir cartoon by a student, on a lecture visit (Leuven, Belgium) 1978.

It has been interesting to experience the different monitoring procedures of grant aid bodies such as the Council of Europe in Strasbourg, the European Commission in Brussels and our own national organisations. Each has its own strengths from which we may learn. Again, each new international door gives access to international rooms; and many friends and visitors from abroad with an interest in common conservation problems now stay in touch, and call on us regularly when in Britain. Every year, the world becomes a smaller place.

We have been extraordinarily fortunate in the way our team and its workload has developed, as its contacts have flowered and flourished. Today, as one of the country's larger architectural teams, we are thankful for all the experience and delight of everything we have already done, and the future shows every sign of busy increase and activity. In the following pages we discuss how we set about and organise the projects we undertake, and illustrate some of the challenging questions our experience has taught us to expect, in this specialised work of caring for historic towns and buildings, and of creating new ones.

24b   A panorama of our past projects by Nicholas Thompson (1996).

Architectural practice today: providing for the future

During all this time, architectural practice has been developing in many interesting ways, and is changing still. Several broad tendencies can be observed, and perhaps some interesting lessons learned.

Within most practices, the advent of new forms of information technology and new skills of computer-aided design have led to more specialisation. So the 'can-do-it-all' architect is a rarer bird and the 'team' concept we have adopted, combining these specialist skills, is today more acceptable.

Beyond the design stage, project and site management has generated its own specialisation; newly developing systems of contract placement such as management contracting have invaded the one-time preserve of the professional architect, already shared with the quantity surveyor and now further extended into managing issues such as site safety.

For all these reasons, and to cope with the increasing costs of professional insurance, of maintaining and updating expensive electronic equipment and of providing specialist facilities and services, the larger office has been given a distinct advantage over the individual. And for the sake of its financial continuity, the concept of the corporate company structure has brought increasing advantages over the smaller partnership or individual practice.

All those trends have been apparent in the developing history of our own young firm. With the encouragement of our accountants, we decided in 1981 to make provision for the future by becoming a small Limited Company (one of the first, in our profession as architects). The four senior Associates agreed to become directors, combining this role with their continuing responsibility as architects actively running our projects. An additional director's post was that of Company Secretary, and our accountant colleague Simon Charrington joined us to mastermind this process. To his distillation of the essence of the Practice, we owe the idea of setting up an Employee Benefit Trust, to which the company ownership is being progressively transferred. Today, together with additional helpers, he looks after all our administrative services including those of the regional offices. And with the passage of time, it has been a delight to be able to hand on the function of Chairman to architect and co-director Nicholas Thompson, for so long a trusted friend and colleague, and to sense the continuing progress of the Practice and company in his capable and safe hands.

Thus our organisation, like most human endeavours, is dynamic and elastic and changing. But the principle has proved an attractive and workable one, and generates and enjoys remarkable team loyalties. Our members combine upon our London base for regular meetings and at occasions such as Christmas, when the annual lunch and mutual screen presentation of our projects has become a major and memorable (if alarmingly numerous) 'family' occasion.

A Practice Associates' discussion-meeting: our growing team.

Living materials: Suffolk oak in Lavenham.

BUILDINGS ARE ALIVE

Buildings and people

The philosophy produced by our training, background and experience is this: a building is not something created at one stroke – a static and crystalline object, incapable of change. Rather, it is the living outcome of an interaction between people and their place – between human beings, each with their own individual dreams and desires, and their daily needs and surroundings.

When it was first born, each building was a direct expression of its locality and materials, responding to the specific conditions of the site. It arose as a concept of the human mind – whether of one person, or a family or a culture. This in turn was executed through the hands and energies of builders and craftsmen, with their own varied skills, and reflecting the traditions and techniques of their day. Ever since the moment it was created, each building has had its own special 'life': surroundings and weather have taken their toll, and the structure has responded to its physical setting and subsoil. Its very purpose may change, even while it is being built; from the moment it has occupants and users, their evolving needs and standards will be reflected in daily changes in form and structure, fittings and furnishings. No building reaches finality, but it expresses its own past and present, intimately bound up with its whereabouts, the needs of generations of users, and the life cycles and renewal needs of its materials.

So our first aim must be to know and understand each building, and the way it came about, how it has altered and changed through its life, to become what it fleetingly is today. Then we can better appreciate what is 'special' and individual about it, and what makes up its essential character and personality. In turn, we acknowledge that as people create buildings, so buildings in turn shape the lives of their occupants. For this is an intimate and mutual relationship, to which each contributes day by day.

Meeting a building is very much like meeting a person; a building is just as fascinating to get to know. Whether for its own sake, or for ours as owners, we can receive and assess what it has to say to us.

Locality and materials

Materials have their own story, and in old buildings speak eloquently of their local origin. Perhaps the commonest are timber and stone. But even a staple constructional diet like English oak, for centuries key to traditional building techniques, displays enormous local varieties. Superb hardwood from the forests of Suffolk, in the hands of assured craftsmen, reliably produced the beautifully accurate work we find in East Anglia's medieval domestic architecture.

27a

27b

27a   The nature of materials: traditional softwood log construction in Scandinavia.

27b   The beginnings of sophistication: jointing in hardwood.

28a

28a Painted softwood weather-boarding in Cranbrook, Kent.

28b Pure form and limewash in Greek sunshine.

28c Classical architectural detailing in painted wood: Bath, Maine, USA.

28b

28c

It stands in contrast with the strong, but relatively perverse-grained and tortured cousin material from the stormier west, from smaller scrubby and twisted trees exposed to gusty sea winds. Similarly, hardwood and softwood construction each have their own characteristic structural patterns and jointing systems. From a craftsmanship and engineering standpoint, the two are almost like different materials. Painted woodwork and weatherboard have produced strong local character in timber-rich areas such as Kent, or indeed in Colonial USA. At home, the place-name of Deal is, after all, synonymous with our word 'deal', as a name for locally imported softwood.

Stone too has its own life-habits, varying with its origins. Limestone was formed from countless shells laid down on an ancient seabed, later thrown up by geological movements. Then it has further weathered,

before and after actual quarrying. As a building material its micro-structure allows it to breathe, absorb and discharge water, but this in turn can carry ice and salts, expanding within its cells, or dissolving its internal structure. Granite was formed by intense heat, so it lacks the layered nature. It presents instead a huge solidity and a demanding weight.

Regional stonework has its own special character, both in design and behaviour. Hard stones such as granite generate bold shapes, rather than delicate detailing. The softer limestones have made possible the respective creations of the medieval mason (29c) and of the classical scholar (29b).

In chalk areas, the clunch stone is soft, while the local pebble flint is hard and intransigent and simply will not bond into corners or span over openings, so walling is frequently laced with brickwork at angles and extremities. Once any surface flints begin to come away, deterioration may be rapid; the flint or pebble-work quickly shows itself inferior to the brick corners and detailing.

29c

29a

29b

29d

29a Roughly dressed but accurate Mycenaean stonework, Greece.

29b Scholarly Classicism at Gonville & Caius College, Cambridge: the Gate of Honour (1575).

29c Entirely in Cotswold limestone – the medieval Parish Church in Cirencester (was the topmost stage a last-moment idea?).

29d Accurately squared clunch stonework with brick quoins and 'galleted' mortar-joints.

30a

30b

30a Flint-pebble walling in lime mortar, with brick patterning and corners.

30b Brick texture, set in lime in a random bond.

30c Clay tiles on contrasting roofs at Florence Cathedral.

30c

Clay-brick areas around the world produce their own characteristic architecture. Where brick (baked or otherwise) is the basic building unit, clay tiles are also a natural choice for roofing. Only in Victorian times, and with the aid of the railways, did Welsh slate roofs overtake clay tiles to cover the country (even since, frequently appearing in areas of natural stone). Other localities developed their own techniques: for example, in Devon and elsewhere one can still find cob and pisé walling made of dried mud and straw. This is perfectly sound under a good hat, even of thatch, but it decays very quickly if it becomes saturated. In some examples in Britain, tiled roofs at steeper-than-normal pitch set between verges may reflect a traditional earlier use of thatch. In time, this has often given way to its replacement by clay tiles, arriving from the Low Countries. In later tiled roofs, an existing eaves-line was often raised to give more headroom in the first-floor rooms. The end gables today betray this change, giving much the same effect as padded shoulders, and still displaying the steeper brickwork verges of an earlier roof line (31b).

Metals such as steel, iron and copper, melted and re-formed as sheets, each behave individually. Some expand and contract more than others in heat and cold. Lead is soft; cast-iron is brittle. The lifetime of each must be taken into account.

Occasionally materials appear in unsuspected localities, prompting questions. A fine balconied façade in Indian teak, encountered unexpectedly in Africa's Zanzibar (31d), may be an international export – especially as the timber joining does not quite fit and suggests it was all prefabricated and then reassembled on arrival.

Local materials and methods bring immense character, as well as occasional weaknesses. They give huge and valued extra character and identity to our historic buildings, and they more than earn their keep.

31c

31a

31b

31d

31a Decorative clay brickwork in Moscow.

31b Flint gable-end with later 'padded shoulders' for added headroom indoors.

31c Local materials – Scottish harling-and-limewash.

31d Teak balconies in Zanzibar – possibly pre-fabricated and imported?

32a

32b

32c

32a   Irreplaceable original craftsmanship: a frieze at Borobudur, Java, Indonesia.

32b   Graffiti on glass: *John Armstead October 12 1789* and *John Moore glazier leded this window August the 20 – 1817*.

32c   Ancient stonework of the Arch of Constantine, Rome.

Crafts content

Architecture is the work of human hands. Vernacular building without any conscious attempts at style can be especially rich in the spirit of the original craftsman, who desired to echo traditional forms, but also to decorate and add his own invention and ornament. In conserving his work, extra importance attaches to the identity of the actual physical fabric – the product of his hands in answer to his favourite tools and materials, perhaps in shaping the whimsical memories and ideas of a now long-past moment. The life this exhibits is, after all, something of an extension of his own life, his desires and his dreams. A copy of it made today can lack the originality and the special human personality of its initial artist. For what we value in his work is like an echo of his voice, and peculiar to him. This ancient fabric, rich in craftsmanship, may well demand that we should prolong its original life, even if that entails accepting a higher degree of deterioration and weathering than would otherwise be acceptable.

Occasionally too, the treasured attribute may be even a feature like significant later graffiti acquired by stonework, or a message scratched on glass by a signet-ring in later life. But even more, this may not last forever.

It is interesting to find that while this honouring-of-evidence is a Western concept; by contrast, in the East – notably in Japan – it is the spirit and form of a monument that may be assiduously copied alongside it, and repeated, but again with this same aim of 'extending its life'. In either case, it is the life that is valued, and the enjoyment of which we strive to extend. The oriental concept seems strange to us; but it lasts longer and the motive is just the same.

33a

33a Two dates – Georgian-marries-Medieval.

33b Period characteristics: the carved voussoirs of a Romanesque arch.

Period characteristics

A neighbourhood or building may be of one date, or of a series of dates. Some of the most interesting have experienced major changes, remodelling or entire reconstruction, and now bear the distinctive signs of each. Style, construction and features may all be highly characteristic of their respective periods. Romanesque stonework, for example, typically used the semicircular arch with repetitive, decorative voussoirs.

An example of a specific period is terraced housing of the early 18th century on the fringes of then-central London (p. 162). This housing was often speculative, inspired by the profit motive. Typically, the bricklayer might erect an outer shell, after which an independent master-carpenter would arrive and frame up a separate carcass within. So a kind of schizophrenia results, producing a pattern of internal loading quite unrelated to the bearing-strength of the outer brick walls. Sometimes, heavy timber beams may be found to collect the load of a whole interior eccentrically onto the narrow brick piers between windows, or even onto a window lintel itself.

Another feature of that period was the generous lacing of walls with horizontal wooden 'bonders', let into the inner face of the brickwork. Especially in places vulnerable to damp, such as the inside of a wall carrying external rainwater pipes, these bonders can be immensely attractive to dry rot by providing it with a perfect and food-lined larder or distribution duct. A century later, another hazard was the use of pitch-pine shipped from abroad, available in big scantlings for structural work, but again offering a ready host for fungal attack.

If one knows what defects are likely in buildings of a particular period, it is easier to spot them. But we must try not to forget the occasional exceptions, for in one luckless country house we encountered, we eventually found that fungus had been rife in the original timber-yard, long before the timber was sawn up for use in the actual completed building.

33b

34a

34b

34a Exposed stonework eaten
    away by cavernous decay
    (Coimbra, Portugal).

34b A 14th-century statue at
    Winchester College, shedding
    its surface; the only possible
    remedy was rescue indoors.

34c Sheet lead has 'walked' down
    a roof-slope and droops over
    the eaves.

34c

35a

35b

35a   Magnificent roof leadwork at Ely Cathedral (the nave pitch is very steep).

35b   With its protective paintwork gone, ironwork rapidly rusts.

35c,d Atmospheric pollution and acid attack: The Bronze Horses, Venice.

35c

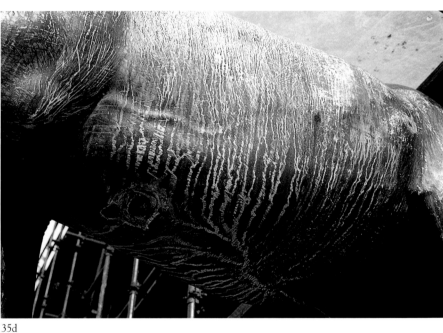
35d

Weather and the elements

The elements are a continuous force in shaping a living building. Winds have buffeted it and worn it away differentially – winter's ice has bitten its north side, and the sun has cooked it on the south. Metal roofs expand and contract and may ride into ridges. Lead roofs at steeper pitches will expand readily in daytime sunlight, but are less willing to contract back upwards again at night, so that by their own weight they tend to 'walk' downwards off a roof. Water has streamed down walls, some of it finding its way inside, especially at open joints or at unprotected ledges, before drying back gradually outwards and sometimes incidentally then depositing damaging salts. Flooding, indeed, may be with salt water anyway. And unprotected ironwork is rapidly destroyed by water and rust.

Any building constantly 'breathes' both air and damp. Walls take up rain with every storm, and later lose it again to circulating air. Within the wall itself, moisture moves constantly, either with gravity or towards a tempting way out. Atmospheric pollution adds to the damaging effects of condensation on cold surfaces. Virtually every problem that a building is likely to encounter is exacerbated by water. In wood, dry rot fungus demands it, then itself carries damp onwards to fresh pastures. In stone, the internal physical micro-structure may be dissolved, while salts are distributed and deposited and further disrupt and erode it. And vegetation takes root in exposed crevices and increasingly disrupts and damages the structure.

36c

36a

36d

36b

36e

36a   Wind erosion attacks a stone balustrade.

36b   Thrusting roots of vegetation destroying brickwork in Myanmar.

36c   Ice, from melting snow on a roof.

36d   Cornice damage by water, and emergency lead protection (earlier attention would have saved it).

36e   Tree-roots from seeds lodged in a roof: nature wins (India).

Structural life and movement

In response to the load of its own weight and its contents, every structure is in a state of constant movement, within its internal and external restraints. So to be able to advise and prescribe for its health, we have to recognise exactly what is happening. We need to understand the system of live loads and thrusts within it, and the compensating and mutually matching movements by which it constantly adapts itself.

The ground itself has in turn reacted in answer to the weight of a building. In places it has compressed or settled, either as a whole or more flexibly (perhaps, as was once charmingly observed by Peter Locke, 'like a broody hen settling on its eggs'), the settlement may have occurred under the greater loads or on soft ground. Any building brings widely differing loads upon it, and the ground reacts in equally varying measure.

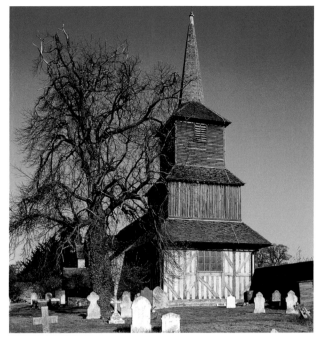

37b

37a

37a   Surprisingly, the lighter porch has sunk more than the heavy main building: softer ground? (Zagorsk).

37b,c   A timber-framed church tower at Blackmore, in Essex (repairs completed 1971) … and another at Hopperstad, in Norway.

37c

38a

38b

38d

38c

The structural system of an entire building presents its own life and movements, which we cannot ignore. Every spire and flagpole sways – if it did not, it would dislocate or snap. Floor structures are inherently springy, whether or not intentionally so. Framed systems behave differently from continuously load-bearing ones, while each moves and reacts to its use.

Construction methods and systems have always generated architectural styles. In well-wooded areas with timber-framed houses, upper rooms were habitually built larger than those below, with their fronts jettied forwards and carried on the ends of projecting floor beams. Here, a common historical change has been to rebuild lower front walls, newly realigned outwards to provide more space indoors. But it may have been forgotten that this weakens the upper floors, whose span has in this way been increased.

Interesting constructional devices abound – consider the expedients developed to span over spaces longer than the average tree. Roof trusses provide many examples – as does the ingenious upper floor at Kelmscott (38a). On the debit side, if one joint fails here, the whole floor is in trouble. In stone localities less blessed with good material, walling was often traditionally built of two fair outer faces with only loose rubble between. A problem that we must expect from this cause is the parting of the face-work and subsequent collapse of the inner core. A variant of this situation arises when loose stone dropping from above accumulates and settles between the two faces to form a live downward wedge, bringing further disruption.

An obvious index of movement is any visible cracking, but we learn to read cracks and to know their language. Movements are usually at right angles to crack-lines.

One or two special effects include vertical cracks in church towers caused by the mechanical forces of 'English-fashion' bellringing, which brings strong horizontal forces upon the structure[1]. Then one may ask: is the movement alive, or arrested, or expended? In which direction and in which plane has this happened? And will current trends in a building's use, and likely future ones, add to or modify this evident movement? In particular, is the effect really damaging, or only disconcerting and perhaps quite safely ignored?

39a Movement outward from plane of a wall.

39b Movement is generally at right angles to the crack: here, both vertical and (mainly) horizontal separation.

39a

39b

[1] See *The Care of Old Buildings Today*, 1972.

Occupants and users

Above all, a building provides for and reacts to its changing occupants. This too is an active and a live relationship, for continuously – daily, weekly and in a thousand different ways – each adapts to the other. Social customs especially change: one generation worships daylight, while another has a window-tax. In one country or century, coal may be cheap; in another, we rely upon undersea oil. Sir Walter Raleigh introduced tobacco smoking; his post-colonial successors sent back air-conditioning to Britain. The string quartet gives place to the hi-fi, and servants to the spin dryer. Furnishings, fittings and services multiply in complexity and ancient structures are remorselessly remodelled to carry and accommodate them. Our perceived needs do change and each generation models and adapts its surroundings continuously, to serve new requirements and to meet new standards.

Occasionally, occupants will have done strange things. Some have carried out whimsical alterations; repairs and maintenance have not always been sympathetic.

Few buildings in turn remain uninfluenced by their adjoining neighbours. Many depend actively upon one another for mutual physical support, and very often for more. A surprising discovery was a wire through a hole, providing a free electrical supply from a meter next door. Houses may find themselves laterally united; and when one of two adjoining premises is rebuilt, no paper agreement or party wall award can secure total immovability, or precisely regain the structural status quo. Even a blocked prospect from an old window, or a newly opened one, will generate changed use-patterns within its rooms. So will tall neighbouring buildings overlooking it, or traffic noise and nuisance – or even damage – from an adjoining road. The changing economic values of a neighbourhood can find themselves closely reflected, whether in money wisely spent on care and maintenance, or in accelerating neglect and decay.

40b

40a   Thoughtless placing of an air-conditioner (Corrientes, Argentina).

40b   A divided window-eyebrow betrays two ownerships.

40c   Some appallingly aggressive repointing.

40a

40c

Multi-date buildings

Occupants and users have generated some particular examples of two-date and multi-date buildings, sometimes with overtones of religious or sectarian zeal, in which work of an earlier period was afterwards deliberately obliterated, or was re-executed in new and more acceptable terms.

A fascinating case was the politically almost fanatical rebuilding of central Warsaw, deliberately destroyed by Nazi dynamite, but where memories were reconstructed. In some instances this included the painstakingly accurate reproduction of buildings of more than one original date.

At Cordoba in Spain the Great Mosque was interrupted by the wholly foreign introduction of a Christian cathedral. Conversely at Nicosia in Cyprus, the gothic cathedral is now recast as a mosque, with its interior reoriented obliquely towards Mecca (42a). A British import was at Highcliffe Castle where a fine oriel window from a French chateau now looks entirely at home in Hampshire (42b).

41a   Painted screen: an older saintly image, seen through later-applied inscription (Binham Priory Church, Norfolk).

41b,c   Warsaw: history re-created. Even two earlier dates are also echoed in this faithful reconstruction.

41a

41b

41c

42a

42b

42c

Materials may be an accurate key to dates. At the rebuilt (1840–47) Palace of Westminster (p. 117) steel screws in the roof construction were still unpointed – the pointed screw was patented immediately afterwards. And iron balusters appeared on site early (assuming they are original?) in Robert Adam's Bridge of 1769–70, which is such a feature in the park at Kedleston.

42a   Changing users: two different religious traditions: once a cathedral, now a mosque (Nicosia, Cyprus).

42b   A French Gothic oriel window translated to England (Highcliffe Castle, Hampshire).

42c   Contrast in dates: late 12th and 11th centuries respectively alongside at St Albans Cathedral.

Multi-date: an example

In England the parish church of St Anne at Kew is a perfect example of the way such buildings can, and do, typically aggregate and grow.

Starting life as a self-contained little building, three windows long and with a clock-turret, it has since been extended stage by stage, until it now occupies at least five times the original footprint.

Despite all these changes, Kew church amazingly retains its identity and has great charm. It demonstrates how strongly a living building can still possess and proclaim so much of its original attraction and character.

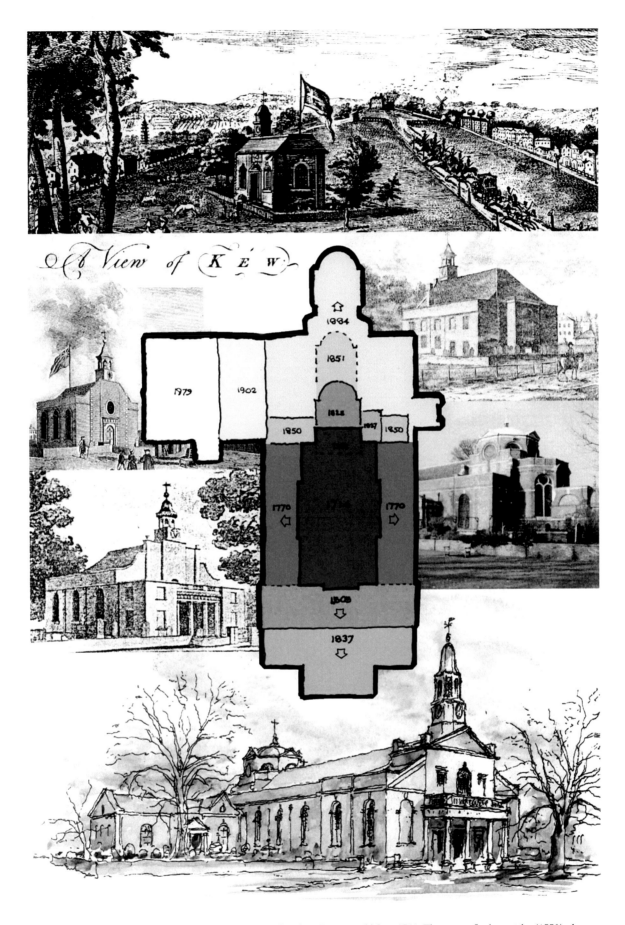

A View of KEW

Buildings are alive, and sometimes multi-date: St Anne's Church at Kew started life in 1714. Then came flanking aisles (1770); then (1805 and 1837) a new west front and portico. In 1850–1 a new mausoleum was added, re-erected further east on the arrival in 1884 of a spacious new chancel and flanking chapels. A choir vestry of 1902 and a parish hall of 1979 complete the church as it is today.

A warped tombstone in Philadelphia, USA.

Lifespan and renewal of fabric

Construction materials, local or otherwise, all have their own characteristic movements and life-cycles. Wood is after all, organic. When trees are felled and converted into timber, they will still behave organically. Wooden beams and boards expand and contract – especially across their fibrous grain. This is why craftsmen have invented the panelled door, in which each rail and panel can accommodate the constant movement of one another. Tongue-and-groove floorboarding behaves similarly. Depending upon the way it is converted, in relation to its cylindrical rings and grain, curling and warping are natural to timber. I have only once, and fascinatingly, seen this effect in stone.

The life span of materials may be long or short. Protective coatings like paint on external joinery are not only more vulnerable but are often the most exposed, and may demand frequent renewal. But without exception none is permanent. Cyclical renewal is part of every building's life and history.

It is this multi-faceted life of a building that is the very core of our message. For buildings are alive. Their opportunities and defects can be a cumulative result of original strengths and shortcomings, whether in construction or materials. Others are the outcome of reactions within, and others still to weather and usage, or to a dynamic history of everyday change and alteration. The architect has to observe and assess the significance of all these factors. He must understand the positive possibilities they offer, and be able to detect any symptoms of ill-health, to diagnose their causes and prescribe for their remedy.

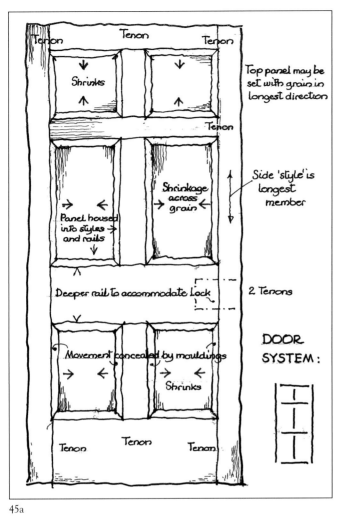

45a

45b

45c

45d

45a Traditional panelled door construction providing for timber shrinkage.

45b An unsophisticated country door of flat boards.

45c Radiating floorboards in Boston, USA.

45d Unusual curved floorboards in the north quadrant at Kedleston.

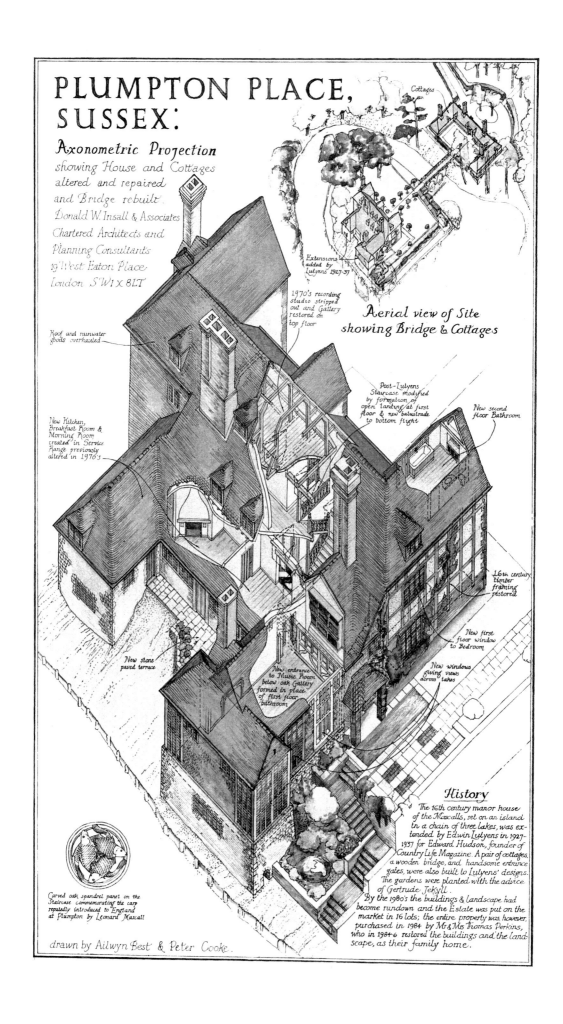

PLUMPTON PLACE, SUSSEX:

Axonometric Projection

showing House and Cottages
altered and repaired
and Bridge rebuilt.
Donald W. Insall & Associates
Chartered Architects and
Planning Consultants
19 West Eaton Place
London SW1X 8LT

Cottages

Extensions added by Lutyens 1927-37

Aerial view of Site showing Bridge & Cottages

1970's recording studio stripped out and Gallery restored on top floor

Roof and rainwater goods overhauled

Post-Lutyens Staircase modified by formation of open landing at first floor & new balustrade to bottom flight

New second floor Bathroom

New Kitchen, Breakfast Room & Morning Room created in Service Range previously altered in 1970's

16th century timber framing restored

New first floor window to Bedroom

New stone paved terrace

New windows giving views across lakes

New entrance to Music Room below oak Gallery formed in place of first floor bathroom

History

The 16th century manor house of the Mascalls, set on an island in a chain of three lakes, was extended by Edwin Lutyens in 1927-1937 for Edward Hudson, founder of Country Life Magazine. A pair of cottages, a wooden bridge, and handsome entrance gates, were also built to Lutyens' designs. The gardens were planted with the advice of Gertrude Jekyll.

By the 1980's the buildings & landscape had become rundown and the Estate was put on the market in 16 lots; the entire property was, however, purchased in 1984 by Mr & Mrs Thomas Perkins, who in 1984-6 restored the buildings and the landscape, as their family home.

Carved oak spandrel panel on the Staircase commemorating the carp reputedly introduced to England at Plumpton by Leonard Mascall

drawn by Ailwyn Best & Peter Cooke.

46

ORGANISING THE PROJECT

1. Assessing the owner's needs

The architect as broker

An architect enjoys a privileged and responsible role, acting in effect as 'broker' on behalf of a building owner, between him and his building. To succeed, he must be able to understand the needs of both, and to advise how each can optimise the benefits and special qualities of the other.

To fulfil this exacting part, we must first try to put ourselves squarely in the place of the owner and occupants (and in town surveys, of a wide number of users), and to study and understand their requirements. Expressed like that, the job may sound disarmingly simple; but like every simple task, its achievement calls for imaginative and wholehearted application.

Before he can undertake this in a balanced way, a wise adviser must be capable of looking inwards at himself as well as outwards for others. Then his appreciation of their problems will be more relevant, and more directed. We seek to approach each building, and its owner, with an open mind. Yet all advice has a certain subjective element, since every counsellor will speak from his own experience, reflecting his own special views and values, individuality and character. So when assessing and evaluating others' requirements, we have first to recognise our own personal balance of awareness, prejudices and predilections, to free ourselves of what is irrelevant and to see each situation as objectively as we can.

Understanding the owner's needs

Once this is accepted, we can arrange to meet with a building owner and together, informally and preferably without undue pressures of time, to explore the particular and sometimes very individual needs and ideas which have now to be given shape, with a real empathy for their relative importance and priority. This will entail establishing and distinguishing between obvious requirements, half-formed wishes and sometimes unforeseen needs; and the best way to learn is always to look and to listen. Human needs above all demand the understanding ear.

Accumulating problems: Diana the Huntress, in trouble, at Kedleston Hall.

Meanwhile, it will be helpful to know and understand the precise status and relationship of an owner to his building, because it is this that colours every response between the two parties. We need to establish whether the owner is a private occupier, already living in his own house, or if he is one of a long family whose home this has been, or perhaps even whose ancestors built it. If so, he will have the advantage of knowing it very intimately; but he may also tend naturally to see it in relation to past circumstances, rather than to an unknown future. He will be concerned with how to deal with accumulating problems of maintenance, and also how to prepare and protect his house for a future he may not yet have contemplated. Then we try to envisage future occupants and their special and

48a

48b

48a Plumpton Place, Sussex – a listed medieval
     house remodelled by Lutyens. In replanning
     for a new owner, new and appropriate
     windows were needed.

48b Interior at Plumpton Place, lit by new
     windows.

changing requirements. What more unforeseen problems may yet come along, perhaps with changing income and tax structures, or with unknown estate duties and settlements which can sometimes take so long to resolve? We must try to look to the future, recognising that circumstances may well continue to change. Even centuries of family ownership may come to their eventual end (see Chevening, p. 137).

Equally, our advice may be to guide a new purchaser, who may have very different views and needs from those of his predecessors. At Plumpton Park in Sussex, a handsome medieval house set in lovely grounds had been extended and altered (1927–37) by no less an architect than Sir Edwin Lutyens, who provided for his then client[1] a music room with relatively windowless walls, as setting for its performers. Alterations to a Lutyens building are undertaken with temerity, so it was necessary in 1984 to design and negotiate – to the satisfaction not only of the new owner, but of the wider world, including the specialist Lutyens Society – a solution to encourage the continuing life and enjoyment of the house, and thereafter to help in effectively realising it.

Leaseholders

If a building occupant is a leaseholder, all his own considerations will be in the context of the likely duration of his tenancy. If this is limited, or if indeed for other reasons such as age, his expectations of its enjoyment are relatively short, another important criterion is the degree of likely disturbance involved in building work. There is no point in ignoring this, which can otherwise so easily result in an owner spending money, but only purchasing years of regret.

Equally, it may be possible to meet the stipulations of a lease while at the same time negotiating its extension, thus setting today's expenditure against a longer future benefit. Conversely, we have advised landowning estates about terms and conditions for lease renewals, which will better reflect the long-term interests of a property. Even public acquisition may on occasion release new funding, as in London's decaying Georgian houses in Camden (p. 164).

Multiple owners or tenants

We may also be called upon to advise not a single owner, but a family trust or a company, a parish, or a public or even a national authority. In those cases there are more people who must satisfy themselves about any proposals, and more elaborate procedures to meet in decision-making, in releasing capital and in budget and income planning. Two prominent current concerns for public authorities are access arrangements for the disabled, and escape provisions in the event of fire. The magnificent Town Hall at Liverpool, dating from 1754 and largely rebuilt by James Wyatt in 1802 had for long been largely unusable. Internal replanning of circulation systems, with fire-resistant doors and new escape routes, has enabled full use of this valuable public building to be resumed (p. 231).

---

[1] Edward Hudson, founder of *Country Life* magazine.

49a

49b

49a London's Banqueting House: the Crypt, as found.

49b Banqueting House: after conversion.

49c Analysis of confused circulation.

49d A new and rationalised use-plan.

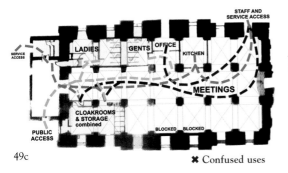

49c

✖ Confused uses

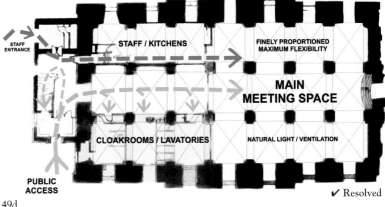

49d

✔ Resolved

While the owner-occupier can often decide for himself about the many details that will affect him intimately, a corporate occupant such as a university or club or society, or office-owning accountants or lawyers, may wish to delegate this power to an independent project manager or to a sub-committee entrusted with day-to-day decisions and perhaps with its own professional advisor.

Historic properties may, by bequest or other means, come into the collective responsibility of a public or private trust. Trustees usually need to satisfy themselves that they have reviewed every alternative possibility, taking every demonstrable and justifiable step to secure what appears to be the best financial value, even if sometimes with less regard for factors of time and personal convenience. Elected local authority members may represent the competing demands of specific minority groups within a cyclical re-election pattern, and may equally be keen to demonstrate clearly how well their electors' views have been taken into full account.

Neighbourhood involvement

In area and neighbourhood studies involving the dynamic forces of a living urban community, the multi-ownership of properties may call for extensive group or local authority participation. Talks, public meetings and discussions about broader as well as detailed issues will enable coordinated and more positive action. So there are great differences in the type of assistance we can be asked to provide; and our services must be tailored to match the scale of ownership, whether corporate or individual.

50a

 *(50b image — architectural section drawing)*

50b

50a At Gonville and Caius College, Cambridge, underused accommodation was converted and equipped as an auditorium.

50b At the request of the College, valuable off-street parking was reincorporated under the new raked seating.

Degrees of assistance

The range and degree of our assistance will also vary greatly. A private owner may able to take his decisions promptly, and without reference beyond his immediate family. But if his building is listed as being of special architectural importance, and particularly if he has to propose significant external alterations, or needs a loan or grant to help with repairs, then the field of necessary negotiations and discussions will inexorably widen. If significant repairs or re-ordering work are to be carried out at a Church of England place of worship, whether historic or otherwise, not only the Parish Church Council's agreement will be needed but a Faculty has to be obtained from the diocese. At a Cathedral a Fabric Advisory Committee and the Cathedrals Fabric Commission for England will also require to be satisfied before any major alterations can be undertaken. In all these directions, building owners and users will need a guiding hand.

Setting priorities

It will help to be aware both of any immediate 'trigger' event, as well as the longer-term incentives that have urged an owner to take action and to start thinking about building work or alterations. A very apparent structural failure, or an event like a fall of stone or a new crack, may have prompted worry and anxiety.[1] Perhaps a long history of inefficiency and confusion may now have come to a head, or an owner's plans for increased use of a building have revealed shortcomings, which must now be met. Changes may be needed when opening a house to the public or to meet increasing visitor demands, as Woburn Abbey (p. 51) or at Knebworth (pp. 170–171). There may be a forthcoming marriage, or the prospect of children. Occasionally a windfall or a legacy will have encouraged an owner or organisation to carry out plans otherwise long delayed.

On occasion too, a disaster such as a fire (pp. 210–220 on the conflagration of 1992 at Windsor Castle) may bring a silver lining by revealing a concealed history, or enabling long-overdue improvements in practical matters such as internal circulation and management.

[1] At the Palace of Westminster in 1980, an evening debate was interrupted by the fall of a wooden ceiling-pendant, which narrowly escaped sitting peers. The ensuing repair programme is described on pages 116–125.

51a,b   At Woburn Abbey in the 1970s, the Duke of Bedford decided to convert wasted basements
as 'Silver Vaults' for a display of family treasures, now made accessible to visitors.

52a

52b

52a,b At Picton Castle, Pembrokeshire, in the 1960s, the private owner was concerned to cure damp problems from permeable stonework, requiring extensive tidying, repairs and repointing.

52c,d A redundant and disfiguring attic storey was removed, simplifying interiors and reducing future maintenance worries.

52c

52d

The owner's aims

Beyond any immediate cause, we ask ourselves what is the real driving force behind the initiative? For some, the initial motive will be financial: the return from a building may not have been covering its proper care, nor the investment it represents. Or a vacant site or some under-used land may have begun to reach a value that stimulates new investment; and surrounding redevelopments and neighbourhood changes may be bringing new opportunities and enhanced market values. For others, the real preoccupations may lie in personal family welfare, and in extending the life of a much-loved building and its familiar inherited furnishings.

In practice, long after initial decisions are taken, an owner's aims will continue to develop and change. Whether the initial stimulus was an appreciation of architecture, with its antiquity and continuity, or simply of exploiting and improving property values, it is surprising how many influencing factors will impinge upon one another. The very activity of planning ahead, and the excitement and drive of the project itself, can expand to become a real part of the exercise. So we must be alive to an awakening spirit of betterment and opportunity, sometimes bringing its own additional pressures for change. A commercial company may suddenly begin to sense the added prestige that its refurbished premises will bring for its public image. Or a local authority may recognise the political goodwill its building-improvement activities are generating, and the 'spin-off' value to the community of encouraging private owners in its area to do likewise. So it is always a help to recognise the main thrust that generates and drives a building project, and also to be awake to these extra motives it attracts, and thus to help to meet them to the full.

Even when the true purpose is clear and appreciated, we have to be sensitive to an owner's special attitudes to any particular building. Its 'image' for him may be compounded by many factors. A house may represent the continuity of a family; a religious building will possess special connotations of significance for the worshipping faithful. A defence installation will contain especially sensitive areas; security aspects are paramount not only in any military building, but in a surprising number of commercial ones. An owner's image of his building will be further influenced by his experience of others he has previously owned, lived or stayed in, as well as by some that he has only seen or even dreamed about. It will help him, especially when he is away from it, to be reminded of its special and unique qualities, and all its plus-and-minus factors. Here, our sequence of survey (observing facts), then analysis (forming opinions) and then plan (generating proposals), in that order, will offer a valuable sheet-anchor among changing opinions, and a reliable way of formulating sound ideas, and then of executing them.

Budget parameters

It is of course vital throughout any project and at every stage to keep it in step with the most important factor of all – the order of cost which an owner is prepared and able to contemplate. An early ranging-shot, however vague, will help him to clarify what degree of works, however desirable, he can at present hope to face and finance, whether from his own resources or with the help of any outside source of aid. There is no point in shaping up proposals and programmes that are likely to stretch beyond ever-available resources. Much potential anguish will be averted by establishing available and reliable parameters on budgeting. In this respect, it may be possible to help with advice on priorities and on the financial phasing of work. Or we may be able to help with ideas on income-raising to help a property to 'wash its own face'. Similarly, it will be important to keep his advisors' own time expenditure carefully in step with an owner's immediate perceptions of sensible outlay.

53a

53a,b Strict economies in post-war reconstruction at Clothworkers' Hall had entailed deferring any finer finishes. The opportunity was taken in 1986, of bringing the Livery Hall into a more appropriate standard for grand occasions and entertainment.

53b

Formulating the brief

Once we have really fully understood the owner's wishes and the reasons behind them, as well as the qualities of his building, we can formulate and shape our own brief, and any specific suggestions about our continuing role and involvement. What particular help can we best now give? How can we best contribute, from experience and from our own brand of skills, to everyone's maximum advantage? An owner's personal degree of involvement in his project is one element in arriving at a formula; so is that of his professional advisors. Where will our efforts be most useful? There may, or may not, already be drawings of the building as it exists; and these will be needed. Historical or other research will almost certainly also be required. One of our most valuable contributions will be to bring a fresh eye and a balanced judgement to bear, in devising solutions to match the problems. It is a rewarding experience to be able to make an independent assessment of a confused and rambling inheritance, to evaluate its merits and its hindrances, generating positive proposals for rational patterns of rescue and management.

The eventual stage of an architectural project will usually be its actual execution. In a majority of cases we will be asked to carry through the conversion and improvement works under our own direction on site. In other instances we can equally hand on the task to selected local architect colleagues, to carry out the work in its final detail. Sometimes too, it can with economies be carried out directly by estate staff, or with the aid of periodical advisory visits by us. The possibilities are many. The further illustrations on pages 229–261 exemplify some of the many varying situations in which the architect can give valuable help.

54a

54a   The new basement staircase under the branching main stair at the Goldsmiths' Hall.

55a   Improvements to Goldsmiths' Hall.

55b   Wasted basement spaces ...

55c   ... now converted as toilets and foyer.

Advising a City Livery Company

For two decades in the life of the building, we acted as consultant architects to the Worshipful Company of Goldsmiths, maintaining and enhancing its magnificent Livery Hall. The Hall, within the handsome 1835 building by Philip Hardwick, was designed by Aitchison in 1892.

Our role entailed attendance at regular House Committee meetings, complemented by extra work from colleagues when needed – especially in the busy annual summer recess.

In 1988–90 a major restoration and adaptation programme was completed in association with the Company's surveyors. This involved the scaffolding, total redecoration and re-carpeting of the historic Livery Hall, while adapting and completely refurbishing previously wasted vaulted basement spaces. A new downward stair, immediately beneath the great branched staircase, has extended the distinguished interiors to the basements in which circulation space, generous cloakroom and toilet accommodation are now provided.

GOLDSMITHS' HALL

The refurbished
Livery Hall

New downward
staircase

55a

55b

55c

Village and town studies: survey data

In studying owner requirements, a special case is the village, town or city survey. Here, the 'team' approach (pp. 15 onwards) has been an essential ingredient. To ease the task of collecting comparable data, we have found it useful to design practical site-survey forms, to stimulate and remind us of our goal. As there is very little point in collecting information for its own sake, these must be tuned to the end-purpose of the particular survey, and the degree and detail of attention appropriate to the immediate task. For having arranged access and embarked upon evaluating places and buildings in a balanced way, one inevitably begins to evolve particular norms and (even unconscious) cross-comparisons and it is next to impossible to return later and fill any gaps.

The best survey-forms are those that provide for immediate on-site completion, whatever the weather, by a minimum of simple pen-work but without excluding anything unexpected. They must stimulate observation and above all, an imaginative and positive response, and always by reference to the wider context. Aspects to be noted may not only be factual but also involve opinion; one needs to be clear which is which. Data such as the number of floors are relevant, but so are physical condition (state of repair), architectural condition (authenticity, quality, potential) and both the facts of ownership (freehold, tenancy, changing hands) and also value-judgements about suitability for purpose, economic validity and the like. Broad comparative estimates of repair-costs, and even suggestions about likely sources of aid, have proved invaluable in programming for a building's continuing use and care. A grading of relative urgencies is equally vital.

Whether we are concerned with individual buildings, a terrace or a whole historic area, every assessment will involve a personal opinion – the mind behind the surveying eye – so the record must include names and dates, and especially a summary targeted upon practical and affordable action.

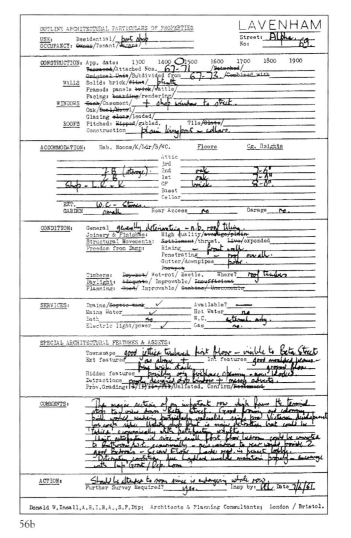

56a

56b

Town surveys

Inspections: Points to watch

1 What structural defects are apparent or inherent? How can they be cured or prevented?

2 What architectural detractions have occurred, or are likely? How can they be remedied or avoided?

3 What may be the effect of likely neighbourhood or ownership changes? How might the building best adapt?

4 Is the building suited for its present purpose? What alternatives might appropriately be allowed or encouraged?

5 How can the economic viability of the building be influenced, to promote its continued use and care?

56a,b Inspection forms: two forms used in collecting survey data (smaller town and larger city).

57a An inspection checklist.

57b Town and village surveys: collecting local opinions (Lavenham, 1961).

57a

57b

2. Befriending the building

Survey and assessment

Once we know and understand the owner's needs, we can devote ourselves to meeting and, as it were, 'befriending' and understanding his building. We have often felt that for us, the encounter is very similar to that of the medical doctor in meeting, examining and diagnosing the health of a patient. The state of health of a neighbourhood or building varies just as much, and in a similar fashion reflects its age and physique and its behaviour, and the way it has been used and treated.

What preparations do we make, what equipment do we need, and how do we go about our task? In assessing a building, we find we must first be responsive and intensely aware. Just as communication with people is not by word alone, so a building speaks to those who listen. In conversation, attitudes and gestures (or sometimes, even omissions) are significant – they convey an unspoken message. In our survey, we can learn much from intense observation, and by being alert to every nuance of information. In practice, we find it difficult to maintain this level of receptiveness for more than two or three days, after which a break is essential, to refresh our depth of awareness.

At the same time, we must never for a moment forget the 'image' that an owner or inhabitant creates from his building, during the relatively short time he shares in its life. The task of the architect is to marry potential with need, to maximise merits and dissolve problems by befriending both the user and his building, acting as representative and agent for both.

Some survey requirements

The first essential is clarity about the purpose of any survey. What may be entirely appropriate for one client could well be useless for another. One of several types of surveys may be necessary:

- The **survey for purchase** is a typical but very particular category. Even here, the relationship of user to building must be borne constantly in mind. Is it appropriate to his needs – or if not, could it readily be made so? And what are its present functional problems, its condition and repair needs, and at what cost can they be remedied?

- Another variant is the **maintenance survey**, where the building is already owned and probably in use and occupied. But whether from a concern at manifest problems or preferably on some more regular management basis (such as the quinquennial surveys now and since 1955 so sensibly required for churches), its condition may now call for a balanced reassessment. Sometimes the subject is a solo building; but it may equally be a group with a single owner, such as a hospital site, a college campus or estate. Then the problem becomes more complex. The buildings may be of varied dates and qualities, with varying demands. Help will be needed in assessing them, not only individually but in relation to one another, and in recognising priorities and programming within a planned budget.

- A more radical requirement is the **feasibility study**, required when conversion works are considered. These may well include repairs; but we must look more widely, and not only at what is visible but also at every latent potential, requiring more exercise of the imagination. In effect, it is the survey for purchase turned inside-out, for it is the building itself that now seeks a user, and it may have to adapt itself to attract a logical function and ownership, with sufficient resources to project and extend its life.

- There are many types of **specialist survey**, such as the scholarly historical or archaeological investigation, or a technical examination for timber pests and decay, or an assessment of compliance with regulations, such as those involving disabled access or escape in case of fire. Specialist surveys can easily become misleading by the inherent narrowness of their viewpoint, so they need to be interpreted in relation to one another, and to the balanced requirements of the building and its user.

Extent and limits

When examining a single building, what are the physical limits of our survey? The question runs deeper than it may seem. A piece of architecture has precise 'edges' but in the mind of an owner, its image goes beyond the centreline of its party walls, and far through the glass of its windows. For the owner, it is inseparable from the external context that includes its neighbours, its view and its garden. Internally too, in the owner's imagination, the decorative schemes, floor-coverings and furnishings are at one with its walls. We must establish how far to look, and just where to draw the line in our analysis, yet recognising these wider aspects of impact and image.

Another dimension we must know, to inform our survey, is its required extent and degree of detail. Sometimes it may be sensible to prepare for the fuller study by first carrying out a reconnaissance, to identify the major queries. In assessing a group of buildings, is each one to be examined, and each in equal degree? In an urban area, even a relatively rapid assessment by the trained eye will establish the relative merits and the condition of building groups, and can many times cover its cost by arresting expensive and rampant troubles. We all seem as yet curiously unconscious of this, and make surprisingly little effort on the well-proven (although not infallible) medical parallel of the mass X-ray.

59a

59b

59c

59a,b,c   An outstanding early example of Gothic architecture survives at Binham Priory church, in Norfolk. The beautiful 12th-century window tracery may even predate Westminster Abbey.
With the aid of an 1860s photograph (59a), it was possible, while replacing rusting ironwork and cleaning the upper tracery (59b), to reinstate the more appropriate earlier pattern of leaded glazing (59c).

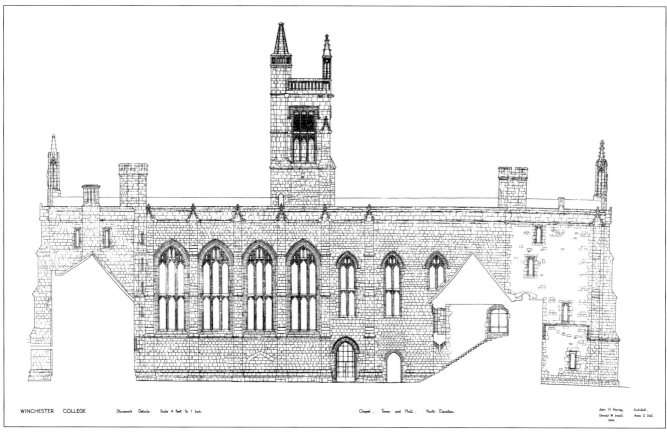

WINCHESTER COLLEGE   Stonework Details . Scale 4 feet to 1 inch.   Chapel , Tower and Hall ; North Elevation.   John H. Harvey,   Architect ,
                                                                                                                                                            Donald W. Insall .   Mона & Dell .
                                                                                                                                                                    1954.

Simple photogrammetry enables the accurate recording of stonework-jointing (Winchester College: a detailed survey for the archivist, John Harvey).

Throughout, we try to assess the changing influences of time – in the past, and with an eye to the future. An understanding of the life-story of each building[1] is essential in outlining and colouring the unique character and personality it has today.

Research, drawings and definitions

Before visiting, we research all available background information. We seek out data, both from central and from local sources, including any old drawings or engravings and early photographs, which can be very revealing about a building's history.

We pursue any previous history of modern planning applications, permissions or refusals. Sometimes public or private files and museum records give a valuable clue to the state of a building and its repairs in the past. We look at its wider context, to see how its history of changes and any past and current planning proposals may affect its continuing life in the future.

If no drawings are available, one of the first tasks on site may be to prepare them, even initially as a basis for the survey. But drawings can all too easily become an end in themselves. We must regard each one at best as an abstraction; it need be no more accurate or detailed than its purpose requires. A simple diagram may be sufficient to identify rooms and spaces. A more

accurate record will enable us to work out detailed conversion possibilities, and, for example, to check the feasibility of any improvement proposals, such as ideas for new access openings or an inserted staircase. When orthographic drawings are needed, we can sometimes measure and plot these approximately on graph paper as we go. For greater accuracy, precise dimensions are taken by tape or rod, noted on site and later plotted to scale in the office. Architects can usefully learn to use basic photogrammetry[2], as employed in our pioneer work for the archivist at Winchester College as long ago as 1954, for recording stonework coursing and jointing.

For certain purposes such as recording the condition of stonework, large rectified photographs can be made, and offer a useful medium for notes added directly by hand. Commonsense will guide the selection of the most appropriate method, with the most sensible economy in time. Incidentally too, the practised eye can achieve remarkable feats of approximate recording – the fruit of a lifetime's experience.

---

[1] A good example is the complex structural history of St Margaret's Church, King's Lynn (p. 127).
[2] See *Architectural Photogrammetry*: a report by the author to the RIBA, 1955.

61a

61b

61c

61d

We must be able to refer clearly to each part of a building, both in our notes and in any later report. So the next decision is how to describe them. A decisive (even if arbitrarily simplified) north-point will certainly help. Precise names or numbering of rooms, coded if possible to express their geographical location, their floor level or their use (or indeed, all three) will enable ready description and avoid mistakes. We sometimes have to devise what is almost a 'vocabulary' for repetitive elements. In a survey of an elaborate wooden ceiling (The Palace of Westminster, p. 117) we had to invent a clear system of names for each repetitive member – in that instance 'major beam', 'minor beam', 'panel', 'trophy' and 'rosette' (61a,b). In this way each observation can be identified accurately and in context, to enable us to carry out a faithful repair or reinstatement.

Access

When arrangements are being made for our survey, we stress the necessity of ready access so that we can look everywhere in logical sequence, without the problems of finding lost keys or an adequate ladder. Occasionally a light scaffold is valuable for closer inspections. Once we know an owner's requirements, we do like to assess a building on its own and unaccompanied, so that we

61a,b   On-site recording. Drawings can clearly identify structural elements for reference purposes.

61c   Inspections can be hazardous!

61d   Danger: loose glass in a skylight …

61e   … and a fallen slate.

61e

can be alert to its message. But inspections can involve site hazards; any single-person survey must avoid all unnecessary risks, especially in dangerous buildings or confined spaces, or when working at heights.

When examining a building in use, it is helpful if occupants are already aware of the survey and its purpose: they may also be able to contribute valuable

62a

62c

62b

62d

62a Exposed chimney stonework dislocated by frost and ice.

62b Built against a hill. A wet internal wall seems here a likely hazard.

62c Trapped water, turned to ice, has separated the outer 'skin' of a brick semidome.

62d Ancient damage caused by the collapse of a long-gone heavy roof lantern (King's Lynn, p. 129).

information. It is also wise to notify all concerned before carrying out a study of an entire village or urban area. This is readily done by a standard letter through every letterbox, or through the local press. Otherwise, the presence of a person with a clipboard looking through windows can be disturbing or even ominous. But we have always found that if people are properly advised, they are amazingly willing to help.

Sequence of inspection

We use pocket recorders for notetaking on site, because we find they free the eyes to observe. We aim to follow a standard routine and discipline, starting our initial examination with the exterior. This enables us quickly to assess and identify the physical form of a building, together with its external relationship with others, the underlying landform and its pattern of exposure. Digital photography is valuable, both as an unstinting aid to the record and memory and later, by providing a ready basis for communicating further ideas and instructions.

First (and incidentally, in case it rains later) we look at the roofs. No building is in better fettle than its hat – the primary protection against the weather. We examine every roof surface, closely noting the condition and likely life of its coverings and any existing or incipient defect. We remember the far-reaching effects of driving rain, wind and snow, envisaging what will happen if any main rainwater route is blocked or if water becomes trapped in the structure. We note the condition of exposed features such as chimneys. Working downwards, we scrutinise the external walls, with each of their window and door openings, taking careful note of their form, materials and present condition. At the foot, we trace and inspect (and where necessary, may also test) the system of rainwater collection and disposal, drains and services, with an eye for past and future trouble.

Moving indoors, we familiarise ourselves with the layout of rooms, and with the loadbearing system of the walls and floors between them. We make enquiries about any invisible spaces such as a sealed-off cellar, or a hidden mezzanine store. The area most eloquent of change is often the roof-space or attic. If a wing has been added, there may be, for example, surviving rafters of an earlier roof-slope, complete with nailholes indicating where tiling battens once were. In one building we examined recently, we found two houses of differing date. Set alongside one another, they had been unified behind a combined brick façade, whose irregular window rhythm this immediately explained.

The unequal roofs had been packed out to present a single front slope, but with a narrow lead flat at ridge-level, quite unseen from below. Inside an old roof space, there are often clues to unlock the whole history of growth and change, explaining inconsistencies in structure, and differential movements between work of one date and another.

After inspecting the roof space, we go on to examine in detail each floor of rooms in descending succession, and in methodical clockwise sequence. Many features or problems only explain themselves when seen in context with others: the lower part of a sagging upper wall may prove to have been removed, without substituting adequate supports. Old damage, or a new and additional load at an upper level, may have caused otherwise unexplained movement and distortion in the structure below. Finally, any cellars can be a mine of information about a house and its structural history. Sometimes even, there may be several successive underground floors at more than one level.

Original shortcomings

In an imperfect world, virtually every building has been heir to its own original shortcomings. Sometimes what we see betrays weaknesses of design, such as local overloading or a failure to balance structural thrusts. Now may be the opportunity to rectify them, giving fresh heart to a sagging beam, or introducing extra ties between unsupported members, or spreading a load over a wider and stronger area of support.

Buttress betrays past structural movement. Cause – perhaps a spreading roof truss?

64a

64b

64c

More frequently, time will have sought out local weaknesses in weather protection. Gutters and flashings may have been skimped or forgotten – countless Georgian terraces today betray the cost of what initially seemed to be savings and economies. And some features like parapet walls are a regular source of trouble. The commonest failures are inadequate rainwater gutters and downpipes, lacking any provision for emergency overflow (see example: 133e). Less obvious but equally harmful shortcomings include copings with unprotected joints, or a lack of any proper throating (a groove on the underside) to prevent run-back under their water-shedding sills and ledges. We watch constantly for such weaknesses in an original construction, whether decades or centuries old. They may result from false economies, or just as often from taking undue liberties with good and straightforward principles of building.

Damaging alterations

While failings are in many cases original, later alterations or disasters are equally often responsible for points of structural weakness we may now discover. So throughout our inspection we keep a wary eye for structural movement, looking for its causes and determining whether the forces it betrays are live or expended. An added buttress may indicate past problems, and cracks and displacements will speak clearly of unresolved movements, dead or still alive.

A beautifully triangulated timber structure may have failed at a joint, or its geometry may have been interfered with, as when a roof-tie has been cut off

64a Rainwater pipe, buried in an angle of walling, and leaking at the back.

64b Parapet gutter in trouble (Wotton House, Bucks).

64c A cracked baluster, caused by displacement of its stone handrail.

64d An important roof-tie has been cut through, probably to provide extra headroom.

64d

65a

in the act of making a new attic doorway. Old stone windows with a succession of mullions may have given place to Georgian sashes, whose wooden weight-boxes were not designed to carry any jointed stone lintels. Past attempts at damp-proofing a wall may conversely have retained water within it – with nowhere to evaporate, the water will have been driven further up. We have encountered endless ground floors in a wet and rotting condition, set over what should have been well-ventilated basements. And once again, external brickwork and stonework exhibit the folly of an over-hard repointing, driving frost and salts to the face of the walling and eroding it.

Conscious alterations and unconscious adaptations are equally to blame; sometimes they compound with an original weakness, and just as often they bring fresh failures to be countered and corrected, if a building is to be kept in good health.

Age and weathering

No building is eternal: every structure bespeaks its age, and wind and weather take their toll. Throughout our survey we watch for the continually changing effects of rain and frost, the natural abrasive wear of the elements and the wear-and-tear of daily use.

The illustrations in this chapter show some of the typical tokens of time that we encounter, bearing in mind their reactions upon one another and upon the building's users, and all within the cycles of decay and renewal of each element and material. A quick review will confirm the adage that every building's enemy is in league with water; it is essential to realise how fundamentally dynamic and changing is the daily pattern of moisture-movement. In effect, each structure constantly 'breathes' moisture both in and out, in sympathy with its surroundings and with the weather and varying with its exposure and use.

65b

65a   Wet bricks have eroded, set in over-hard mortar.

65b   Movement in a crenellated parapet, the Great Wall of China.

Accommodation and potential, services and equipment

We like to ask ourselves what use each space receives, and what functions it can now most usefully meet. Could a roof space be adapted and used, if some inconvenient pipes were re-routed and if access were improved? Is the use-pattern logical? Or would it help to rethink and improve the circulation layout, and perhaps provide for useful new possibilities? If it is true that any building includes its own outward views, are these enjoyed to the full? Or might an extra window add value to a room? We may by now know whether the owner has considered the effects of passing time upon his own life, and of future changing family patterns. His architect may be able to help him to do this more objectively, and to recognise future needs to which he has previously given little thought.

66a

66b

66c

66a,b,c   Outdated domestic equipment may be of historic
value. An old wooden kitchen sink; a fine wall-
clock and house-bells for servants long since
vanished; and some handsome plumbing.

This attack of dry rot is well-advanced, and could be fatal to its building. Emergency attentions may be vital.

Services such as piped water, gas and electricity, together with new mechanical and electronic equipment, have revolutionised domestic life. Much of our building stock has yet to catch up. A castle was designed to function around its precious water supply – its well – and discharged the soil to its moat. A country house collected its own rainwater to storage tanks, usually in the roof or sometimes in the cellar. Lamps burning candles and oil had to be serviced. There would have been an icehouse in the grounds and a knife-cleaning machine in the kitchen. Coal fires in every room provided warmth; tending them created a great deal of domestic employment. Before mains electricity arrived, coal-gas was piped in, or a petrol engine generated a private supply. Some of the more antiquated services and fittings may still have their own special interest and value.

Yet already, only decades later, we have already the chimneyless housing estate. Technical development has accelerated over recent years to such a degree that in almost every building we see, improvements in

equipment and services can immediately be suggested. We try to observe and to use our imagination, with both the latest and potential future equipment in mind. Even if a much-needed lift cannot be afforded now, it may still be wise at least to reserve the only possible space for it.

Completing the survey

Finally, we ask 'what have we so far missed?' Are there questions still not addressed, or are a further opinion or urgent remedial work needed? Should we recommend specialist surveys dealing in more detail with pests, wood-borers or disinfestation, or the testing of the electrical or heating installations, lightning conductors and similar services? These important matters may demand fuller exploration or assessment and more urgent attention than is possible on an initial visit or only by eye.

Before taking our leave from our survey visit, we establish that everything necessary has been examined, that no stone – or indeed key – remains unturned, and that any helpers have been thanked, security staff informed, lights turned off and ladders returned to safety. A day-long state of hyper-observation can be immensely fatiguing: on one occasion I turned to leave the building, said how happy we were to help, and 'goodbye'; then I exhaustedly opened a door and almost walked into a cupboard. But like all pursuit of knowledge, careful survey is curiously satisfying; and the reward of arriving at reliable results will soon outstrip in the memory, any pain of the process.

Ten conservation maxims

- **Observe** what is there
- **Understand** it
- What are its **merits**?
- What **detractions**?
- What should we **keep**?
- What to **remove**?
- What may we **add**?
- In what **character**?
- And how to **relate**?
- Finally, how to **provide** continuing care?

3. Analysis and report

The primary purpose of our survey has been to arrive at a balanced understanding of a building's merits and demands, in relation to its owner's needs. Our assessment will include both positive and negative factors, calling attention to any assets that may have been baulked by handicaps we could overcome.

We return from the survey with a rich but mixed harvest of information that has next to be marshalled into a more useful shape. Here we again try to identify ourselves with an owner's special personal wishes and requirements, our ultimate criterion being to ask ourselves, 'What would I do, if I were he, and if this building, with all its opportunities and problems, were my own?'

In assessing the origins and history of the building and learning of its subsequent life history, we begin to understand its living structure and the effects of its locality and construction, materials and changing uses. As we critically examine its health and its potential, some revealing patterns may begin to emerge.

Drawings and graphics

From the dimensions taken, we will first transfer the shape and arrangement of the building safely onto paper. This is simply now a job of converting digits into comprehensible plottings, whether by hand or computer. For sensible economy, it is essential to know the likely purpose of our drawings, what degree of accuracy they may ever be required to show, and what measure of reliance they may accordingly carry. They should preferably appear no more accurate than they are; the graphics may well be freehand, but we shall keep all measurements and sketches, to act as a reliable basis for any continuing or future assessment. Original data are a valuable record of accurate dimensions at a given

date, so we may in a few instances even keep a legible copy of them for the record. Site photographs are similarly an invaluable continuing source of evidence. Modern computer-aided recording and reproduction processes are extraordinarily helpful and have their huge advantages, although we find that informal explanatory sketches, such as analytical diagrams

68a,b   Computer and hand-drawings.

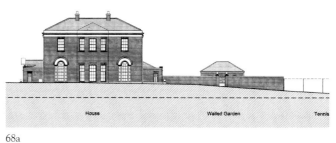

68a

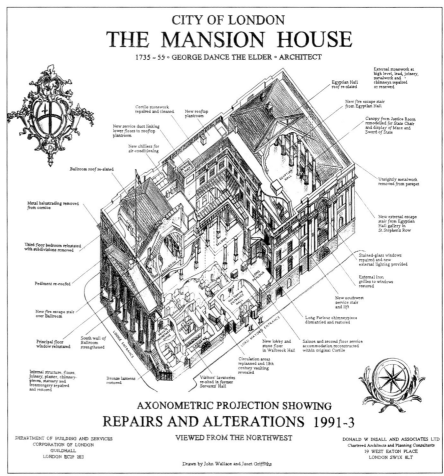

68b

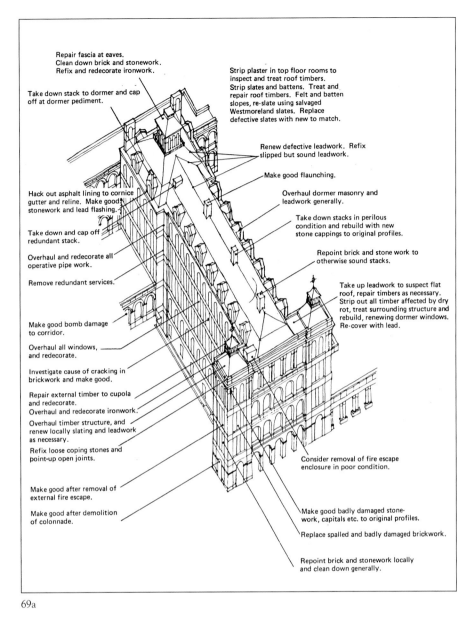

Repair fascia at eaves.
Clean down brick and stonework.
Refix and redecorate ironwork.

Take down stack to dormer and cap off at dormer pediment.

Strip plaster in top floor rooms to inspect and treat roof timbers. Strip slates and battens. Treat and repair roof timbers. Felt and batten slopes, re-slate using salvaged Westmoreland slates. Replace defective slates with new to match.

Renew defective leadwork. Refix slipped but sound leadwork.

Make good flaunching.

Overhaul dormer masonry and leadwork generally.

Hack out asphalt lining to cornice gutter and reline. Make good stonework and lead flashing.

Take down and cap off redundant stack.

Overhaul and redecorate all operative pipe work.

Remove redundant services.

Take down stacks in perilous condition and rebuild with new stone cappings to original profiles.

Repoint brick and stone work to otherwise sound stacks.

Take up leadwork to suspect flat roof, repair timbers as necessary. Strip out all timber affected by dry rot, treat surrounding structure and rebuild, renewing dormer windows. Re-cover with lead.

Make good bomb damage to corridor.

Overhaul all windows, and redecorate.

Investigate cause of cracking in brickwork and make good.

Repair external timber to cupola and redecorate.
Overhaul and redecorate ironwork.

Overhaul timber structure, and renew locally slating and leadwork as necessary.

Refix loose coping stones and point-up open joints.

Make good after removal of external fire escape.

Make good after demolition of colonnade.

Consider removal of fire escape enclosure in poor condition.

Make good badly damaged stonework, capitals etc. to original profiles.

Replace spalled and badly damaged brickwork.

Repoint brick and stonework locally and clean down generally.

69a

69a,b   Isometric and section drawings (St Thomas's Hospital): defining original buildings and successive additions and indicating recommendations for repair.

of constructional details, can still be very useful. Often, impressions and jottings onto a plan direct from site may be perfectly acceptable in clarifying instruction drawings and giving flesh to their artificially rectilinear bones.

Given good basic plans, we like to plot and interrelate our ideas and observations in a way we can share; this has produced a method of graphic analysis that many owners find extremely useful. Structural aspects, for example, can be emphasised, distinguishing between load-bearing walls and non-supporting partitions. Plans can group and regroup rooms and areas by date, or by floor level, ceiling height, or by degree of architectural or any other merit. They can identify and underline the access and circulation pattern, drawing attention to positive horizontal and vertical links, and to negative elements such as barriers or any impediments to easy movement. They can isolate features such as daylighting and aspect, or the prospect from windows, or any groupings of plumbing and services, and factors such as use-patterns and their interrelationships, clearly indicating them for comparison in simple coloured diagrams. They can simply set out needed repairs, or they can express and bring forward latent potentialities, often as yet unrealised. By direct comparisons

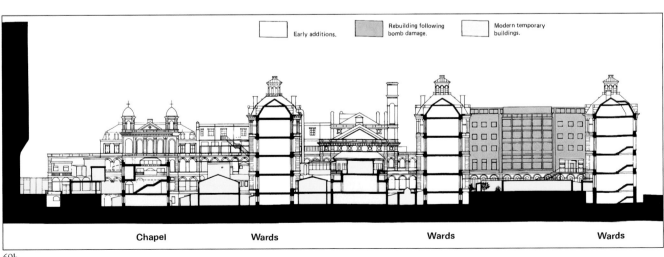

Early additions.

Rebuilding following bomb damage.

Modern temporary buildings.

Chapel   Wards   Wards   Wards

69b

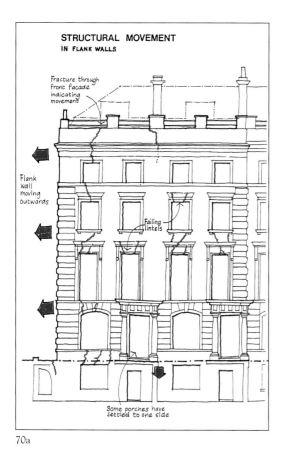

Fracture through front facade indicating movement

Flank wall moving outwards

Failing lintels

Some porches have settled to one side

70a

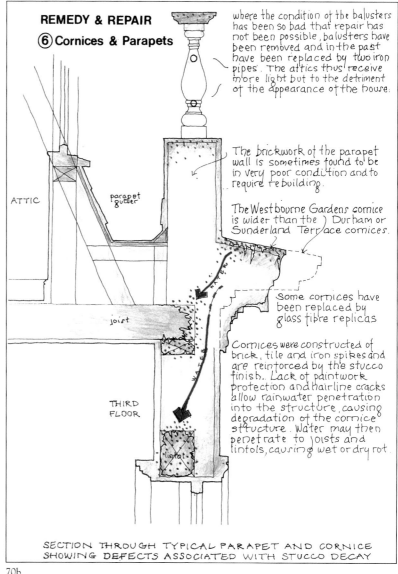

REMEDY & REPAIR
⑥ **Cornices & Parapets**

where the condition of the balusters has been so bad that repair has not been possible, balusters have been removed and in the past have been replaced by two iron pipes. The attics thus receive more light but to the detriment of the appearance of the house.

ATTIC

parapet gutter

The brickwork of the parapet wall is sometimes found to be in very poor condition and to require rebuilding.

The Westbourne Gardens cornice is wider than the Durham or Sunderland Terrace cornices.

joist

Some cornices have been replaced by glass fibre replicas

THIRD FLOOR

Cornices were constructed of brick, tile and iron spikes and are reinforced by the stucco finish. Lack of paintwork protection and hairline cracks allow rainwater penetration into the structure, causing degradation of the cornice structure. Water may then penetrate to joists and lintols, causing wet or dry rot.

SECTION THROUGH TYPICAL PARAPET AND CORNICE SHOWING DEFECTS ASSOCIATED WITH STUCCO DECAY

70a   Diagrams: structural movement in flank walls at Westbourne Grove, London.

70b   Water seeks out vulnerable timbers.

70b

between one diagram and another, all these aspects of a building can readily be studied and related, even when they are much less apparent on site. In our initial study of Windsor Castle after the fire, we prepared a series of transparent overlays from historic plans, enabling us to obtain a valuable appreciation and understanding of the building's developing history.

Our aim is to make simple drawings that speak for themselves; it can prove a revelation to an owner or a valuable talking-point to a neighbourhood amenity group to have observations plotted and set down in this way. We strive for a clear notation, perhaps amplifying colour by symbols, such as added ticks for good features or crosses for weak ones, or a simple question mark to pinpoint a problem.

Clear analysis sketches are extremely useful, because they enable the thinking behind all our discussions to be quickly checked, demonstrated and understood.

They are valuable too, in helping an owner with continuing explanations and negotiations, or when trustees or committees are involved, or with complex matters of estate and financial planning. The impact of good drawings is immediate and more comprehensible than words; and if they are based on well-observed data, they will enable everyone to arrive at clearer and wiser decisions.

The report

At this stage, a formal report is likely to be needed. The content, emphasis and format will again vary greatly with its purpose and with the real aim of the project constantly borne in mind. The report should effectively promote the real aim of the project.

For order and consistency, we like to work from the general to the particular, and from fact to opinion. In this way, detail falls within its broader framework,

PLANNING ANALYSIS

sunshine - or lack of it

good and poor outlook

bad feature

significant blocked window

State Apartments

Good quality rooms

Domestic suite

Poor quality rooms

Remote rooms

Museum rooms

Single storey addition

Dining rooms

Circulation and communication (on elevations)

Circulation (on plan)

71a

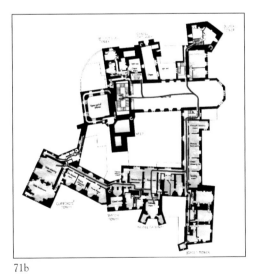

71b

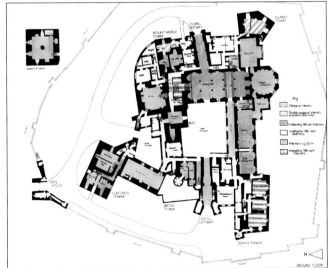

71c

71a   Analysing a magnificent aggregation of centuries of history:
Raby Castle.

71b,c   Access and circulation problems identified in analysis plans at
successive floors.

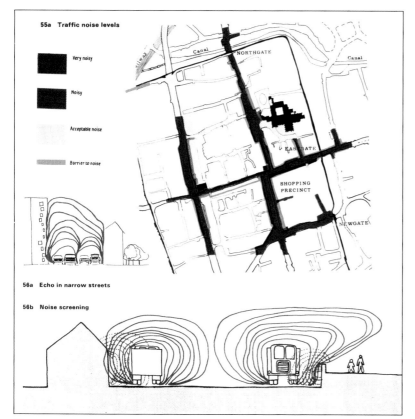

55a Traffic noise levels

- Very noisy
- Noisy
- Acceptable noise
- Barrier to noise

56a Echo in narrow streets

56b Noise screening

72a

Fire spread

72b

72a   Traffic noise in Chester: plotted and analysed.

72b   Clear diagrams: danger of fire-spread (Thaxted).

72c,d Battle Abbey Gatehouse: proposals for displays and
       new visitor facilities (English Heritage); access and
       circulation diagram.

72c

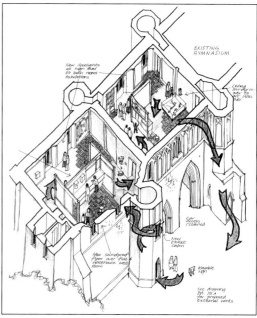

72d

both in historical sequence and in terms of spatial layout. Inevitably, every observation made will in part be subjective, reflecting the ideas and criteria of a surveyor; this is especially true of the comparisons, assessments and judgments he will make. We try in our reports to distinguish clearly between facts and assessments, moving from the known to the tentative, and from the observed to the proposed. Facts will come first, then observations; while any rapidly changing conditions will be separately noted for immediate attention.

In any study from the historical and architectural standpoint, descriptive writing will have its own particular place. A well-observed assessment demands accurate and careful expression, encapsulating and communicating real understanding. In this field, the tradition of reports by official architects investigating grant applications for historic buildings can provide an absolute model. When the aim is merely identification, there is less need for description. Even so, it seems a shame for the expert to resort to the average 'listing' catalogue of facts, with its finger-counting references to 'elevations of three floors with 23 sash windows on each flank'. If a visit is made, it is always rewarding to record the immediate reactions of the viewer: the trenchant comments of a Pevsner come immediately to mind. If a building is already well known, recorded and described, we can simply then refer the reader to the best available sources, and concentrate our time upon effectively outlining the actual problems to be solved.

The format of our report deserves careful planning. Is to be read at one sitting? And in context of the building, or away from it?

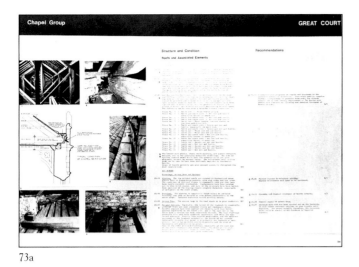

73a

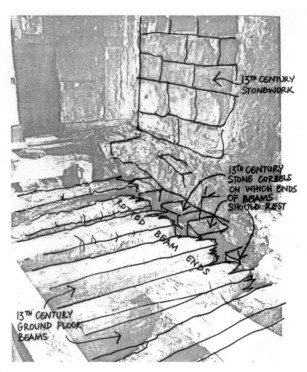

73b

73a   A three-column report: description, illustrations and recommendations.

73b   Explanatory overlay based on site photograph ('The Falcon', Chester).

Who will consult it, and how many copies will be needed? Some studies are simply 'one-off'; others will be published. In that instance, the cost of reproduction is significant and in turn affects the layout. Clear illustrations are always immensely telling and helpful. Photographs are quick and economical, and can be annotated directly. We need to remember that not every owner is able to climb onto roofs, or may be familiar even with readily accessible parts of a building. An ambassador will not necessarily be familiar with his embassy's kitchen, but he may well need to understand and provide for its improvement. Good illustrations help an owner to envisage problems and remedies, in a balanced way and with better knowledge.

Sketches or diagrams may 'locate' and explain observations we make, and will help in subsequent measurement and costing. In town survey reports, an example is the continuous street elevation (pp. 206–7), accompanied by overall measurements and occasional height checks. When referring to an individual building, a quick diagram defining either a removable addition or valuable vestige will speak volumes.

We state any initial assumptions we have made, because if these change in the future, the recommendations must also be varied to match. Examples in town surveys are current parking provisions and projections of traffic volume, or in individual buildings, a continuing standard of regular maintenance. We also record any limitations, such as conditions that make access difficult: close-carpeting of floors, or the loss of old

keys (this one is surprisingly frequent). We owe it to a building's owner to recommend any further or more detailed or specialist surveys needed, and what will be the right time for them.

We have in some instances used for certain reports (for example at Jesus and Trinity Colleges in Cambridge) a format of columns: description, comments and recommendations are set out side-by-side to avoid repetition, and are illustrated by photographs in close juxtaposition. Devices like transparent overlay pages can also be remarkably helpful in setting out analyses, or in making comparisons between proposals.

The recommendations we make will be phased according to urgency, the use of the building and current cost planning. Our conclusions will outline main repair items or improvements, in the context of the quality of the buildings and their use, and will set out relative priorities in a rational sequence. The cost dimension is vital. Very early financial checks on proposals are an essential element in any study; we involve the quantity surveyor as early as possible. In our report on the City of Chester (1968) (p. 195) we hazarded rough budget allocations to repair each of the 435 buildings we inspected. Although individual estimates were of necessity at that stage only offered as a guide, the report presented perhaps the first truly quantified assessment of the financial problems and requirements of any historic area at this scale.

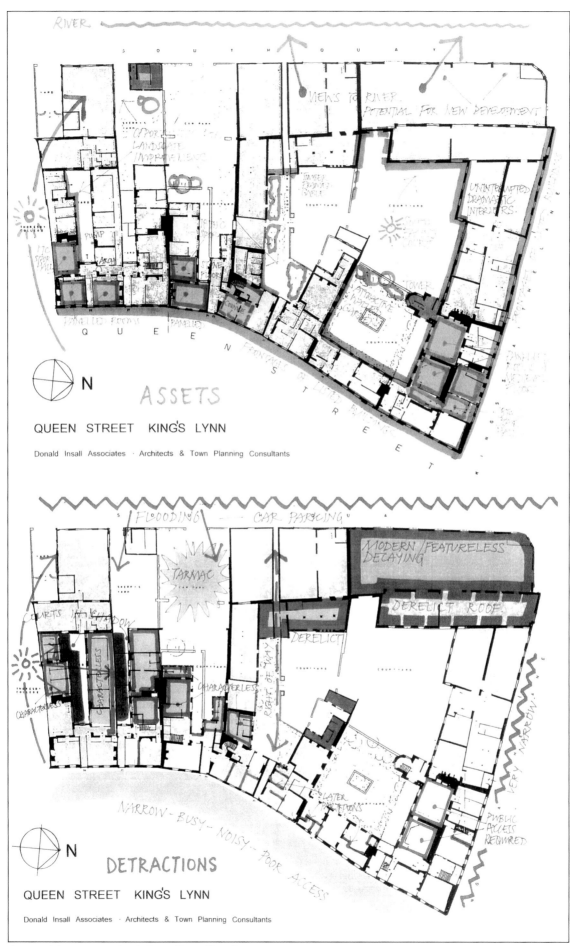

Assets and detractions analysed: Queen Street, Kings Lynn.

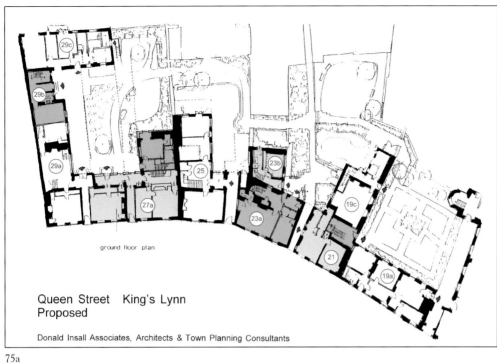

ground floor plan

Queen Street   King's Lynn
Proposed

Donald Insall Associates, Architects & Town Planning Consultants

75a

75a,b   Proposed conversions,
        moving entrances from busy
        street to combined rear
        gardens.

75c   The resulting conversions
        completed.

The result was that the bull could be taken by the horns, with high confidence of achieving real success, and free from the budgetary doubts that otherwise feed political uncertainty and dissolve the will to act.

We find that sometimes in addition to the written report, an informal visual presentation and discussion of ideas can greatly assist an owner in arriving at firmly based decisions. This especially applies to a gathering or committee of people. Presentations enable direct comparisons to be made immediately between two alternatives shown side-by-side, or between paired photographs of problems and ideas for their remedy.[1]

Above all, and whatever form of report is produced, we strive to make it a real action programme, leading the reader to a clear understanding of the way ahead, and saying what can be done and what should be done next. It sets out any immediate first-aid measures, and outlines the next steps to be taken, such as completing supplementary surveys, consulting with specialists or negotiating for statutory approvals or grant help.

Never must it become 'just another book on a shelf'.

---

[1] Experience helps: within our team, at office lunchtime talks and meetings, we try to give younger members the opportunity of presenting their schemes to their colleagues. The ability to communicate ideas is just as important as having them.

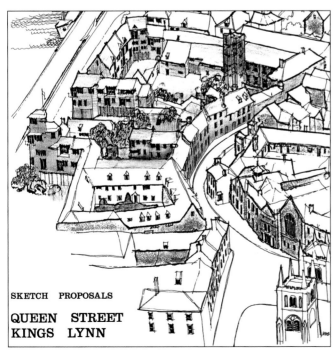

SKETCH PROPOSALS

QUEEN STREET
KINGS LYNN

75b

75c

4. Planning the project

If the first and essential step, and the secret of success, is to *identify* oneself – first with the *owner* and his requirements, then with the *building* and its problems and opportunities – then the next step is to identify with those *people*, the contractors, specialists and craftsmen, whose skills and hands will execute the work.

If our analysis and report on a building or architectural venture has done its job, an owner will now be able to see the future to some extent through our eyes, as well as his own. He may also now know more about the needs and possibilities of an existing building, of which he was previously unaware. Sometimes our verdict will simply be reassuring, but sometimes it will be more stimulating, identifying problems to be reconciled between the respective needs of the building and of its users. Although the receipt of our report may on occasion be met by instructions simply to 'go ahead with the work', more often time will need to be spent in discussion and on site, in exploring the art of the possible, to decide just what can be done, at what cost, and when.

The range of options may be wide, and clear-headed discussion is necessary. It is useful at this stage to keep accurate notes, especially when committees or other bodies such as resident groups are concerned, and to circulate clear minutes of all meetings, ideas and decisions.

Financial aspects and statutory requirements will of course colour every issue. The advice and input of technical advisors on problems of cost, structures and servicing will be helpful in avoiding wasted time and money. We always like to initiate consultation as early as possible, and to make early and informal contact with grant-giving bodies about financial aid, or with planning authorities, avoiding any later unfortunate misunderstandings and consequent loss of energy and momentum.

When the owner has decided on his course of action and is able to signal his wish to go ahead, our next task is to prepare the actual instructions – the drawings, specifications and schedules accurately describing the work to be done, in enough detail to allow us to obtain competitive prices, and to guide and control it.

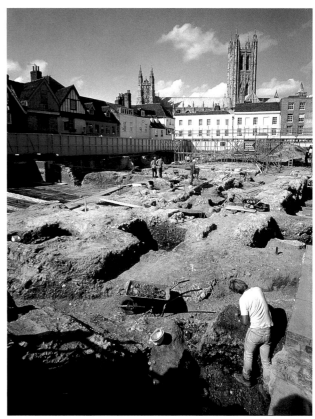

Preliminary investigation: phasing is important – redevelopment here in Canterbury awaited urgent rescue archaeology.

In preparing these, the essential tools are experience and knowledge, and an open and flexible approach. Every problem brings its own individual response. Experience may have built up a bank of useful answers for familiar conditions, but each and every specification must be tailor-made, and this is a special art. Any unknowns, such as the likely result of preliminary archaeological investigations, must be named and foreseen. The builder's estimator, and later his foreman, will need to be able to plan the sequence of subsequent operations, and to envisage exactly what is wanted. Traditionally this may be set out for new buildings on a trade-by-trade basis, or in an existing one, room-by-room, which is very often more satisfactory. The work must be very clearly envisaged, in the sequence in which it will happen. Otherwise a confused specification may arise, as in describing the reuse of a door which has not yet been removed from

77a

Phase III   Phase II (Hall)   Phase I

77a   Sequence and phasing of
      contracts (Speke Hall).

77b   'Unknowns' – exploration in
      progress: a succession of
      fireplaces.

somewhere else, and hanging it in a doorway that is not yet made. The specification has to be exhaustive, yet clear and comprehensible as a working set of practical instructions on site. Increasingly too, work may need to be described in separate packages, which a contractor can reliably delegate to subcontractors he may employ.

In specifying standards of workmanship and finish, we find it is important to set out exactly what is appropriate to the particular building. The desired standard is often determined by that of the original old work we are trying to match. Absolute perfection may be beyond achieving, let alone at affordable cost. But equally if the condition, for example, of old paintwork, has been steadily deteriorating with each successive coat, it may not be even a 'match' we are now seeking, so we must be very clear about exactly what it is that we expect.

We find it particularly important to say exactly what samples of material and workmanship we shall require, and what details like the routing of pipe-runs and wiring will need our prior approval on site.

Unknowns and contingencies

Old buildings frequently contain a high proportion of 'unknowns' in suspect areas where obviously something needs to be done; but where until they are opened up, no one can say exactly what. Traditionally, these are usually covered by an overall 'provisional sum', but our experience shows that this can be altogether too global, and with retrospective accounting may make effective cost control impossible. Instead, we have successfully used a scheme for allocating to each 'unknown' its own individual provisional sum; and by code-numbering it,

77b

referencing this on key drawings to the point in the building to which it is allocated. By this means, everyone knows how much can be afforded for the item when it is opened up; and by insisting on similarly coded daywork-sheets for it, effective cost-control becomes possible. 'Peter-and-Paul' items can then to some extent borrow if necessary from one other within a defined and controlled total. Where bills of quantities are used, we have also developed with quantity surveyors a practicable method for quickly finding the sums estimated for particular items, by sometimes combining the specification and bills as a single document in which the items run page-by-page together.

Contract information varies from the freehand to the computer-drawn diagram and must convey accurate and lucid information. It can be lavishly annotated with notes – for this, clear handwriting is perfectly

78a,b   Old buildings can be very crooked.

78c   Excluding dust: traceried window stonework cut away and repaired from outside avoiding indoor disturbance.

78a

78b

adequate. Dimensions must be stipulated from zero-points that are to remain, and not from anything likely to be removed or taken away. Since old buildings may be very crooked, we need to convey whether new elements are expected to be correctly rectilinear or plumb, or if not, what existing line they are to follow. Otherwise perfectly level shelving will 'read' as running very much uphill in relation to a strongly downhill floor; aggressive right-angles will shout their newness within a skewed parallelogram of old walls. We try to avoid over-elaborate drawings, or excessive information about areas that will remain unaltered. A large-scale illustration or freehand sketch may be useful,

78c

with only the actual area of alterations worked out. Occasionally, it is even easier to draw directly onto a photograph; and in the last analysis (and although they cannot well form any basis of tendering) drawings in chalk 'on the wall' will be a great help on site.

Practicalities: occupied buildings

Hand-in-hand with the physical needs of a building structure are the practical constraints that will come into play during work on it. A building may remain wholly or partly occupied during the work, when life will differ from its normal quiet tenor rather as does war from peace. Excluding dust may be important; in ordering a contract for a vacated room, we must be sure it does not contain a hot-water cylinder supplying the man next door, and who may still be at home.

Repairs and remedies

Our survey concentrated upon *diagnosis*. Now is the opportunity to think our way through alternative *remedies*, and what these involve in terms of work to be done. In particular, the great enemies of buildings are structural movement and damp.

Movements

We ask ourselves about the movements we noted – are they live, or expanded? If live, are they indeed to be stopped? Or localised, and allowed to continue? If we want to restrain them, we look for the exact line along which an economical restraint such as a tie can be introduced, with the least disturbance to the building and its occupants. A tie along the direction of restraint may be more economical than a buttress, because it is

79a This tie-bar, unusually, acts at a diagonal to restrain a weak corner.

79b Massive cross-braced strutting against structural movement at Beauvais Cathedral.

more effective to pull than to push; a tensile member is more efficient than a compressive one. Sometimes, although less often, sheer added weight may be useful in bringing a force within control, like the heavy stone pinnacles that help to 'steer' the thrust of a gothic vault along through a flying buttress and down to the ground. They may still need to be strutted laterally. If buttressing is the only answer, we must remember that newly loaded ground will in turn compress and 'give'. Many an added buttress has pulled its wall over. Some buttresses are decorative – some are a nuisance, such as one we found that only contained a nest of snakes and was removed, contents and all.

Damp

What action shall we take in remedying damp? This will need fuller study now, as we look more closely into alternative ideas. Sometimes it may be possible to redirect underground water away from or around the building: certainly it will be better to guide, rather than to attempt to dam it. Since a wall is never totally dry, we shall further investigate whether its degree of damp penetration is acceptable; and if not, whether it is best diverted by a barrier or damp-proof member, or isolated – perhaps by a ventilated cavity and dry inner lining. But we must remember that the floors still take their bearing from the walls, from which timber may have to be distanced or carried on dry brackets. It may well be worth re-forming and simplifying the roofs, the better to cope with their function. In roofs and floors, timbers may have deformed and split: are they still doing their job? If not, it may be possible to splice a new end on a rotten beam, or we can suggest details like added metal plates or timber splints, or the insertion of a new steel

80a

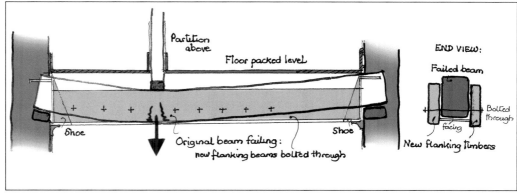

80a   Roofs may have to be
      re-formed and simplified.

80b   New flanking timbers to
      reinforce a failed beam.

80c   Scarf-joint: a new beam-
      end, securely spliced,
      scarfed and bolted on.

80d   Lightweight diagonal
      ties within a roof-space.

80b

Partition above

Floor packed level

Shoe

Shoe

Original beam failing:
new flanking beams bolted through

END VIEW:

Failed beam

Bolted through

facing

New flanking timbers

80c

80d

Replacement stones: should the lost original mouldings be reinstated?

beam or a system of ties. We must then remember to take into consideration the effects of extra weight, and plan how the finishes will be adapted around it. An important factor is the exact way everything can in practice be put into position without any excessive disturbance. For example, a decayed timber awaiting renewal may originally have been framed in, and tenoned at both ends into its supports. If the process cannot now be repeated, we must specify a device such as a 'swung' tenon, to get the timber in. In a similar case, a sagging and failing beam could only be strengthened by a pair of new timbers alongside it, themselves bearing on steel shoes or 'hangers', the whole being bolted together to serve as one.

Replacement materials

In our work we are constantly dealing with ageing and changing materials, and all the detail of everyday replacement and renewal now comes under review. Will stone replace stone, and be similarly jointed? And was the stone used the right one for its position? Is the same quarry still producing good material? Or must we find a substitute, and if so, what will be the most suitable alternative? Will replacement stones be inserted to their original line, or matched to weathered ones alongside? (This is a riddle calling for endless practical compromise.) While the scaffolding is up for

access to a damaged parapet, will any repointing work from it be useful and sensible? When the roof slating is off, will we have to replace some roof rafters, and if so, which ones? Is the beetle damage serious enough to justify treatment while the roof space is exposed; and can we afford it?

Conversions

Continually changing requirements mean adapting buildings to today's demands. We try to aim at reducing further maintenance, and to make the building as useful as we can. Then we are likely to win for it a longer future. An additional staircase or a new doorway for readier access may help the circulation pattern. Wasted attics or basements can perhaps be brought back into daily use, if suitably daylit and insulated, heated and serviced. Given central heating, it may be possible not only to remove an unwanted chimney but to provide useful space in the area of the previous stack. At the same time, we may be considering whether to replace any valuable features the building has lost. A missing fireplace may be restored as the focus of a room, or a later dividing door removed from a fine staircase. Folding shutters earlier sealed up can be returned to their original use and attractive appearance, or other architectural features uncovered for enjoyment again.

82a   Roof carpentry under cover.

82b   Planning access routes from
one side and across under a
temporary cover-roof.

82a

Sequence

Finally, in specifying how the job is to be carried out,
we shall need to give careful thought to every way in
which the contractor will be able to ensure a smooth-
running job. Here especially, there are many obvious
differences between work on a virgin site and in an
existing and occupied building. Access routes may for
example need to be planned.

The succession and interrelation of trades and skills
the work demands, and the resulting critical path for
action, can have the complexity of a military
campaign, and can as easily result in rout as in victory.
During the work the contract's job-organiser – a
jobbing foreman, or a director with his ear to the
ground – will be a valued and experienced ally; upon
him its success or otherwise will ultimately depend.
But long before he arrives on the site, we must try to
imagine his priorities, the availability of trades, and his
physical resources and requirements. Where will he
start? How will he ensure the best continuity of work?
And within what margins of error? What access will he
need? Would the cost of a temporary cover-roof justify
itself? Or would it at the same time make the job too
hot, or too dark? Can everyone get good natural
daylight, or electric lighting or power just where it is
needed? And where, while roofs are stripped and in
process of change, will the rainwater go? While a
building is open, its interior will be extra vulnerable
and its contents at risk. If, in turn, a permitted

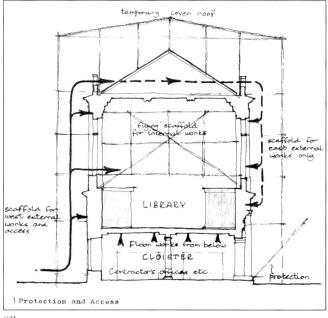

82b

rainwater route gets accidentally blocked or interrupted
(which can happen) where else would it go – inwards,
or outwards? Where will the foreman's site office be, to
allow him adequate control with the least confusion
and effort? And where will the operatives wash and eat,
and recover when it is cold? All these factors and the
sequence and phasing of work must be carefully planned,
more assiduously even than in a new building, and
especially if there will still be occupants at home,
or allowance made for busy continuing use.

TRAFALGAR SQUARE

1. AT THE START OF EACH PHASE, CRACKED, UNEVEN & PATCHED PAVING WAS TAKEN UP & OLD DECAYED SERVICES REMOVED.

2. EXCAVATIONS WERE THEN CARRIED OUT FOR NEW ELECTRICAL & DRAINAGE SERVICES, FOUNTAIN PIPEWORK & NEW HYDRANTS FOR CLEANING.

3. SERVICES HAVING BEEN INSTALLED, A NEW REINFORCED CONCRETE SLAB WAS CAST TO SUPPORT NEW STONE PAVING.

4. SUCTION PADS WERE USED TO LOWER THE SLABS INTO POSITION ON PRE-SOAKED WOOD BLOCKS.

5. AREAS OF UP TO 20 STONE SLABS WERE THEN FLOODED BENEATH WITH GROUT. COMPLETED, THE PAVING CAN WITHSTAND A TEN TON LOAD.

6. NEW PAVING LAYOUT INCORPORATING NEW CROWD BARRIERS AROUND NELSON'S COLUMN PLINTH.

7. PREVIOUSLY, FOUNTAIN PIPES HAD BEEN FAULTY, BASINS HAD LEAKED & THE VANDALISED LIGHTS HAD BEEN ABANDONED.

8. FOUNTAIN LIGHTING HAS NOW BEEN RECESSED INTO NEW WATERPROOFED R.C. SLAB, WITH NEW SERVICES & TILED FINISH

9. THE NEW LIGHTING & WATER SUPPLY ARE BOTH CONTROLLED FROM THE NEWLY FITTED-OUT SUBTERRANIAN PUMPING CHAMBER

Sequence of operations in repaving Trafalgar Square.

5. Working on site: contractors and craftspeople

As early as possible, we must find contractors with the requisite skills to meet the special demands of each job. In work carried out on older buildings, success will then largely depend on teamwork and mutual trust, personal skills and involvement.

Institutions and buildings, contractors and their craftspeople come in every shape and size. Even in different parts of the same country, local habits and customs vary from place to place; operatives will be just as different in their knowledge and skills. Together with the owner, the architect must identify and consider the resources of the most appropriate building team to execute the work. One has to remember too that all organisations do change – they shrink and grow, and can lose or gain their best employees, or may sometimes diversify into new and more profitable work. The same, of course, is true of architects. We need to know where the right people can be found, and at the right time.

Increasingly, the traditional builder with his own staff of full-time tradesmen is a scarce commodity; and contractors increasingly tend to be structured as management teams, with a supply-chain of many independent (sometimes and arguably, less committed) subcontractors and suppliers. Whether large or small, the aim is to hold together a team that is sufficient and balanced enough to attract work, to complete it and to cover its costs. At its best, the small, often family-based firm achieves this simply by establishing and jealously maintaining its local reputation. The ideal for such firms is a steady sequence of work, to offset any inherent lack of resilience and coverage. While there are limits upon the scope and availability of staff and skills to these family firms, especially for work on humbler vernacular buildings, they can be unbeatable. The continuity of an established local connection may also bring extra future dividends, in terms of ready availability for everyday repairs and maintenance.

The best firms are well and efficiently organised and take pride in maintaining a stable and skilled regular workforce. The reputation of the whole team will stand

84a

84b

84a Skilled tradesmen – a slater at work on a roof valley.

84b Sensitive work: reinforcing a failed plaster ceiling from the floor above.

or fall by the quality of its basic tradesmen, and strength in all relevant departments is equally vital. The success of a huge but largely hidden repair job can still be spoiled by the poor quality of that last lick of paint. And a scribble of surface wiring makes nonsense of delicate stone mouldings.

In the case of hitherto unknown firms, we not only obtain and follow up references but also visit offices and workshops, to see some recently completed

85a

85c

85b

85a Paint spread beyond its window-bars onto glass.

85b Restoring elegance to a Georgian fanlight.

85c Crazy wiring by an otherwise conscientious electrician (Belgium).

alarmingly as an element in the budget, not to speak of wasted time. A nearby firm can bring an enormous advantage in being able to give continuing future attention from first-hand knowledge. Similarly, past experience in comparable work, or the availability in the team of specially trusted or experienced tradespeople, may justify the extra distance in daily travel from further afield. On occasion, we have negotiated with firms we knew, to select and organise a labour force prepared to live on site or nearby, working on a fortnightly or other cycle through long hours daily but then with longer weekends away.

In selecting firms to approach, much will depend on the size and complexity of the job, what equipment, what office and what on-site management is required. All of these must be appropriate to the scale of the work. Scaffolding nowadays is readily hired almost anywhere, but a good arsenal of traditional and mechanised tools will be needed. A reliable availability of supplies and basic materials will result in a tidier site and building programme.

For the simplest jobs, direct labour may sometimes be cheaper. If the work of a single trade is called for, and if little coordination is necessary, the owner can save much money if there are good on-the-spot site arrangements, such as an estate office to supervise the work. Similarly, other continuous 'Forth Bridge'-type of projects, such as maintaining the stonework of a

projects and get some feeling of everyone's skills and capacities. Contractors will readily name examples of similar jobs recently undertaken; it is our responsibility to follow up these informal references personally with other owners or architects. This will enable us to determine what a builder is likely to be best at, his special strengths or any weaknesses, and how well a contract will be run. It may also be necessary to take formal business and financial soundings about a lesser-known firm. Sometimes we, or an owner, may already have established a valued working relationship, or can nominate someone who has previously proved his worth. Many contracts have been placed from a continuing personal contact in this way.

We are often asked whether it is best to choose a local builder. Certainly, he will have the lowest travelling costs; mileage rates on daywork can mount up very

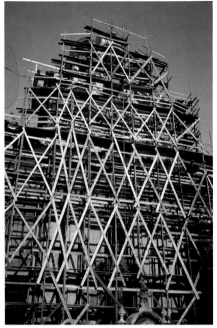

86a

86b

86c

86d

cathedral, may well justify a site yard with directly employed staff. The difficulty in that case is how to provide the incentive to keep moving, when a job has no end in sight. Much depends upon the efforts of a reliable senior hand, or a really good clerk of works.

Above all, it is vital to know exactly who will be organising and running the job. Who will be the site foreman, the site agent and the contract manager? It is not unusual to seek a commitment from tenderers that a named key individual will be allocated and reliably retained to work on a project and to see it through to completion. It will be his responsibility to secure the effective coordination of his labour force, planned as an integrated operation. To maintain firm control, but at the same time to run a happy site, he will need to continually look ahead and think positively. To cope with the ever-changing demands of a repair job, he will have to be resourceful, organising or sometimes also resisting changes in personnel, timing in advance the

86a,b Scaffolding and access equipment take many forms, varying with the locality, scale and complexity of the job. Examples of traditional heavily triangulated wooden scaffolding, and of modern lightweight access staging.

86c Equipment well-matched to its task: tractor crane with suction pads to carry and reposition heavy paving slabs (Trafalgar Square).

86d Shanghai: bamboo scaffolding.

need for specialist labour and requisite materials, and with reasonable caution but enough zest, tackling the problems and opportunities as they arise.

87a

87b

87c

What of specialists? One example of a long-established task requiring very particular abilities (and insurance cover) is that of the steeplejack. In other trades such as dry-rot eradication, there are now well-established firms with a number of local branches, carrying the knowledge and backing, and often the guarantee, of the parent organisation. This can be especially useful in buying peace-of-mind about adequate protection against timber troubles, but it is also necessary to check the real significance of any warranty, setting it in a long-term context and remembering that no firm can guarantee a whole building, but only the specific area actually treated. So we need to be sure that the details are accurately and properly on record.

In most instances, skilled tradesmen such as masons and slaters, or specialist crafts such as those of stone carvers, artists and picture restorers may be called for, whether working on site or at their own specially equipped premises. Specialist firms now offer country-wide coverage in some trades such as leadwork, and are able to offer the advantages of major centralised equipment and services. Lead-casting was for centuries carried out locally on site on the equivalent of a travelling billiard-table (p. 88), but this traditional skill has now been commercially mechanised. Heating, electrical and service engineers usually cover a broad area, and are generally ready to travel. Wider enquiries may be involved when finding highly technical crafts like clock repairs or millwrighting.

87d

87e

87a Special tasks may call for special aptitudes: steeplejacks at work.

87b Delicate work: re-laying marquetry.

87c A fine art: tincturing heraldry on-site …

87d … or in a studio (panels from the Lords' Chamber ceiling, pp. 116–125).

87e Work under cover: a sculptor in his studio.

Traditional lead-casting in the 1950s, now mostly superseded by mechanised methods.

At the outset of a job, separate demolition contracts can be useful, to dispose of unwanted structural elements in advance of the main start. But this expedient does feel rather like inviting a vulture into one's nest; it must be ensured that nothing important has been removed, whether accidentally or otherwise, in this initial clearance.

In issuing formal invitations to tender, we meet each builder on site to explain the work, indicating any special circumstances and conditions of the job. For example, during church work, there may be weddings and unexpected funerals to accommodate and plan around. In a busy public building, work may only be possible for certain parts of each day, or between set dates. We send out identical documents and follow up with circulated answers to any queries. It is of course only fair to ensure that competing tenderers making their respective visits do not arrive on site at the same time, but this is often difficult to manage – we have met one competitor handing on his measuring rod to the next – and it is perhaps unlikely that in the building trade, total secrecy can ever be assured. We ask for identical data: prices, timing, daywork rates for unmeasurable work, travelling costs and the rest, and sometimes for fixed prices in times of high inflation. It is important that everyone tendering can trust you to be fair.

The tenders obtained should be strictly comparable, so that like is considered with like – this is not always as easy as it sounds. Certainly we must be happy that all the necessary trades are reliably to hand, and will not be supplemented by temporary 'cowboys', whether local or imported. Clues to quality can appear in unexpected ways – the choice of one contractor was clinched by the knowledge that when sending a pair of operatives onto site to remove a valuable wrought-iron screen, he had supplied not only skilled and careful men, but a pair who were respectively left-handed and right-handed and able to work together, one on each side of the screen. Not often is such foresight and choice available.

Briefing and directing the contractor

Once the decision has been taken and the contract has been placed, whether by competitive tendering or based on owner preference and negotiation, time is well spent in again going systematically around the site with the site manager and/or foreman. Regular continuing visits are thereafter essential. All building contracts are complicated and work within an existing building can be especially so. No specification, however precise and detailed it may be, can exhaustively express the exact standard of work required in an old building, the needs of which have to be interpreted on the spot. Crooked doorways and sloping floors demand an unexpected response from anyone trained to expect geometrical rectitude. These and a multitude of similar aspects are best sorted out on site, and by example. The standard of finishes is never easy to define: how do you 'match existing paintwork' when this varies so much?

From the moment of commencement (and avoiding any questionable starting date, such as the week before Christmas), we pay regular site visits to review progress. Formal minutes are then kept and circulated to record the labour force on site, the state of current progress and any difficulties anticipated, encountered and cleared. These notes form an invaluable record of any hassles, otherwise forgotten when all is complete.[1]

89a

89a Regular site visits include close inspection from
     scaffolding.

89b Mechanical lifting equipment enables direct delivery
     to work on roofs.

89b

In occupied buildings, it helps if the owner and agent can establish a mutual understanding with everyone on site. During building works, it is highly understandable if the patience of occupants, deprived of their normal peace and security, occasionally grows thin. It is important to maintain good relations between builder and owner, and indeed with his daughter and his dog.

Our specification will have stipulated bounds for site staff, setting firm restrictions on disturbance, within which their needs take efficient priority, but beyond which owners can feel relatively safe and undisturbed. A sensible deployment of scaffolding and mechanical equipment will ensure efficient handling of material on site, with minimum disturbance to occupiers. Quiet equipment such as electric hoists and mixers will have been specified, but building workers are a merry crew; and their banter and badinage can be startling to anyone of more monastic demeanour and habits.

Good access and protection, often sensibly combining scaffolding and a temporary cover-roof, is a primary necessity. A building site can also be a dirty and dangerous place. Adequate safety measures are essential to avoid accidents, and damage to existing fabric must be avoided. It is entirely vital (and surprisingly difficult) to maintain continuous anti-fire protection, compartmenting, alarm systems and watchfulness on site, during what is in practice one of the most dangerous periods in a building's life. Ladders blocking doorways, interrupted services, deliveries of materials and half-completed installations have been responsible for many major disasters, so this cannot be over-emphasised.

Debris, dirt and belongings will have accumulated in old rooms, cellars and roof spaces. Their clearance must be thorough, but not so over-enthusiastic as to destroy valuable evidence of the building's origins and history.

---

[1] In our early days, following site visits, 'Architect's Instructions' were confirmed simply by handwritten notes, formally rubber-stamped and issued to this effect. A copy was kept and these were duly committing but avoided delays.

90a

90b

90c

90a Safety first: insecure structure presents risks of collapse.

90b Protecting site staff: a careful contractor insists upon meeting health and safety requirements.

90c Fire extinguishers – a highly necessary precaution – maintained on site for easy accessibility.

Once, and unhappily, I saw the recently painted-out vestiges of a family's unique record, marked on a door, of the increasing heights of their children. Unnecessary losses are a pity.

We must remember too that if a door is accidentally left open while powdered plaster comes off a wall, every book in a library will need vacuum cleaning. Conversely, a craftsman may quickly take umbrage at excessive complaints about what he sees as 'his' area of work. A great deal of compromise is essential. But we try to keep the peace by forewarning both parties and stipulating any areas of extra care. One or two particular hazards include hob-nailed boots, scaffolders on piece-work, the inadequately sheeted and delicate mechanism of a church organ, and blowlamps on Fridays, but experience does enable extra vigilance. A spirit of mutual cooperation in an occupied building under repair can save so much friction both now and later.

Especially in larger works, site organisation and programming arrangements need to be clarified and quantified, and recorded in clear charts or critical-path programmes, kept constantly updated and displayed on site. To an owner, progress seems never to be continuous but to jump between long periods in which nothing appears to happen, and in which nothing actually looks quite like it did in the drawings. The foundations of a new room, for example, look so deceptively small at first, when set out on the ground. An owner may wish to be personally involved, but it is not always easy for him to see the progress beyond these apparent series of static 'plateaux' through which all work seems to pass. Contentment comes more easily when the decorators are in, the finishes are beginning to show, and the whole effect is suddenly taking shape.

In our cost control arrangements, we make specific allocations for items that unavoidably, being not fully seen or measurable, could not possibly be costed in advance. It is an advantage if the least predictable of these can be undertaken early, enabling further budget allocations and planning for the remainder. We always recommend including allowances for such likely contingencies (although surprisingly, one or two grant-giving local authorities will not accept them) because in work on existing buildings, a number of unknowns will almost always arise. But we must hold this fund appropriately and reserve it for these items alone, and not be tempted to use it to cover any additional instructions received. The planned duration of the work is a quantified factor in the overheads tendered and contracted; beyond these, financial as well as time extensions may fairly be claimed. Although it is natural for an owner living in his building to find unplanned extras, he needs to be protected from interrupting a programme and thus unconsciously increasing its cost.

The architect's progress visits to the site will be varied to match the needs of the particular work in hand. Some tasks demand exceptional care, and these include fully tracing the extent of a dry-rot outbreak. If an organic growth is making its way through a structure, unless it is systematically tracked and destroyed, any remaining traces could rapidly revive. Anything removed, but evidencing fungal growth, must be marked and held for inspection alongside its source, then destroyed.

In the long run, everything depends on teamwork, and upon a ready adaptability to changing demands.

Principles of repair will have been established by clear specifications and drawings, augmented by details showing typical remedies – a carpentry example is the scarfing of a new end onto a damaged beam. But decisions may still be needed on site, about questions such as whether to form a top or a bottom scarf, for the maximum retention of original timber. Both carpenter and foreman must then be present, to ensure that a structure will first be safely propped, and that, for example, any saw-cuts can physically be made, when the work is hampered by the surrounding structure.

We use extensive photography to assist with our record keeping for each job. The responsibility of recording and handing on this information is often forgotten, and cannot be remedied in retrospect. Photographs help future generations of architects and builders, just as we in turn have been helped by really adequate past records. Very occasionally, it may prove valuable to make an actual cast or replica of decorative items such as elaborate carved plasterwork, which may never again be accessible after the scaffolding has gone.

Close supervision helps to show by example that the work of everyone on site is a joint effort with a common positive aim. The range of items on which the architect must advise is immense: he may, on the same site and scaffolding, be involved both with problems of likely collapse and with minute details of the emblazoning of heraldry. He must give equally careful professional guidance on each. The results may not be showy: in the most restrained conservation work it may be a real compliment to know that 'you can just see where the work was done – but only if you look carefully'. In every case, we try to lose nothing original of real value, and to contribute good new work in the materials, techniques and spirit of our day – in short, to respect, complement and extend the history of what is already there.

The concluding days of any contract can be a particular challenge, because the on-site team will be disbanding – some will already be in demand elsewhere. The foreman or site manager has a special duty to ensure that final tasks are all tidily coordinated and finalised. When all is complete, some celebration is both appropriate and appreciated by all those who took part. After the post-fire reinstatement work at Windsor Castle, the Queen gave (and attended) a generous party for more than 1000 people of every rank and trade. An example to us all.

91a   Recording: a professional photographer at work on site.

91b   Casting a fibreglass archive copy of carved woodwork, at normal times inaccessible.

91c   A talk on site is often better than a letter on file.

91d   Celebrating 'topping-out' at the end of a contract.

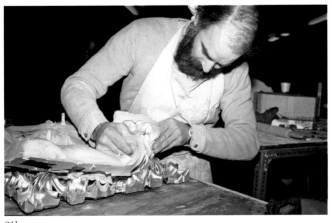
91a

91c

91b

91d

History – the place where Becket fell: Canterbury Cathedral.

TEN DEGREES OF INTERVENTION:

Criteria for care: Philosophy in Action

Selection

To make or to keep; to change or to save?

Our philosophy of conservation is based upon resolving a simple dichotomy. The life of places and of buildings is conditioned largely by two contrasting human motives. These two instincts, somewhat akin to the philosophical Chinese male and female energy factors, can be isolated and identified as 'making' – the aggressive principle that implies change (sometimes indeed, domination), and 'keeping' – protecting and saving things unchanged. These two notions run very deep in human nature and they do conflict.

Virtually all we set out to do involves change. When we set out to plough a field, or make a clearing for ourselves in a forest, we change it. We may create a shelter, or improve it, enlarge and equip it. We may set out to acquire or sometimes to attack and possess something, believing that our own way is the best way (for we all suffer from the conviction that 'we' can do things better than 'they' can). These activities reflect one instinct – the 'make' principle.

The second instinct – the 'keep' principle – is the wish to save and protect, which may be summed up as 'leave it alone – don't alter it!' We like it: we know it. It is part of our experience; and 'I love it like that', we say. This desire is equally strong and fundamental. Yet, 'keeping' is the direct opposite of 'making'; and only when we recognise these two deep instincts at work in ourselves can we understand and wisely manage our dual drives to conquer and yet to conserve.

More subtly, we may well acknowledge that even 'restoration' in the Victorian sense – and this idea still tempts and engages our attention – is really the same 'change' principle, still just as active but sublimated. We long to make a change and to make something into our own, even if in this case it is by changing it back into what we think it used to be.[1]

A village scene, unspoilt (except for health-and-safety-conscious handrail?).

To take a typical example of today, suburban man may take a fancy to a place in the country – a pretty village, an 'unspoilt' cottage – an Elysium, without a telephone. But how long is it before the rusticating city-dweller begins to dislike the spiders and the smell of the pigs, and before he sophisticates his rural retreat? Soon, he will cook by electricity, go to bed late and get up late, and generally behave as a townsman again. For how long will he accept and project the inherent nature of the place that attracted him, without imposing his own ideas?

To attempt to preserve any place, literally and totally, would demand preserving its way of life, and that of the people who inhabit it. Logically speaking, it would demand that we deny every opportunity of improved education, or the benefits of public health and relief from the terror of disease, or of today's increasing blessing of a longer life. And it has to be asked: how many of us would really wish to preserve our slums and every shameful ancient hovel, entirely unchanged and entirely unaltered, or attempt to impose a preservation order on cholera?

Change is a part of life – we cannot avoid it. All we can agree upon or argue about is merely the degree and direction of that change, and its relation to what has gone before. Indeed without change, there could have been no history, nor can it continue. Accepting the

---

[1] The 19th-century architect sometimes expanded this as 'what it should ideally have been …'

inevitability of change, we can still however set out to guide and influence it. This we can only achieve by intervention. The question then becomes 'what *kind* of intervention, and how much intervention?' And indeed, 'when does that intervention begin to become interference?' This too is a matter of circumstance and degree. It is also essentially founded upon the conscious and unconscious criteria that in fact underlie and govern every human choice, and every decision we make.

Principles and criteria

If making choices results from holding certain values, what values underlie our own judgements? For they will govern and colour every selection we make. Initially they will result from our background and above all, what training we have had.

94a

94b

94a   The historian's preoccupation (most architects would hate it!): earlier windows exposed as 'continuing evidence'.

94b   Craftsmanship, and the way people in the past made everyday things.

94c   Local materials give identity: clay tiles and traditional roof pitches in Siena, Italy.

94d   Identity again. Oolitic limestone of the English Cotswolds at Chipping Campden, Gloucestershire.

What we value and appreciate most is in some measure born in us, but develops further from the cradle onwards. Our family life, our childhood and our schooling colour all we do. Our professional education may focus us even

more. An historian or an archaeologist will have acquired one particular and specialist outlook, and an architect or a town-planner another. In the same way, a sociologist or a teacher will have different viewpoints. And whether an atheist or a monk, we are all biased. In turn, our choices reflect life's ever-changing experience: and our own set of values will continually develop and change.

So what will be our guiding star, in selecting those buildings and features worthy of conservation? How do we make decisions about the merits or otherwise of cleaning, improving, restoring, replicating, moving, demolishing, rationalising, or sacrificing buildings, or making them economically viable? Our personal instincts and opinions will vary. We all must agree to differ, yet still to see merit in other people's viewpoints, in some cases at variance with our own. We have to acknowledge our narrowness of view, but then widen it by working together.

Let us start from the standpoint that *each place has an identity* and that each deserves respect. When human beings are motivated by the two opposing poles of desire – desire for change, and desire for protection – there will always be conflict and competition. In selecting what we wish to save, we must first recognise our basic criteria as being subjective and selective. Then in our response, given so wide a range of available degrees of intervention, we can put our task in its true perspective.

94c

94d

In setting out to intervene in a building's life-process, which we know cannot be reversed, but which we can still influence, the aim will be to extend one function – that of pleasing our personal or collective sense of history and continuity. But this has many facets, varying from a joy in past craftsmanship to a delight in design, or indeed in sheer historical knowledge for its own sake.

In repairing the fabric of an ancient building, we must first recognise just what it is we respect and value. In a medieval church for example, this may be its craftsmanship, evidencing the work of ancient hands more skilled than our own. Here, what we are striving to maintain is the continuing enjoyment of the evidence of that skill. Or in a Renaissance palace it may be the unalloyed visual beauty of architectural design that drives our instincts of attention and care. Here the identity of the fabric itself may be secondary; it is the unity and harmony of architectural form that is paramount and quite independent of any renewal of its constituent materials.

In a historic townscape, a building that has little intrinsic interest may still have place-value, for example, in closing a vista or continuing a crescent, to the huge benefit of the wider place. In a terrace, our criterion may be simply the design unity of the whole. If what we value and seek to save is in fact a frontage line or skyline, individual design variations within this may be relatively acceptable.

When it is the evidence of history that we set out to save, Ruskin's principle of Memory enters the picture. Under the flag of 'the building where …' may lurk a series of claims on our emotions, extending continuously from a building's origin into its subsequent history over centuries, and even into today. Within this particular category, almost any replacement by copying will inevitably affect the sense of continuity. Yet we may not wish to remember and recall each and every phase of that history, as in the interior decoration and furnishings of each successive President and First Lady at Washington's White House. Each case has to be carefully considered on its merits.

We have a vast spectrum of choices, but it must be remembered that the music of each instrument takes its place within an orchestra of control and guidance. Although the vitality of a historic city cannot be arrested, it can in some measure be steered. The weathering of a granite monument or war memorial will be slow – that is why such a long-suffering stone was employed for it in the first place. The demands of the crumbling paintwork on a wooden window will differ from it only in timescale. We polish the granite, we renew the paint, and it is futile to argue about either. These are all simply cyclical necessities in time.

The debate arises mostly about what aspect of a building we seek to affect and tamper with. Is it the physical form, or is it the use? Or is it what we choose to see as historical 'evidence'? Or is it even the accidental charms of a chance townscape, including yesterday's contrasts between neighbours, which our town-planning controls might never have allowed to happen today?

This wide range of aspects that we can influence is all based upon subjective choice. So we must be clear in our minds as to the criteria to guide those choices.

95a   Local history exemplified – Durham Cathedral.

95b   Contrasts – tall new buildings in Singapore with restored 'shop houses' at their feet.

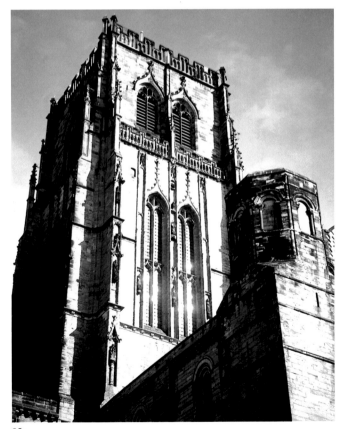

95a

95b

A jewel of its period: English Perpendicular Gothic architecture in the Henry VII Chapel at Westminster Abbey.

Very similar criteria are recognised in other international studies. For example the highly significant and influential ICOMOS[1] document known as the Burra Charter (1979–1988, revised in 1999), summarises 'cultural significance' as arising within four categories: aesthetic, historic, scientific and social values.

In applying all of these criteria, it has to be acknowledged that inevitably, much still depends upon individual judgement and opinion – in turn inherently subjective – and thus open to variation and change, if only in emphasis.

An equally fundamental and less-realised factor to bear in mind is that the shape and identity of an object or building or neighbourhood we are seeking to conserve is itself not limited to physical bricks and mortar. Rather, it extends from the very mind of its creator into the minds of generations of others who have influenced it and changed it throughout its life, and in turn into its impact on the minds of people today. And these links and relationships between people and buildings change subtly and surprisingly with time and circumstances.

As the pilgrim succeeded the crusader, so the tourist has succeeded the pilgrim. It might even be admitted that the 'make' and 'keep' principles in protection and preservation are just as much expressed in the impression of each building within people's minds. Love for a building – or for the image it has in our minds – can be just as significant and valuable as the physical form of the fabric itself. We need to take a wide and observant view about the boundaries within which every intervention can have its effects.

In practice, legal powers for building protection almost always vary from one nation to another. The most successful are those that concentrate upon selected aspects or elements of the heritage, enabling a community to acquire only essentially significant features. Purchase may, for example, take up entire ownership of a property, but still provide for continued occupancy (perhaps by leaseback) of its owners or occupants. Or legal control may extend over an owner's 'right to develop' and involve only control over future change. The guiding principle is that the public's involvement and investment should as far as possible be focused upon just what it wants to protect.

Intervention

A matter of degree

The next variable is simply one of extent and degree, from replacing a lost tile to renewing a roof. The art is in knowing just what it is that we and others value, or may value in the future, and then just how far to go.

This range of choices and decisions to be taken might well be expressed as a graded spectrum or scale between extremes. When extending a building's life, we all have to select between alternative degrees of change, varying from simple retention to total replacement. And in the last analysis, every philosophical difference and every battleground of public opinion about preservation will usually prove to be about either the selection criteria, or about deciding at what point in this spectrum we are to stop, or to act.

At one end of the range the most literal task of preservation, such as the repair of a memorial, will still from time to time involve at least some renewal. Even simple cleaning may remove the patina of time, and together with it what some will see as the evidence of history. At the other end of the scale, change may be total. The new replacement may incorporate conscious memories of its predecessor, or may even deliberately contrast with it. Between these two extremes, all repair involves at least some local renewal of fabric, and the cyclical replacement of living materials.

There are parallels in nature, where life and continuity are in varying measure self-renewing. The basic elements of a landscape are made up of successively larger units, each in turn with a life of its own – a leaf is part of a tree, and a tree part of a changing forest. In man, the cells of our human features and frame are subject to replacement at a bewilderingly fast rate; yet we remain recognisable even while continually changing, as when a child's finger lives on into the hand of the adult. The growing child still has his place within his family, and the family within a community, while each in turn is changing and developing in its own way. Just the same pattern presents itself in any human institution like a company or club, whose members succeed one another in cyclical fashion, all within a recognisable but developing organism.

[1] ICOMOS: International Council on Monuments and Sites

In buildings and towns, this life principle is just the same. Materials decay and are renewed, although at varying rates. Whole parts of buildings are replaced and adapted. The structure settles, weathers and wears. In towns, individual buildings perish and are replaced by others, each within a neighbourhood that is itself undergoing cyclical change.

The case studies of actual and completed conservation projects in this book may help to illustrate not only the varying criteria we seek to apply in practice, but also the widely ranging scale of 'degrees of intervention' in the life of buildings that may pass through an architect's care. These may be viewed in something of a broadly increasing order of degree, ranging from total no-change preservation to complete renewal. In practice, projects rarely fall into neatly defined and exclusive categories. Each project will exhibit the need for flexibility when we take our decisions about this fundamental balance between stasis and change.

In some cases, construction methods and materials will have changed the most. Some of these may be seen as having greater intrinsic merit or interest, while others may now be unobtainable. Or newer and more effective replacements may logically be suggested. Equally, architectural and social requirements will have changed, so that what was once desired or accepted may today have become irrelevant or unacceptable. Or indeed, changing past attitudes may have become of new interest, but specifically now as social history.

To examine these principles, the following case studies illustrate ten successively *increasing degrees of intervention*. Each will encompass its own set of values and decisions, reflecting a balance between differing criteria of assessment. For each building is unique.

Some selection criteria

What is it that we all value? What categories are we to save, and what are we to lose? Surprisingly many nations of the world, each with their own valued architectural heritage, have yet to face up to this problem, and for many, the basic criteria are still evolving and may remain unclear.

In the UK, the principal national criteria for selecting buildings or areas for protection have so far mostly included the following, all in varying degree:

Architectural values:
- Masterpieces of design
- Outstanding works of building craftsmanship
- Examples of the work of particular architects/designers acknowledged as outstanding
- Buildings within which major historical events have taken place
- Birthplaces and homes of important historical persons (occasionally even of fictional characters, but honoured by long tradition)
- Known architectural interiors of special significance/importance
- Examples of characteristic aspects of a particular period or school
- Important links in the chain of architectural and constructional development
- Unaltered period buildings, deemed of importance as research material.

Urban values:
- Outstanding examples of conscious town-planning and layout
- Elements in planned architectural groups of high merit
- Features that are the essence of a specific locality and define its character
- Significant street and pavement surfaces and public street furniture
- Outstandingly important trees, planting schemes or landscaped gardens
- Dominant elements in skyline composition
- View-lines towards local and national monuments (in turn, subject to 'selection')

Missing elements:
- Paradoxically, but usefully, attention may on occasion be drawn to the absence of earlier significant elements, now lost or missing from a conscious architectural or townscape composition.

Day-to-day care (Mexico).

1. Day-to-day building care

At one end of the ascending scale of intervention in the lives of historic buildings is simply their regular maintenance and daily care by owners and architects.

Each building has its own problems, but there are similar basic elements to watch for. The first to demand attention is almost always the 'hat' or roof. In Britain the roof will traditionally be covered either in overlapped tiles or slates, which are individually vulnerable but quite easily replaced, or in sheet metal – lead, copper or zinc – or occasionally in felt or asphalt.

Unit materials such as tiles and slates suffer mostly from failure of their fixings – pegs or nails, or sometimes of the battens that carry them. In the short term, individual slipped slates may be slid back into position with a copper hook or tab (not lead, which is too soft and bends). But if there are many, it is time to plan for more comprehensive attention. Metal coverings are always prone to failure from thermal movement,

99a

99b

99c

99a   A very tired roof.

99b   Beautifully re-laid stone roofing in diminishing courses.

99c   A stitch in time – renewing a lead gutter.

especially if they were laid in sheets of excessive size. Their day-to-day expansion and contraction then induces hardening and cracking, directly admitting wet and weather. Leadwork is the easiest metal to repair, if this is well executed by lead-burning and not by soldering, which may break away. Sometimes an extra cover-flashing can be introduced. Any emergency patching akin to bandaging should only be adopted when plans can be made for a fully adequate repair, with proper steps and drips and expansion-joints.

Asphalt and similar materials are less forgiving and typically fail at any abutment or junction between solid walling and wooden roof-structure, such as the point where a roof-deck meets a parapet. Surprisingly, an adequate second line of defence at weak points such as this seems to have been very rare – although perhaps it need not be so, now that sheet plastics are so cheaply and readily available.

The point to appreciate is that all roofing finishes, like any building material, eventually call for cyclical renewal. Meanwhile it is the unattended hole or defect that can be so lethal to carcassing timbers and trusses within, especially when softened by any admitted water and unventilated, and particularly at their joints and bearings. Hence the need for regular and attentive vigilance.

Roof care is often compromised by the complex layouts that have developed in older buildings, presenting vulnerable hidden slopes and internal valleys, not always easy to access. And the rainwater routes from these may in turn be tortuous and frequently overloaded, or sometimes even carried in open troughs from one roof through another. Parapet gutters are a particular source of trouble, and soon collect silt and leaves (and sometimes even dropped slates), demanding frequent

100a

100b

100a   Deteriorating roof leadwork, in overlarge sheets with inadequate drips.

100b   Expert renewal of leadwork in progress: narrow sheets, jointed over wooden rolls: good drips.

100c   Roof leadwork in good fettle.

100d   Patched leadwork, but solder will come away. A better response is to burn-in lead patches.

100c

100d

101a

101b

101c

101d

101e

101f

101a Complex roofs bring heavy maintenance problems.

101b Wooden rainwater-trough carried through a roof space, with danger of blockage and overflow.

101c Roof gutters need regular clearing (but avoid steel shovels).

101d Fallen slates demand replacement, and duckboards may need attention.

101e Autumn is painful for roof gutters.

101f Parapet gutters lacking expansion-joints and inadequately patched.

clearance. Good emergency overflows can be a real help in avoiding disaster; attention to a single obstruction can save much future outlay on repairs.

After the roof, it is the eaves, gutters, downpipes and rainwater disposal systems that mostly fail. Blockages and failed fittings are the main culprits, but unattended rust, cracks and holes have much to answer for. So have any thoughtless constrictions, including inadequate

102a

102b

102c

102d

102e

102a   Overflowing and rusty cast-iron rainwater-head.

102b   Tell-tale crack in a downpipe.

102c   Physical damage and lack of fixings.

102d   Neglected blockage – a wet outside wall encourages dry-rot indoors.

102e   Overgrown churchyard at foot of tower.

103a

103b

103a   A well-tended dry area surrounding a parish church.

103b   High-quality flooring, damaged by an over-zealous electrician.

outlets, sharp bends, and layouts and falls incapable of coping with emergencies. Some amazingly over-optimistic systems show us how a water disposal system can be no better than its weakest point.

In the main walling, elements such as weather-shedding copings and cornices, ledges and sills are most at risk; the whole day-to-day pattern of water absorption and evaporation deserves to be recognised. In wet weather, rain and atmospheric damp are continually absorbed into every wall, especially where directed over it by impervious features like glass windows, or absorbed from surrounding vegetation. In the same way, water will be evaporated away, either internally (especially where drawn towards evaporation points at heat sources such as radiators) or back outwards again in dry weather or sunshine. Few materials are totally dry; and most will at any time in effect be 'breathing' moisture, whether in or out.

Water movements will be complicated by any open gaps or cracks, which provide a ready path for entry. But these also represent reduced strength and may show up significant movements, which need to be analysed and either resisted or at least controlled.

Joinery and woodwork features such as doors and windows in buildings take the brunt of human use, and by occurring in wall openings they may have had to adapt themselves to any structural movements. Natural expansion and contraction of woodwork is endemic and cannot be stopped, but allowance needs to be made

for it. Door furniture including hinges, locks and bolts, together with mechanical elements including sliding sashes, all need continual attention – especially in buildings such as greenhouses and conservatories, where broken glazing may also be likely.

Floor structures and surfaces receive heavy wear, and are also especially vulnerable to attack by plumbers and electricians when installing or altering services, often with a completely unnecessary degree of disturbance and damage. Loose, unfixed and thoughtlessly refixed boards can be a menace and deserve regular attention. Any 'piecing' with new wood is best confined to the individual boards, without attempting to bridge natural gaps between them.

Wall and ceiling finishes, such as damaged plasterwork, will bear witness to any movements of the underlying structure, or to failures in plumbing or services, and sometimes merely to wear and tear. Depending upon the degree of finish sought, skilful repair may be required before redecoration is contemplated.

Mechanical services including electrical and gas, heating, plumbing and drainage services invariably age the quickest, and suffer most from alteration and frequent updating – not all of it sufficiently expert. Any resultant damage as a result of leaks, and especially any safety problems or fire risks, will demand an urgent response and cannot wait.

The shortest lifecycle of all is probably that of exposed external and even internal paintwork – in many cases

104a

104b

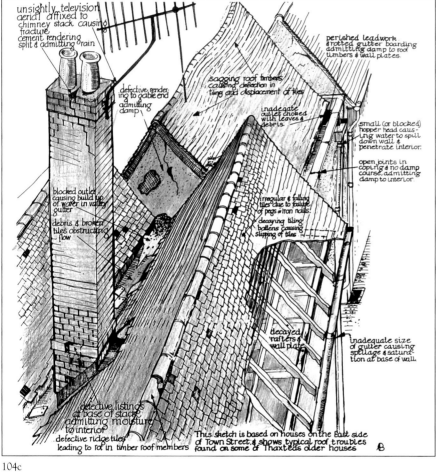

unsightly television aerial affixed to chimney stack causing fracture

cement rendering split & admitting rain

defective render-ing to gable end admitting damp

perished leadwork & rotted gutter boarding admitting damp to roof timbers & wall plates.

sagging roof timbers causing deflection in tiling and displacement of tiles

inadequate outlet choked with leaves & debris

small (or blocked) hopper head caus-ing water to spill down wall & penetrate interior.

open joints in coping & no damp course, admitting damp to interior.

blocked outlet causing build up of water in valley gutter

debris & broken tiles obstructing flow

irregular & falling tiles due to failure of pegs & iron nails.

decaying tiling battens causing slipping of tiles

decayed rafters & wall plate

inadequate size of gutter causing spillage & satura-tion at base of wall.

defective listings at base of stacks admitting moisture to interior

defective ridge tiles leading to rot in timber roof members

This sketch is based on houses on the East side of Town Street & shows typical roof troubles found on some of Thaxted's older houses

104c

104a   Electrical dangers.

104b   Peeling paintwork betrays overdue redecoration to protect a sash-window.

104c   Typical roof troubles.

104d   A dropped floor – tell-tale evidence of dry rot in floor joists and hidden timbers.

104d

not only decorative, but protective as well. Interim attention to repainting any ready failure-points such as windowsills can extend life and bring surprising economies.

Last and above all, daily care must keep an open eye for any sign of dry rot – especially in warm, damp spaces or on the inside of a wet outside wall. Caught in time, this 'cancer of the house' can then be dealt with as the emergency it truly is (104d).

Although there is some truth in the advice of a canny transatlantic philosopher, that 'If it ain't broke, don't fix it', there is no excuse for costly neglect. Maintenance, in a way, may be simply repair writ small, but its absence can result in emergencies and rapidly builds up a large and more serious claim.

The words of William Morris still ring true, in stressing the huge benefits of 'daily care' and minimum but regular intervention.

Maintenance manuals

Our team has experimented with developing 'maintenance manuals' for daily care in a number of historic buildings, especially within university programmes of planned building care (pp. 107–115). Here (and usually in summer, when builders too will take their holidays) a tight calendar of activities calls for a regular annual onslaught of concentrated disturbance. Manuals are designed to provide simple diagrams and checklists, in which regular tasks are detailed, and initialled by those responsible as each is completed. The most difficult aspect of day-to-day maintenance is the ability to envisage the capabilities of a sometimes-unknown staff, perhaps untrained in observing a building's problems. The system thus works best under the direction of a qualified clerk of works or building supervisor. An old building requires a ceaseless round of attention, from replacing its long-term materials such as stonework to frequent and regular repainting. Daily attentions are much more successful when set within an accountable framework, and as part of a regular pattern of care.

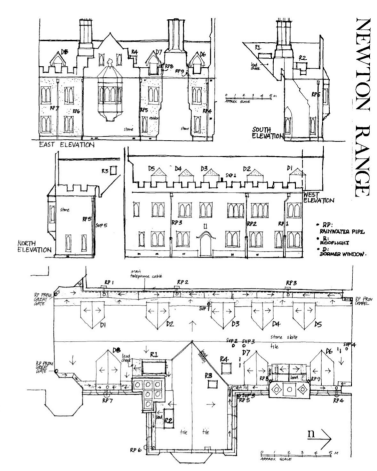

Trinity College   Standard Maintenance Checklist

1. ROOF COVERINGS AND ASSOCIATED ELEMENTS	SLATING & TILING – Slates/tiles missing, slipped, cracked or laminating; ridge tiles open-jointed
	LEAD RIDGES, HIPS & VALLEYS – Splits, defective fixings or joints, holes, ridging or movement
	LEADWORK – Splits, holes, ridges, dislodged flashings, slipped soakers
	GUTTERS & OUTLETS – Blockages, inadequate falls, "ponding"
	LEAD RAINWATER PIPES – (ACCESSIBLE – Splits, holes, defective joints or fixings / (INACCESSIBLE – Signs of spillage or leakage
	IRON RAINWATER PIPES – Splits, holes, broken collars, defective fixings, corrosion, defective paintwork
	IRON EAVES GUTTERS – Splits, holes, leaking joints, defective fixings, insufficient falls, corrosion, paintw
	IRONWORK: GENERAL – Defective fixings, corrosion, defective paintwork
	CHIMNEYS – Decayed bricks/stonework, fractures, open jointing, loose pots or flaunching
	STONEWORK – Decay, spalling, fractures, displacement, open-jointing
	BRICKWORK – Fractures, decayed bricks, open jointing
	RENDERING – Cracked or missing areas, hollow sounding areas
	WOODWORK – Decay, damage, defective paintwork
2. WALLS: EXTERNALLY	STONEWORK – Decay, spalling, fractures, open jointing, displacement
	BRICKWORK – Fractures, decayed bricks, open jointing
	STONE WINDOW MULLIONS – Fractures; displacement, spalling, open jointing
	LEAD RAINWATER HEADS & PIPES – Ladder inspection for splits, holes, defective joints or fixings
	CAST IRON RAINWATER HEADS & PIPES – Ladder inspection for cracks, holes, corrosion, defective fixings, leaking joints, defective paintwork.
	WINDOWS – Frames, Glazing, lead cames.
3. PAINTING: EXTERNALLY	IRONWORK – Wire brush and rub down, derust, spot prime & special prime, undercoat and two top coats
	WOODWORK – Rub down or burn off, prime, undercoat and two top coats
4. ROOFS: INTERNAL	ROOF TIMBERS – See under individual buildings
5. INTERIORS	INTERIOR ELEMENTS – See under individual buildings

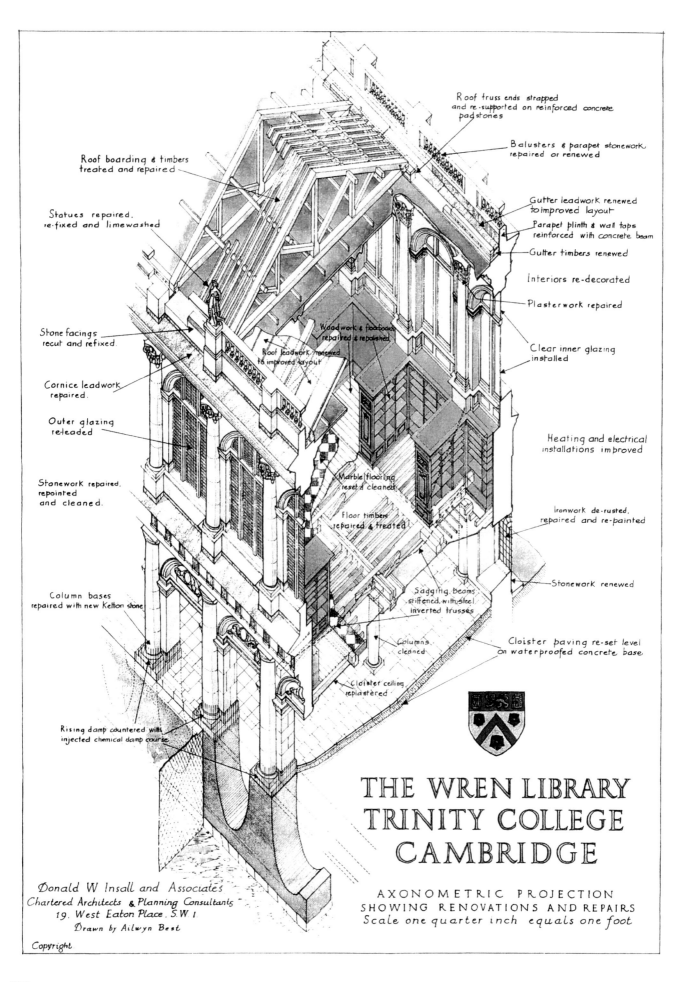

Roof truss ends strapped and re-supported on reinforced concrete padstones

Balusters & parapet stonework repaired or renewed

Gutter leadwork renewed to improved layout

Parapet plinth & wall tops reinforced with concrete beam

Gutter timbers renewed

Interiors re-decorated

Plasterwork repaired

Clear inner glazing installed

Heating and electrical installations improved

Ironwork de-rusted, repaired and re-painted

Stonework renewed

Cloister paving re-set level on waterproofed concrete base

Columns cleaned

Cloister ceiling replastered

Sagging beams stiffened with steel inverted trusses

Floor timbers repaired & treated

Marble flooring reset & cleaned

Woodwork & floorboards repaired & repolished

Roof leadwork renewed to improved layout

Roof boarding & timbers treated and repaired

Statues repaired, re-fixed and limewashed

Stone facings recut and refixed

Cornice leadwork repaired

Outer glazing releaded

Stonework repaired, repointed and cleaned

Column bases repaired with new Ketton stone

Rising damp countered with injected chemical damp course

THE WREN LIBRARY
TRINITY COLLEGE
CAMBRIDGE

AXONOMETRIC PROJECTION
SHOWING RENOVATIONS AND REPAIRS
Scale one quarter inch equals one foot

Donald W Insall and Associates
Chartered Architects & Planning Consultants
19. West Eaton Place, S.W.1
Drawn by Ailwyn Best

2. Programmed maintenance

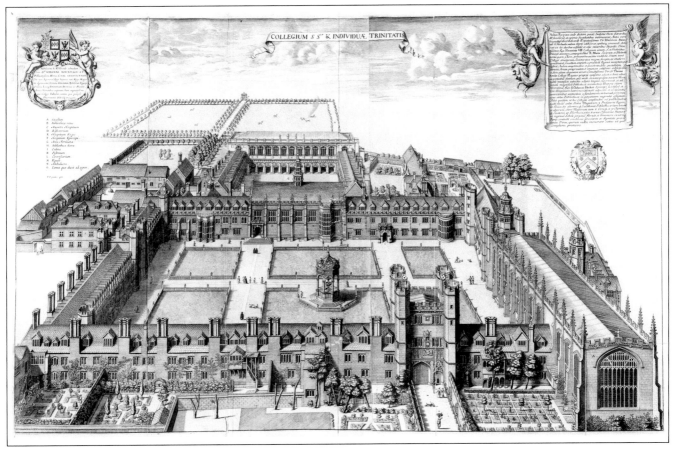

Trinity College, Cambridge: Loggan's superb drawing (circa 1690).

Trinity College, Cambridge

Regular maintenance is best achieved within a planned programme of systematic review and repair, such as that carried out since 1972 for the buildings of Trinity College, Cambridge.[1]

The Courts of the College present a noble pageant of historic architecture almost unparalleled in scale and quality. Covering 5 hectares, and representing five centuries of distinguished building, the College attracts visitors from all over the world. The tranquillity of the Courts is, however, a deceptive façade as the College is an intensively used functional unit. Throughout the academic year, it continues to fulfil and develop the purposes of research and teaching for which it was founded; the older buildings currently house more than 100 graduates and undergraduates and provide residential and teaching 'sets' for more than 150 Fellows. In vacation periods, the emphasis changes to accommodating conferences and seminars of many kinds. The functions of the Trinity buildings are thus multiple and continuous.

The problems inherent in maintaining a large complex of historic buildings are magnified by their intensive use. Within such tightly knit and sensitive surroundings, neither the loss of College accommodation nor the inevitable disturbance caused by major works can be easily reconciled.

---

[1] During some three decades of work, planning and supervision were continuously under the able direction of our now-retired director and co-founder Peter Locke. I am grateful for his most valuable contribution in providing this summary.

108a

108c

108b

108a The Wren Library in 1969, urgently in
      need of repair and refurbishment.

108b The library windows, given extra
      insulation by inconspicuous secondary
      glazing.

108c External scaffolding and cover-roof,
      erected half-by-half for economy in
      storage and scaffolding.

108d A stone half-collar to re-dress a damaged
      column.

108d

When we were first consulted, this problem had been met by confining repairs mainly to summer vacations, although aided by vigilant day-to-day maintenance. But a growing backlog of problems may accumulate until only a determined and phased programme of repair can retrieve old buildings to a healthy and manageable state. A particular crisis did arise, which was to have far-reaching results. Because the structure of the great Wren Library had for some time been showing obvious deterioration, we were commissioned to carry out a thorough survey and prepare a programme for its repair. The radical decision was taken to give over that building to a continuous two-year renovation contract.

This work on the Library revealed its serious and deep-seated defects, alerting the College to the possibility that other buildings might be harbouring similar problems only detectable by detailed individual study.

Accordingly, we were re-engaged to carry out a further and wider survey; the brief this time was simply to examine the structural condition of the whole complex of historic buildings that make up the College. The needs of each could then be incorporated into a practical and phased conservation programme.

The Trinity College Report of 1972 ran to well over 100 pages of analysis, illustrations and recommendations upon the 38 major buildings and ranges that form the College nucleus. Noting the weaknesses inherent in structure and design at their various dates, and their acceleration by natural decay and usage or sometimes by alteration, it set out a relative assessment of current demands and needs. The review that emerged was gathered into phased repair recommendations, expressed as no less than 97 major items, each allocated by relative urgency. The overall message was clear: the compound

109a

109a The Library's restored interior (1972).

109b Programmed maintenance: guided by a balanced assessment and report.

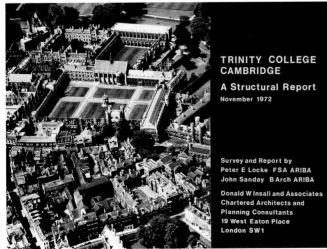

TRINITY COLLEGE
CAMBRIDGE

A Structural Report
November 1972

Survey and Report by
Peter E Locke FSA ARIBA
John Sanday B Arch ARIBA

Donald W Insall and Associates
Chartered Architects and
Planning Consultants
19 West Eaton Place
London SW 1

109b

effect of building decay had begun to outrun the holding capabilities of normal piecemeal repair and maintenance, and many of the College buildings were reaching a critical state.

In planning ahead, a balanced strategy was clearly needed. The sheer size of the overall problem, and of each individual building demanding attention, meant that the situation could only be retrieved by a programme of systematic and continuous major repairs. The College accepted the fact with determination, and a phased repairs programme was launched. On this basis, work proceeded for more than three decades, without a break.

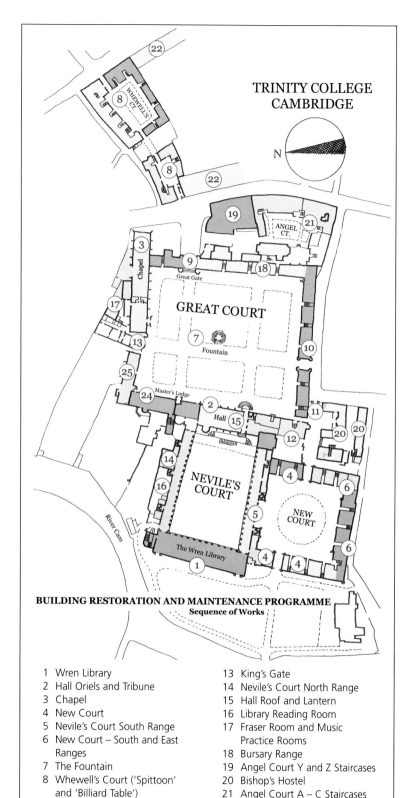

TRINITY COLLEGE CAMBRIDGE

N

WHEWELL'S CT.

GREAT COURT

Great Gate

ANGEL CT.

Chapel

Fountain

Master's Lodge

Hall

NEVILE'S COURT

NEW COURT

River Cam

The Wren Library

BUILDING RESTORATION AND MAINTENANCE PROGRAMME
Sequence of Works

1 Wren Library
2 Hall Oriels and Tribune
3 Chapel
4 New Court
5 Nevile's Court South Range
6 New Court – South and East Ranges
7 The Fountain
8 Whewell's Court ('Spittoon' and 'Billiard Table')
9 Great Gate and Newton Range
10 Great Court – South Range
11 Nevile's Gate
12 Essex Building and R Staircase, Great Court

13 King's Gate
14 Nevile's Court North Range
15 Hall Roof and Lantern
16 Library Reading Room
17 Fraser Room and Music Practice Rooms
18 Bursary Range
19 Angel Court Y and Z Staircases
20 Bishop's Hostel
21 Angel Court A – C Staircases
22–3 T and I Stairs, Blue Boar Court
24 Master's Lodge and Senior Combination Room
25 Old Library Range

Principal buildings of the College: a planned programme of major continuing attentions.

Initially, three main problems called for solution. The first was to reconcile the disturbance of major repair works with the daily needs of Trinity life and work. A second was to ensure a continuous, flowing handover of buildings for repair and return to College use at the optimum time. Third was the need to ensure continuous work on site at the required standard, to be carried out with maximum productivity and economy. The answers to these interdependent questions emerged from constant consultation and liaison between everyone involved.

The Wren Library contract thus formed in effect a useful 'audition' by bringing together the College authorities and clerks of works, the architects and other professional consultants, and introducing contractors; several of the team have worked together ever since.

The essence of the programme was to select and match each section of work with the working resources needed to execute it, all in a sequence and timing enabling the College to accommodate it with the least practical inconvenience. In the event, it has proved possible to relate this equation quite consistently to the academic year. So the work cycle has run from the beginning of the long vacation in one year to the end of it in the next, labour being gradually transferred from phase to phase during the vacations. Disruptive relocation of site establishments and scaffolding could thus also take place during this relatively quiet period. In the case of the residential buildings, the College has, in effect, created an 'empty block' of accommodation, which has been successively decanted and filled again at either end of a repairs phase. This has involved considerable reorganisation of College life and not a little forbearance, especially on the part of resident Fellows asked to leave home temporarily.

Careful pre-planning has been vital; and phases have been organised at least one year ahead, but with a degree of flexibility to cater for any opportunities and problems inherent in the life and condition of the buildings.

111a

111b

Given programmed maintenance, progress can be constantly monitored: labour, plant and materials can be planned and scheduled well in advance. An essential requirement of continuity of work was met during one period of uncertainty by making special contractual arrangements between the College and an established contractor. When it was impossible to foresee what would be found as each structure was opened up, the costing was based upon agreed rates with a negotiated profit margin. In this way financial risks for both parties were reduced, and an uninterrupted operational flow was made possible.

The assurance of available work in the long term helps to ensure a stable and skilled workforce, while a long-standing involvement can achieve consistently good productivity and standards of work. Even so, the competitive element does help to keep down costs, and the vagaries of buildings will quite frequently demand additional and specialist skills and tailor-made repair techniques beyond the capacity of a single contractor.

Both cost-plus and tendered figure contracts can have their own advantages. Tenders may be invited, and contracts placed, either at cost plus a negotiated profit margin or at fixed figures, or indeed sometimes involving a combination of both, and whether in open competition or from selected contractors.

The demands of old buildings are wide-ranging and detailed. The principles guiding their daily care could be summarised as: achieving a good and manageable state of repair, at a standard to which they can be realistically maintained; respecting and valuing the signs of their age; preserving what can be sensibly preserved; and carrying out honest and appropriate work to secure them a living future.

When work of this kind is finished, there may be little really visible difference. This has been especially so in the College, because the majority of problems have been hidden, for example below ailing roofs and gutters with their timbers attacked by dry rot, or in high-level stonework fiercely exposed to the punishing Cambridge micro-climate. A tenet of the work has also been strategic planning for those who will have care of the buildings in the future, as well as the present. In gauging an extended lifespan for buildings, our target has often been to secure at least a century that will be trouble-free, except for normal maintenance. The sheer extent and size of these buildings (reflected in heavy access scaffolding costs alone, as well as in their loss of use) can make it unrealistic to expect repeated attention within a shorter cycle.

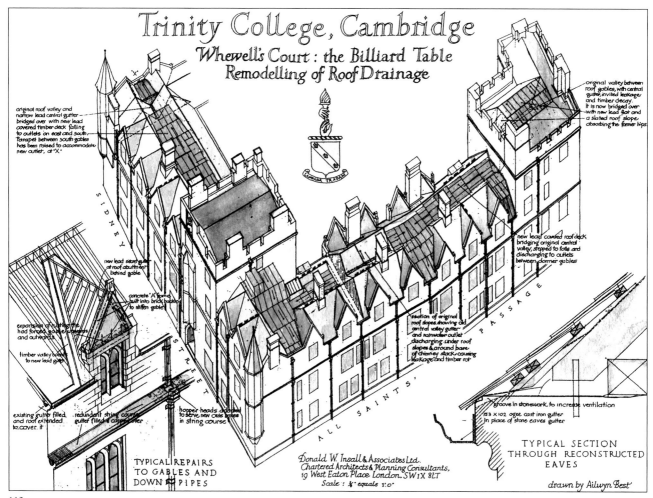

Trinity College, Cambridge
Whewell's Court : the Billiard Table
Remodelling of Roof Drainage

original roof valley and
narrow lead central gutter
bridged over with new lead
covered timber deck falling
to outlets on east and south.
Parapet between south gables
has been raised to accommodate
new outlet, at "X".

original valley between
roof gables, with central
gutter, invited leakage
and timber decay.
It is now bridged over
with new lead flat and
a slated roof slope,
absorbing the former hips.

new lead sexet gutter
at roof abutment
behind gable

concrete "A" form
built into brick backing
to stiffen gable

new lead covered roof deck
bridging original central
valley, stepped to falls and
discharging to outlets
between dormer gables

expansion of rusting tie
had forced gable outwards
and outwards

timber valley board
to new lead gutter

section of original
roof slopes showing old
central valley gutter
and rainwater outlet
discharging under roof
slopes & around base
of chimney stack causing
leakage and timber rot

existing gutter filled
and roof extended
to cover it

redundant string course
gutter filled & covered over

hopper heads added
to serve new cess pipes
in string course

groove in stonework to increase ventilation

153 x 102 ogee cast iron gutter
in place of stone eaves gutter

**TYPICAL REPAIRS
TO GABLES AND
DOWN PIPES**

Donald W. Insall & Associates Ltd.
Chartered Architects & Planning Consultants,
19 West Eaton Place London. SW1X 8LT
Scale : ⅛" equals 1'.0"

**TYPICAL SECTION
THROUGH RECONSTRUCTED
EAVES**

drawn by Ailwyn Best

112a

Ensuring that buildings are handed back for a long future of no more than gentle ageing, while treating them with sensitivity and respect for their historical conservation needs, can be a hard course to steer. In selecting repair methods and techniques, we tend to rely heavily upon those that have proved their worth through the practical trials of time and experience. All elements needing care are best dealt with while within reach and without repeated disruption. Each element is assessed strictly upon its own requirements; it must be the state of the buildings themselves that speaks most eloquently of their needs.

Trinity's buildings offer an extraordinary encyclopaedia of building behaviour. Each in its own way has told us much about the success and failure of its structural forms, components and materials. In some cases, no amount of careful repair could cure the ills inherent in their structural design, and radical attention has been needed. For example, Anthony Salvin's 19th-century work in Whewell's Court was all but crippled by a nightmare spaghetti of buried internal rainwater pipes, charged with

112a   Whewell's Court: remodelling of roof drainage.

112b   The 17th-century fountain in Great Court, with its delicate stonework.

112b

112

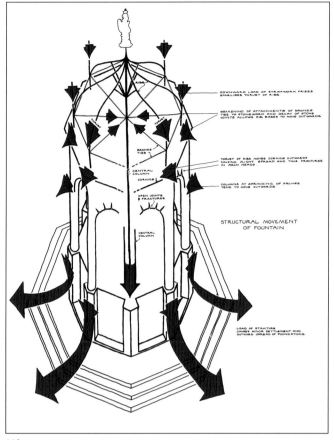

113a

113a   The fountain structure is analysed, noting its thrusts and movements.

113b,c   The Essex building, before and after programmed repairs.

At the other end of the spectrum, the 17th-century fountain in Great Court is a marvellous example of structural logic made manifest in architecture, but is crowned with a delicate tracery of fragile stonework. The crestings were gradually wasting away, but the whole structure is comparatively accessible for any continuing timely attention. Historical patina may take precedence over immediate replacements, and more limited conservation techniques have deliberately here been adopted.

A policy of 'preventive' repair has been central to the programme. This involves looking forward to a time when even carefully fashioned new lead gutters will age once more, and again expose the structure beneath to water attack. We have done our best to ensure that this can no longer find and seize upon vulnerable enclosed timber, by providing a well-ventilated structure, carefully protected with damp-proof barriers at any points that could form natural water-paths. In really dangerous situations, and where this is architecturally acceptable, timber wall plates and beam ends have been replaced with resistant materials such as concrete, which can also aid the stability of otherwise gradually weakening walls.

In the shorter term, much attention is paid to helping regular future maintenance, by simple measures such as providing more and better inspection traps and arranging systematic access routes over roofs, helped by fixed ladders and safety harness anchorage-points. Here too, as in other examples, a series of maintenance manuals will aid in the informed and systematic aftercare of each building.

The art of securing good continuing care is simply to make possible regular and correct attention when and where it is needed. Upon this basis, the daily needs of each repaired building within the programme have been systematically defined in notes and drawings designed to be handy and practical. In addition to listing the jobs to be done, these can serve both as routine reminders of

the hopeless task of discharging rainwater safely from the internal valleys between continuous double-pile roofs. Failure was all too evident in the massive outbreaks of dry rot discovered. The basic problems could only be successfully solved by bridging over the concealed internal roof from ridge to ridge, and providing an entirely new external rainwater disposal system.

113b

113c

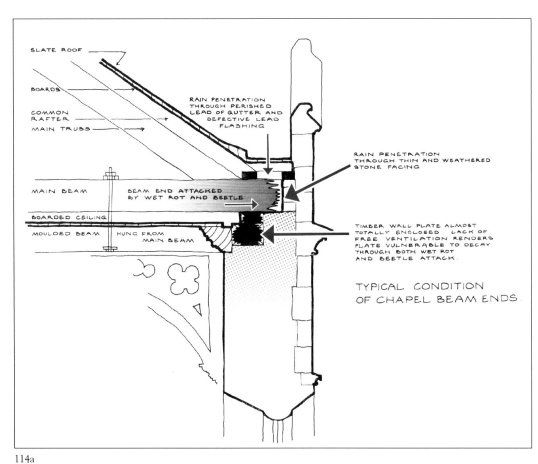

Diagram labels:

SLATE ROOF

BOARDS

COMMON RAFTER

MAIN TRUSS

RAIN PENETRATION THROUGH PERISHED LEAD OF GUTTER AND DEFECTIVE LEAD FLASHING

RAIN PENETRATION THROUGH THIN AND WEATHERED STONE FACING

MAIN BEAM

BEAM END ATTACKED BY WET ROT AND BEETLE

BOARDED CEILING

MOULDED BEAM

HUNG FROM MAIN BEAM

TIMBER WALL PLATE ALMOST TOTALLY ENCLOSED LACK OF FREE VENTILATION RENDERS PLATE VULNERABLE TO DECAY THROUGH BOTH WET ROT AND BEETLE ATTACK.

TYPICAL CONDITION OF CHAPEL BEAM ENDS.

114a

114a The chapel's decayed beam-ends and wallplates – a result of leaking gutters and lack of ventilation.

114b Trinity College. A planned maintenance programme provides for regular care and repair.

114b

their timing, and as records of action taken. Attentions are planned around practical maintenance routes, and the whole programme is wall-charted in the clerk of works' office, as a day-to-day guide in building care (p. 105).

The repairs programme has offered a good example of concentrated and continuous work, within an outstanding complex of historic buildings in single ownership. The College now firmly holds the initiative in controlling the natural forces of ageing, which had threatened a number of its historic buildings. The approach adopted, and the practical realisation of planned building care techniques, are as applicable to the smaller, humbler and less privileged buildings as to the greatest.

Trinity College. A planned maintenance and enhancement programme.

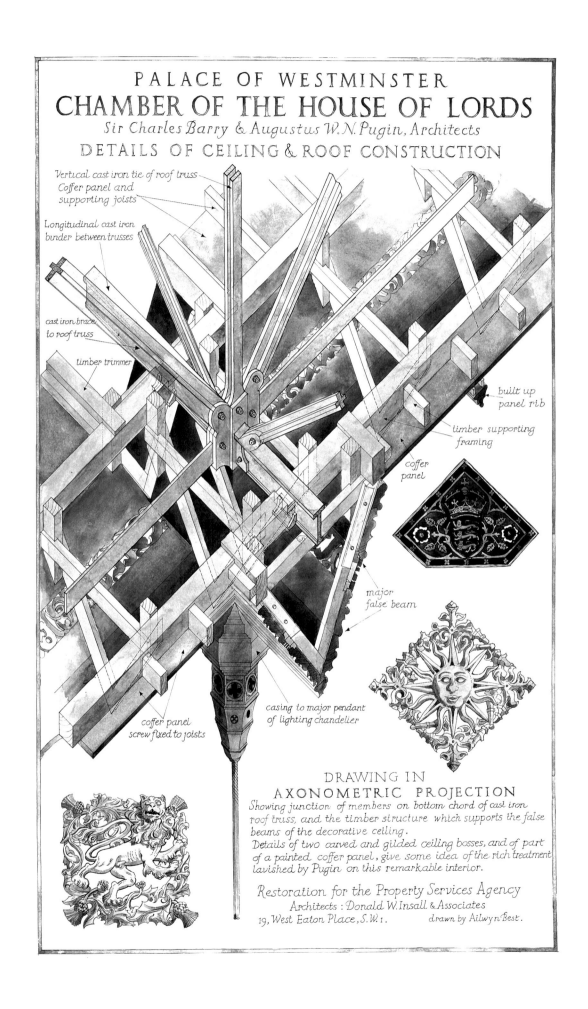

PALACE OF WESTMINSTER
CHAMBER OF THE HOUSE OF LORDS
Sir Charles Barry & Augustus W. N. Pugin, Architects
DETAILS OF CEILING & ROOF CONSTRUCTION

Vertical cast iron tie of roof truss
Coffer panel and supporting joists

Longitudinal cast iron binder between trusses

cast iron brace to roof truss

timber trimmer

built up panel rib

timber supporting framing

coffer panel

major false beam

coffer panel screw fixed to joists

casing to major pendant of lighting chandelier

DRAWING IN
AXONOMETRIC PROJECTION
Showing junction of members on bottom chord of cast iron roof truss, and the timber structure which supports the false beams of the decorative ceiling.
Details of two carved and gilded ceiling bosses, and of part of a painted coffer panel, give some idea of the rich treatment lavished by Pugin on this remarkable interior.

Restoration for the Property Services Agency
Architects : Donald W. Insall & Associates
19, West Eaton Place, S.W.1.   drawn by Ailwyn Best.

116

3. Conservation

117a

117b

117c

117a   The Lords' Chamber: interior with its ceiling.

117b   Inspecting the ceiling timbers from above.

117c   Danger! A falling pendant narrowly missed a sitting peer.

The Lords' Chamber, Palace of Westminster

The restoration of the magnificent but damaged wooden ceiling of the Lords' Chamber at the Palace of Westminster was a contract that exemplified the degree of care essential in strict conservation work, and the wide-ranging technical skills available for accurate and correct historical repair. This superb architectural achievement, probably the greatest work of Augustus Welby Northmore Pugin, was completed in 1847.

We were urgently called in to advise when during a late-night debate in July 1980, and without warning, a heavy wooden boss fell from the ceiling to the benches below. Mercifully, no one was killed. Scaffolding was erected and four architects, working in pairs and probing from above and below, first carried out a very thorough inspection. The ceiling proved to be, in effect, a decorative wooden canopy slung from

the iron structure above; we found it had become seriously degraded, in an unpredictable and haphazard way. Samples of the damaged timber were sent for examination to the Building Research Establishment. It was pronounced to be suffering from a serious loss of physical nature, which was interestingly identified as 'brashness'. It seemed this phenomenon could only have been caused by decades of 'toasting' during the 19th century, by the open jets of gas lamps hanging only a metre or two below the ceiling.

As soon as further instructions were received, the next step was to analyse carefully the structural hierarchy of the ceiling, devising a system of nomenclature to identify each element. A thorough photogrammetric and photographic record of the whole Palace had recently been made and this proved especially useful.

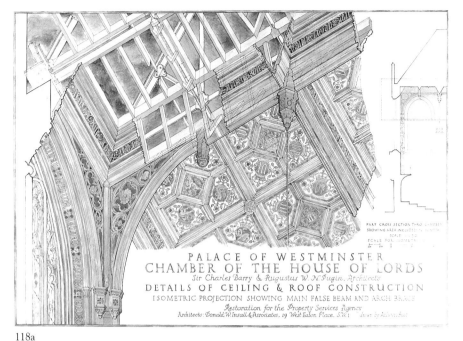

118a

118c

118b

118a Ceiling construction, seen from below. V-shaped 'beams' carry fretted ventilation slots in their flanks.

118b Dismantling a sample panel of the ceiling in reverse order of original assembly, and numbering each member for reference.

118c The hollow v-shaped softwood 'beams', seen from above.

A sample bay of the ceiling could then tentatively be dismantled, unit-by-unit. Photographs were taken and drawings made to record the construction methods and evident sequence of the ceiling's original assembly. The roof space above, with its iron structure, was subdivided by a hollow-tile floor into two 'decks', and had served in effect as a giant extract duct. Into this, vitiated air from the Chamber was drawn through a series of open frets in the flanks of the V-shaped ceiling beams, each carved in the form of the Garter inscription 'Dieu et Mon Droit'. A series of heraldic wooden panels was suspended from a supporting carpentry grid and was set between major and minor V-shaped beams. Although these appeared from below to be very solid, they proved on examination each to be made up of pairs of thin, moulded boards, supported on a lightweight carpentry framework, and hollow within. All this elaborately moulded woodwork was in short lengths of yellow pine;

it had been cut by early steam-driven machinery, and assembled moulding-by-moulding with roughly scribed butt-joints, glued and screwed together. Curved arched 'braces' from the walls gave apparent support to the major beams, and were again in yellow pine.

Moulded and decorated, all these timbers had suffered the same strange attack, now found in unpredictable, scattered areas of varying size. There was no evidence whatsoever of fungus or beetle, but the damage had made the ceiling timbers highly friable, lacking the normal fibrous strength of wood. When crushed in the hand, they reduced to powder and gave off the strong spicy smell now very noticeable in the enclosed roof spaces above. The only way to reinforce, strengthen and supplement the weakened structure would clearly be by replacing entire timbers, or by cutting out defective areas and piecing them in with new and matching woodwork.

The richly decorative ceiling had been completed by a wonderful assemblage of carved wooden details: pendant coronets (like the one that had fallen), bosses and rosettes. Five hundred and forty three of these beautiful carvings, executed under Pugin's personal direction, were affected; each was important as a specific work of art. It was established that if they were now to be renewed, the task would occupy expert carvers for at least 35 man-years. Set in the middle of each panel were a series of handsome carved and gilded trophies based on heraldic and similar motifs. The problem, if a suitable and reliable method could be found, was how much to renew and replace, and how to save intact all the more elaborate elements of craftsmanship.

Advice was sought from the Building Research Establishment, where a programme of research was carried out to identify a resin with all the necessary characteristics of penetration, setting-time, stability and strength. Eventually a suitable epoxy resin (butanediol diglycidyl ether) was found, but a practical technique of impregnation and treatment had to be devised. We negotiated with industrial chemists, who were able to demonstrate how to impregnate each carving under vacuum with the epoxy resin. After curing in mild heat, its chain-molecule formation could then replace the lost cell structure and restore some of its strength. The consolidated timbers carry no significant increase in weight, yet they have become once again capable of repair, re-decoration and re-gilding.

119a

119b

119a   Dismantling revealed only roughly scribed butt-joints against the moulded beam faces.

119b   Timber carpentry within the roofspace had lost its fibrous nature.

The next elements were the heraldic painted panels between the beams. These were of canvas mounted on wood and had likewise not escaped the attack of brashness. Painting conservation specialists were located and appointed. With them, we devised a technique of routing away the backs of the panels, leaving a thin facing with its irregular surface exactly as found, but remounting this under vacuum onto birch-faced plywood. Then they could be carefully cleaned and retouched, and brought back for reinstatement.

Having identified the main decorative elements and taken decisions about the degree of renewal or intervention necessary, we could number and set aside every element capable of reuse. Then the structural ceiling could be dismantled and eventually rebuilt. The unseen and unworked carpentry members could be renewed, to their exact original model. Likewise, the straight moulded work of the beam facings would be run anew, while every member of craft significance, like the curved work of the braces, would be carefully treated by 'dentistry' methods, cutting out damage and piecing it in with matched softwood.

A major challenge was to see how the operation could be carried out in practice, given this sensitive and busy situation. Our main concern was to ensure that if at all possible their Lordships should be able to continue undisturbed, occupying the Chamber in the normal way, over the entire time the work was in process.

120a

120a   Defective backing of the panels is routed away, to leave a thin original facing.

120b   Reverse of the panels, attacked by 'brashness'.

120c,d Nails removed and surface of panels protected, for remounting on new backing.

120b

120c

120d

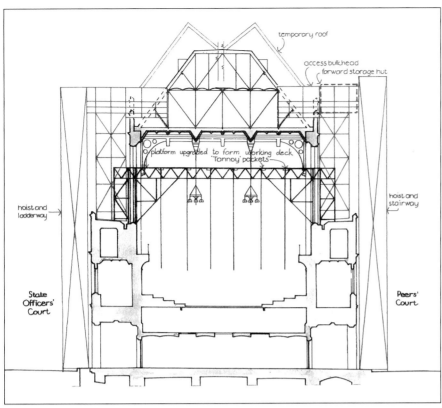

121a

temporary roof

access bulkhead
forward storage hut

platform upgraded to form working deck
'Tannoy' pockets

hoist and
stairway

hoist and
ladderway

State
Officers'
Court

Peers'
Court

121a   A working deck below the ceiling, with access from above and avoiding disturbance to the busy Lords' Chamber.

121b   The scaffolded interior.

121c   One of the two alternative access lifts to the roof.

121b

To achieve this, the temporary inspection deck was first strengthened to form a solid working platform, incorporating services such as air conditioning, suspended microphones and the like. In this way, work might be concentrated into busy mornings before the sittings of the House, confining major disruption to vacations. A further challenge was to incorporate an acceptable access route, a working compound and proper protection within this intensively used building.

We arranged a system of scaffolding incorporating two alternative external lifts, giving quiet access into the roof space, and from there downwards to the ceiling. To provide a local storage reservoir for returning woodwork and newly treated timbers, an air-conditioned hut was incorporated at a high level.

121c

A carefully considered programme was devised, to be executed over three years. A schedule of works was also drafted and costed in discussion with our quantity surveyors, identifying budgets for agreement. Following competitive tendering, a main contractor was appointed to direct and carry out the main timberwork renewal and repairs, and to coordinate the many specialists engaged. Skilled subcontractors would be needed; these in turn were invited and selected in competition. Following wide enquiries, some excellent firms of wood carvers were located, three of whom were selected. The partly experimental process of chemical consolidation would be more difficult to assign, but we found a small firm that was prepared to undertake the task on negotiated rates. So now, the team was in place.

The first task was the recording and dismantling of this great ceiling. The carvings were taken down, as the time needed for their treatment and restoration was critical to the whole programme. Then the heraldic panels were removed for specialist repair. Finally the remainder of the woodwork could be carefully dismantled. For a while, there would be no ceiling.

The arched braces were boxed and taken to the main contractors' joinery workshops off site, where damaged areas could be painstakingly cut out and renewed. They were then vacuum-treated with insecticide, for later return. Meanwhile the great wooden supporting frames of the superstructure were re-made. The new Scots pine for carcassing was specially felled and supplied from the Cawdor Estate in Scotland. The construction replicated

122b

122c

122a

122a   Consolidant is introduced into one of the carved fretwork panels, supported on a carrying frame.

122b   Carvings treated with the consolidant are cured in a practical 'oven'.

122c   Eventually, the whole defective ceiling structure is dismantled.

123a

123b

the original, although an improved system of fixings was introduced, incorporating slotted stainless-steel brackets. The original straight beamwork suspended from it had been run by steam-driven machinery and not by hand, so it was run again by modern machinery and in selected Canadian yellow pine.

Back on site, the scaffolding was further reinforced. Then, item by item, all the new frames and the pieced and repaired work were returned. Gradually, and element by element, the whole main structure was reassembled as a ceiling. Taking advantage of a parliamentary recess, the heaviest work was done in the summer, when the restored ceiling could at last be reinstated and prepared for redecoration. Following careful research and microscopic sampling, and in close discussions with historic decorations consultant Dr Ian Bristow, it was re-coloured and re-gilded exactly on the original model, and again with 23¼-carat gold leaf. New gold, being a metal, cannot be varied in colour; but we found it could be 'tuned' by a traditional but reversible surface treatment employing parchment size and pigment, to perfectly match the new work with the restored original.

The whole process was recorded in detail by accurately scaleable photographs of each item of carving. As a record and as

123a Craftsman and apprentice work together on piecing-in a carved wooden brace.

123b A wooden boss is repaired.

123c The beam-work is repainted in a careful match to the original colours and re-gilded.

123c

124a

124b

an experiment, glass-fibre casts were also made of selected trophies, where this proved safe and possible without damage. From these, and using a three-dimensional pantograph, carved wooden copies could be re-created if this ever became necessary in the future. The available funds did not however permit the precaution of making a complete set.

This was a highly complex programme of work. But by identifying its component elements – structural carcassing, straight moulded beamwork, curved braces, elaborate carved ornament and painted heraldic panels – all in turn reunited by expert redecoration and re-gilding, the task could be planned and executed as a series of carefully coordinated specialist items. We were fortunate to have the great expertise of all the skilled craftsmen, contractors and specialists, to whose enthusiasm and exemplary zeal this magnificent work may today be credited. The project was safely completed for the Royal Opening of Parliament on 6 November 1984, and within the budgeted cost.

A project of this magnitude and complexity may call upon every degree of intervention, ranging from retention to renewal. Decisions can only be taken as each problem arises, but can be safely united within a sure and trustworthy conservation philosophy.

124a The Lords' ceiling repaired: the pendant that had fallen to the benches below.

124b The completed ceiling: moulded beams, heraldic panels, carved decorations and frets, and their final painting and gilding.

124c A treated and re-gilded 'trophy' from the centre of a ceiling panel.

124c

The restored ceiling, under television lighting at the completion ceremony.

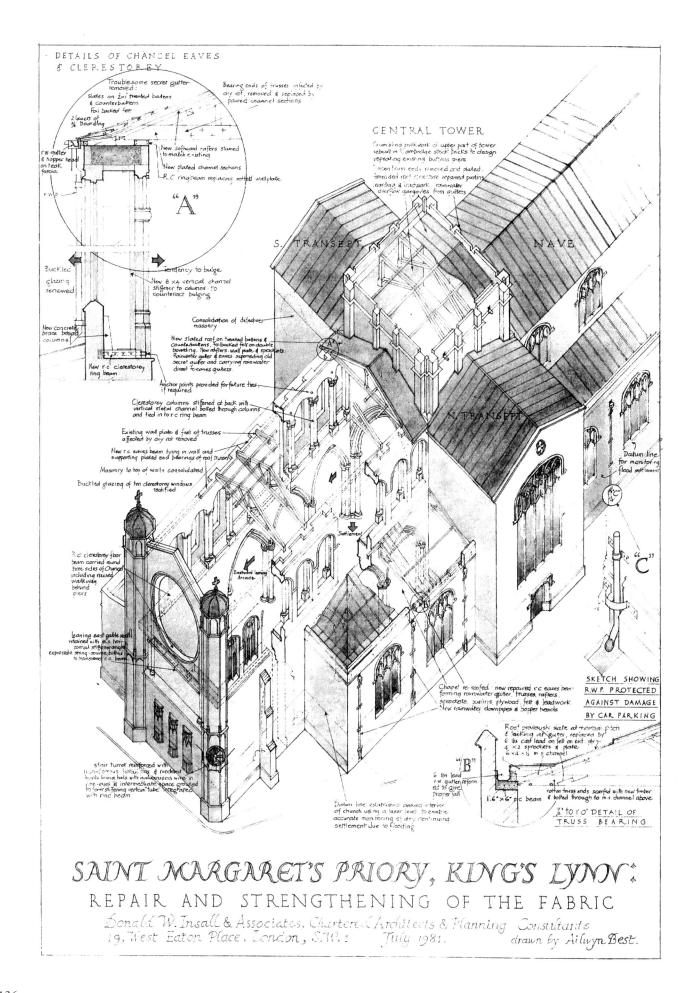

DETAILS OF CHANCEL EAVES & CLERESTOREY

Troublesome secret gutter removed:
Slates on 2x1 treated battens & counterbattens
Foil backed felt
2 layers of ¾ boarding

Bearing ends of trusses infected by dry rot, removed & replaced by paired channel sections

r.w gutter & hopper head on teak fascia

New softwood rafters stained to match existing
New plated channel sections
R.C ring beam replacing rotted wallplate

"A"

r.w.p

Buckled glazing renewed

Tendency to bulge
New 8 x4 vertical channel stiffener to columns to counteract bulging

New concrete brace behind columns

New r.c clerestorey ring beam

CENTRAL TOWER

Crumbling brickwork of upper part of tower rebuilt in Cambridge stock bricks to design repeating existing buttress piers

Rotten truss ends removed and plated. Remainder of roof structure repaired, purlins, boarding & leadwork, rainwater overflow gargoyles from gutters

S. TRANSEPT   NAVE

Consolidation of defective masonry

New slated roof on treated battens & counterbattens, foilbacked felt on double boarding. New rafters, wall plate & sprockets. Rainwater gutter & eaves superceding old secret gutter and carrying rainwater direct to eaves gutters

Anchor points provided for future ties, if required

Clerestorey columns stiffened at back with vertical metal channel bolted through columns and tied in to r.c ring beam

Existing wall plate & feet of trusses affected by dry rot removed

New r.c eaves beam tying in wall and supporting plated end bearings of roof trusses

Masonry to top of walls consolidated

Buckled glazing of ten clerestorey windows rectified

N. TRANSEPT

Datum line for monitoring flood settlement

"C"

"C"

Settlement

Eastward leaning Arcade

R.c clerestorey floor beam carried round three sides of Chancel including raised walkway behind piers

Leaning east gable wall retained with m.s horizontal stiffener angle expressed as string course, bolted to transverse r.c. beam

Chapel re-roofed: new repaired r.c eaves beam forming rainwater gutter, trusses, rafters, sprockets, purlins, plywood, felt & leadwork
New rainwater downpipes & hopper heads

SKETCH SHOWING R.W.P. PROTECTED AGAINST DAMAGE BY CAR PARKING

Roof previously slate at minimal pitch & leaking at gutter, replaced by: 6 lbs cast lead on felt on ext. ply; 4 x2 sprockets & plate; 6 x4 x½ m.s channel

"B"

6 lbs lead r.w. gutter reformed to give proper fall

stair turret reinforced with non-ferrous fixings, pins & rendered thumb lining held with galvanised wire in ring-eaves & intermediate space grouted to form stiffening vertical tube integrated with ring beam

1'6" x 6" r.c beam

rotten truss ends scarfed with new timber & bolted through to m.s channel above

½" TO 1'0" DETAIL OF TRUSS BEARING

Datum line established around interior of church using a laser level to enable accurate monitoring of any continuing settlement due to flooding

SAINT MARGARET'S PRIORY, KING'S LYNN:
REPAIR AND STRENGTHENING OF THE FABRIC

Donald W. Insall & Associates, Chartered Architects & Planning Consultants
19, West Eaton Place, London, S.W.1   July 1981.   drawn by Ailwyn Best.

4. Major repairs

St Margaret's Church, King's Lynn

Next in the ascending scale of a building's health requirements comes the cyclical renewal of its materials, resulting from age, weather and changing circumstances.

Despite a natural reluctance to replace the original structure and workmanship, the owner and his architect must accept that virtually no building element can possibly be eternal. What we must first carefully evaluate is the relative significance of both original work and any subsequent changes.

In a few instances, the workmanship itself may be more important than the design. In these cases, the only decent answer is to sustain, extend and protect the life of this fading craftsmanship, as far as this is humanly reasonable and at sensible cost. But where the hand of the craftsman is less in evidence, original materials may simply have to be replaced as regularly as they also repeatedly decay. The new materials used may then be either identical or similar, or may incorporate technical advances and improvements.

Weathering and the ravages of time meanwhile bring their own message; sometimes they even add subtly and irreplaceably to the attractions of architectural form. Every copied historic element and feature is something new, and each loss of the original element brings changes in identity. Meanwhile, time moves on, and in the life of a building, the periodical major repair programme is a fact of that life. In practical terms too, the extent and timing of work undertaken will take into account the cost of access and the inevitable nuisance of disturbance. Sometimes a concentrated or localised programme brings real benefits in efficiency or economy, or by avoiding unnecessary damage.

Examples of major repairs include replacing whole areas of roof leadwork and re-hanging slate or tile slopes, repairing and re-pointing stonework and brickwork, renewing worn stones now admitting damage to their neighbours, and carrying out necessary joinery repairs. In many cases, other works such as removing harmful or misguided alterations and additions can be carried out at the same time.

Periodical 'major servicing' is as essential to a building as to a machine; the age-old maxim about 'a stitch in time' is just as relevant.

The system of quinquennial inspections now adopted by the Church of England for all places of worship and all parsonage houses enables incipient troubles to be detected before they become too damaging, and before their cost grows too crippling. It is probably true to say that since this routine was introduced in 1955, our churches as a whole are better maintained than ever before. This is not to claim that emergencies do not or cannot arise, but at least they may be seen in perspective, so that proper budget provision can be made on a planned and phased basis. A great number of other buildings, notably country houses, could benefit from a similarly prudent programme of regular surveys; a great many have been lost in the absence of such a programme.

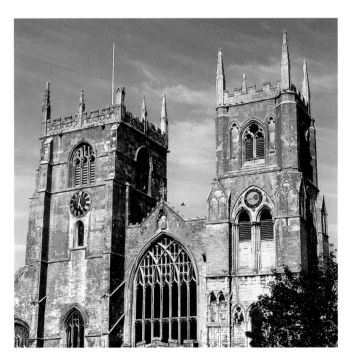

Northwest tower (left) rebuilt externally in 1453; a spire was added to the southwest tower but was lost in a storm in 1741.

From time to time however, every building passes through a period when major structural repairs become essential. The cause may be simply an accumulation of neglect in many areas, but action is often triggered by a more urgent item like a rapid attack of dry rot that cannot be ignored. This combination of circumstances occurred at a magnificent Priory Church in King's Lynn.

Sited in the Saturday Market Place, this great building is nearly 80 metres long and is one of the major monuments in the town. It dominates the local skyline with its squat twin towers, and closes the vista along the pedestrianised High Street. Located near the river estuary, the church has repeatedly been flooded with salt water (the latest occasion was in 1978, to a depth of more than one metre), and the chancel roof had also become visibly dangerous after prolonged damage by gutter leaks.

This church has a complex and fascinating structural history. The oldest part dates from the 12th century, but after the two massive west towers were built, they evidently began to lean. The top of the northwest tower was removed and rebuilt, and at the same time its vertical alignment

128a   The nave after flooding in 1978.

128b   Drying-out: salt residue on floor.

128c   Inside, arches lean strongly to the west.

129a

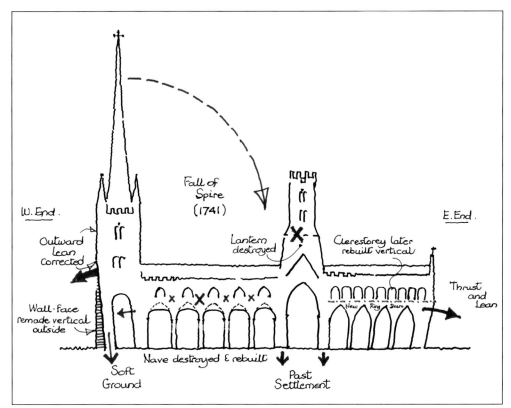

129b

129a   From the south, when
       complete with southwest
       spire and central lantern.

129b   Diagrammatic history.

130a

130b

was extended downwards to ground level, towards which the west wall now thickens. So while the tower's exterior appears true, the internal arches lean quite dramatically to the west. The second and southwest tower originally carried a tall spire, and contained a ring of bells. No doubt following a progressive weakening, this spire collapsed dramatically in a thunderstorm in 1741 and fell about the nave and transepts, largely destroying them. It also wrecked what

was evidently a somewhat Ely-like lantern, which crowned the crossing. The nave was soon rebuilt, with a new elliptical arcade springing from the older pier bases; but puzzling misalignments remained at the crossing (even apart from settlements), and these were inexplicable until we knew about the existence and destruction of the earlier heavy lantern.

In the 19th century Sir George Gilbert Scott drew up elaborate plans for a new octagonal lantern tower, as well as for the complete refitting of the interiors of the church, but these evidently proved too expensive and were never built. To the east, the chancel arcades had in turn spread and produced an increasing outward lean in that direction. Here in similar fashion, the clerestory had been dismantled and again rebuilt, set vertically and to a new design but re-using original mouldings. Yet more changes appear in early photographs, for they show the nave and aisles with deep galleries returned across under the great west window, in front of which a large organ was installed. All of these had since been removed.

130a   Arches at crossing still 14th century: but nave rebuilt, with semi-elliptical arches.

130b   13th-century bases remain, in rebuilt nave arcade.

The net result is a large and handsome church on uncertain ground, subject to periodical flooding, and with both west and east ends leaning outwards in opposite directions, each partly disguised by later building and compounded by continuing alterations. Throughout, it displayed settlements and cracking, partly due to foundation movements and flooding and partly to the earlier fall of the spire onto the lantern, in turn removing its own historical evidence.

We decided to establish at least a firm basis of knowledge about any continuing and future movement. Trial drillings were taken, to learn more about the subsoil. A new horizontal datum was next established with a laser level, to extend throughout the church, and permanent plumb-line points were set up for future regular checks on verticality. Reliable readings can now therefore be taken over a period, with a very clear knowledge about what relative movements have occurred.

In exploring the dangerously dropped roof of the chancel, we noted that an irregular loading of the greatly weakened, heavy structure was in turn causing new distortions of its own, compounding those of earlier damage and settlement. Under the load of the remaining sound roof trusses, the slim inner shafts of the chancel clerestory, separated from their windows by a narrow walkway, were beginning to bow inwards, while barrel-fashion, the corresponding windows were distorting outwards.

131b

131a

131a   Movements distorting window tracery.

131b   Establishing a laser-based datum level, to monitor future movements.

132a

132c

132b

132d

wallplate. Here all damaged woodwork was removed, and a continuous restraining beam of reinforced concrete was cast along the top of the wall to stiffen it; this being also carried into the eastern gable to link the whole together. Along the flat walkway below the windows, a reinforced concrete girdle was then inserted, carried across inside the leaning east wall, this time below the rose window and with ties to an external brace. At the springings of the chancel arch, concealed hooks were provided, in case any future movement might demand a tie-wire or rod to complete the entire circuit.

In the outer east corners were a pair of narrow spiral staircases, weakening the angles between the walls, but providing access to the clerestory. Thanks to a resourceful building foreman, their thin outer walls were lined from the inside with expanded metal mesh, and grouted up to create in each a vertical stiffening tube. This was linked with the reinforcement at clerestory walkway level, so that the whole system adds a three-dimensional cage of restraint against the compound pattern of movements observed in the chancel. Finally to stiffen them, the bowed clerestory shafts were backed by light vertical steel channels, invisible from below (132c). So a great deal of extra strength has been inconspicuously introduced into a very lively structure.

Given a knowledge and understanding of the particular circumstances, the next necessity in any conservation contract is that of adequate access and protection. A carved reredos was sheeted to avoid damage. The chancel and its flanking chapels were scaffolded, and an external hoist was installed to provide a working access route inwards through the clerestory, without disturbance to the interior below. The scaffolding also carried a temporary roof, affording continuity of work; the roof slating under its cover was stripped to expose the construction. Rotten trusses and timbers were repaired, splinted and plated as necessary, and a double opportunity was taken in removing the rotten

133a

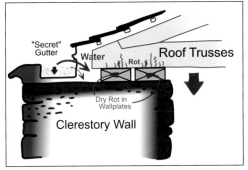

"Secret" Gutter — Water — **Roof Trusses** — Rot — Dry Rot in Wallplates — **Clerestory Wall**

133b

We found that the cause of the roof trouble had been the existence of 'secret' gutters, which were now constantly blocked by pigeons' mess (King's Lynn is a grain port). As a consequence of faulty original detailing, these gutters had repeatedly overflowed inwards into the church. The slopes were re-slated to an improved design to dispose of the rainwater, and new external eaves gutters were provided. These are of stout cast-iron to resist ladders, and a visible emergency overflow spout is provided at the head of each downpipe.

In reinstating the clerestory windows, their leaded glass was repaired and re-formed as far as the budget would allow. The square base of the lost lantern had been only roughly made up in 19th-century brick, which had severely eroded. Now it was rebuilt in a cream-coloured Cambridge brick to harmonise with the stone, stepped and buttressed to match the base.

What we were unable to undertake is perhaps as significant as the work completed. From our inspection, we estimated that essential work called for a budget that in architectural terms might represent the demands not so much of a parish church as of a mini-cathedral. But the appeal fund aimed lower than this, and could not reach even its lesser target. We had therefore to dismantle falling pinnacles on the west towers, but could not at the time rebuild them. Essential

133a Exploring decayed timbers inside the 'secret' eaves-gutter.

133b Roof water driven inwards by blocked gutters causes dry rot in wooden wallplate and trusses.

133c Roof-truss given sound new bearing by a steel shoe.

133d The remedy: 'secret' gutter roofed-over, and a new and visible outer eaves-gutter.

133e Emergency outflow at each new rainwater head.

133c

133d

133e

134a

134b

renewals of roof leadwork had to be restrained within budget. An alarming fruiting-body appeared above the nave arcade, warning of likely dry rot in the aisle wall-plates, which could endanger the wide timber roof above. External stonework was repaired only locally, and a long-term task of essential stone repairs was still accumulating.

In many of the greater churches in the land, immense efforts are now needed to catch up with their daily physical deterioration and decay. At the time we were involved with this building (1977–1981), it was heartbreaking to share in the positive ideas of the vicar, a man of taste and vision, for the enhancement and improvement of his church as a powerhouse of worship,

and a fundamental resource for parish work. It was just possible financially to undertake some items including the new ironwork gate for a side-chapel, and the cleaning of a single panel of a magnificent Bodley reredos. But the heating and lighting improvements remained outstanding, as did many other worthy improvements.

A small and very successful gesture was the re-use of a dangerously fallen stone pinnacle from the tower to form the base of an altar for a new temporary chapel, with a simple curtain backdrop and a single spotlight trained upon it. The question of 'degree' of intervention has sometimes a deep financial and economic undertow.

134a   A 19th-century red-brick replacement of the wrecked roof-lantern, now itself in trouble.

134b   The central tower re-roofed, and termination rebuilt.

134c   Emergency: stone pinnacle distorted by old rusting cramps.

134d   Another tower pinnacle, already collapsed into the parapet-gutter (one stone had also fallen to the Nave roof below).

134c

134d

The repaired chancel clerestory, given additional invisible strength.

TEN DEGREES OF INTERVENTION   135

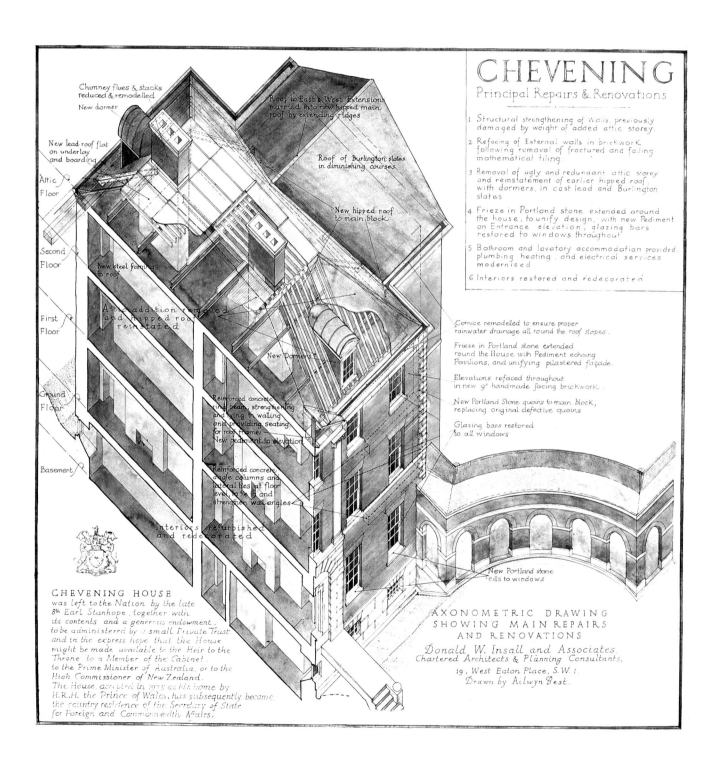

CHEVENING
Principal Repairs & Renovations

1. Structural strengthening of walls, previously damaged by weight of added attic storey.

2. Refacing of External walls in brickwork following removal of fractured and failing mathematical tiling.

3. Removal of ugly and redundant attic storey and reinstatement of earlier hipped roof, with dormers, in cast lead and Burlington slates

4. Frieze in Portland stone extended around the house, to unify design, with new Pediment on Entrance elevation; glazing bars restored to windows throughout

5. Bathroom and lavatory accommodation provided, plumbing, heating, and electrical services modernised

6. Interiors restored and redecorated

Chimney flues & stacks reduced & remodelled

New dormer

Roof to East & West Extensions married into new hipped main roof by extending ridges

New lead roof flat on underlay and boarding

Roof of Burlington slates in diminishing courses

Attic Floor

New hipped roof to main block

Second Floor

New steel framing to roof

First Floor

Attic addition removed and hipped roof reinstated

New Dormers

Ground Floor

Reinforced concrete ring beam, strengthening and tying in walling and providing seating for roof frame

New pediment to elevation

Basement

Reinforced concrete angle columns and lateral ties at floor level, to tie in and strengthen wall angles

Interiors refurbished and redecorated

Cornice remodelled to ensure proper rainwater drainage all round the roof slopes.

Frieze in Portland stone extended round the House with Pediment echoing Pavilions, and unifying pilastered façade.

Elevations refaced throughout in new 9" handmade facing brickwork.

New Portland Stone quoins to main block, replacing original defective quoins

Glazing bars restored to all windows

New Portland stone cills to windows

CHEVENING HOUSE
was left to the Nation by the late 8th Earl Stanhope, together with its contents and a generous endowment, to be administered by a small Private Trust and in the express hope that the House might be made available to the Heir to the Throne, to a Member of the Cabinet, to the Prime Minister of Australia, or to the High Commissioner of New Zealand. The House, accepted in 1974 as his home by H.R.H. the Prince of Wales, has subsequently become the country residence of the Secretary of State for Foreign and Commonwealth Affairs.

AXONOMETRIC DRAWING SHOWING MAIN REPAIRS AND RENOVATIONS
Donald W. Insall and Associates, Chartered Architects & Planning Consultants.
19, West Eaton Place, S.W.1.
Drawn by Ailwyn Best.

5. Radical improvement

Chevening House, Kent

On occasion, a situation develops in which even major structural repairs are insufficient, and a more radical programme of changes and improvements to a building is the only possible successful remedy. In 1967, such a case arose at Chevening, near Sevenoaks in Kent, when the house was left to the nation in the will of the last Lord Stanhope. The will also established a trust, with appropriate experts as trustees, and a fund from which repairs could be carried out without recourse to public funds.

The trustees were faced with a furnished house in severe disrepair. Lord Stanhope's wish was that it be offered for use by a member of the Royal Family or a leading Minister of the Crown, but the house lacked the qualities to make the offer either viable or tempting. An early approach had received a discouraging response; the house seemed to have little at that time to commend it but its privacy. We were appointed to investigate its history, and to recommend whether there might be a positive way forward.

Chevening was initially built between 1616 and 1630; the original design is often attributed to Inigo Jones. We found that the house incorporated vestiges of a slightly earlier building within the cellars. Originally it had been a tall and imposing four-square block, an early example of the double-pile plan, with a basement and three upper storeys, all set with big casement windows. According to the inset drawing in an early estate map of 1679, there had been a tall hipped roof with a balustraded corona. But very early in its life, the house had experienced a succession of major changes. First, the main entrance was switched to the north side, and between 1717 and 1730 two flanking projections were added. A pair of handsome red brick pavilions by Thomas Fort (1718) were built, facing one

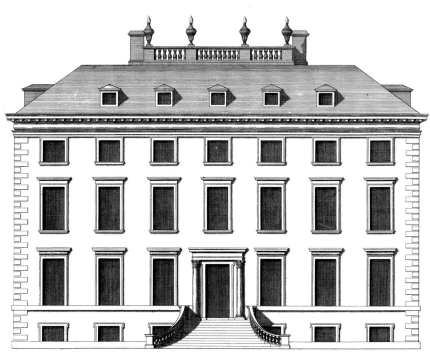

137a

137b

137a   Vitruvius Britannicus (Vol. II: 1717) illustrates the 'Elevation of Chevening House in Kent'.

137b   Chevening House: from the corner of an estate map of 1679.

another across a forecourt, and linked to the house by two curving quadrants. The forecourt was then enclosed within a wrought-iron screen and gates. This was all the concept of the Stanhopes, who acquired the house and estate in 1715. In 1721 the main block acquired a superb 'flying' spiral staircase, the work of Nicholas Dubois, one-time master-mason to the Crown; but what followed was less happy. Towards the end of the century (1776–1796) a box-like attic storey was added (possibly by James Wyatt) to provide sufficient accommodation for servants. The front and back elevations were given stone pilasters and the cornice was remodelled. A large projecting porch was later added at the entrance; between 1855 and 1860 the glazing bars were removed from the sash windows, substituting blank planes of clear glass.

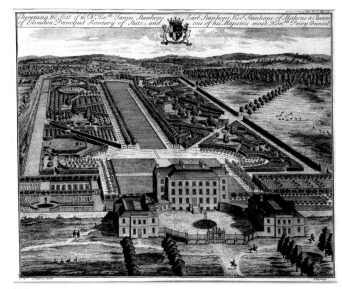

138a

138a   Flanking projections, two pavilions and an enclosed forecourt: a new concept for the Stanhope family in 1715.

138b   The House by 1968: pilastered treatment, mathematical tiling, added attic storey and porch (and loss of glazing bars).

138b

The complete exterior of the main block up to cornice level, which at first appeared to be of dun-coloured brick, proved on closer inspection to have been clad between 1789 and 1796 by the Third Earl in stone-coloured mathematical tiles, fixed with great iron spikes driven deeply into the original soft red local brickwork. But these were now causing cracking at the building's angles and were falling away like leaves in autumn. The interior had splendid rooms but lacked modern bathrooms; the distant kitchen in one of the pavilions was piled high with old memorabilia and unwanted furniture. In short, the house had become something of an architectural enigma. Many relatively

recent improvement proposals, such as ideas for re-facing the house entirely in stone, had offered no acceptable answer. It seemed essential to revert to first principles, so that the trustees could decide what was now to be done.

We prepared an analysis of the merits of the house, outside and in, and set about assessing its problems, starting with the falling external wall tiling. This had all too easily come away; our first surprise was the motley mixture of brickwork behind. Above the windows were deeply radiating brick arches of an engineering type, and curious lines of differences could

139a

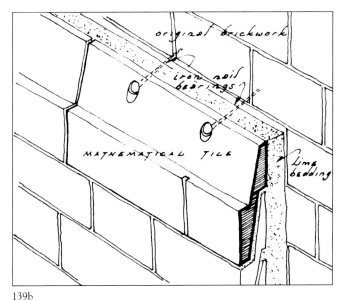

139b

139d

CHEVENING · KENT
SOUTH ELEVATION

KEY

■	1630 - 1650 BRICK WORK		INIGO JONES c 1620
	1630 - 1650 STONE		
	1720 BRICKWORK		1717 CHEVENING BOUGHT BY LD STANHOPE
	1789 - 1798 BRICK PIERS TO TAKE TILES		3RD EARL STANHOPE
	1789 - 1798 PORTLAND STONE		
	1817 ATTICS (RAISED 1776)		4TH EARL STANHOPE

139c

139a Falling mathematical tiles; and brickwork damage by iron spikes.

139b Tiling detail and rusting iron fixings.

139c The walling analysed: original soft red brickwork and later alterations, found hidden behind tiles.

139d Radiating brick arches could not have been original, and match altered window surrounds.

be detected in the red brickwork, which was evidently of more than one date. From research in the archives and from direct observation, we came gradually to the conclusion that when the house was clad with tiles it had evidently also been heavily adapted to receive new sash windows, and that the brickwork around these had been completely rebuilt, leaving original red facing-brick only in the irregular piers between them. The whole of the main walls below a re-made cornice had been covered by the mathematical tiles on a bed of lime. A few traces of stone remained to show where original string-courses had been cut away; the stepped quoin stones were also riven by the rusting iron nails. Crowning the façades, an attic storey had been added in place of the sloping roof. Its front was of brickwork rendered in cement; but its flanks were made of timber carrying gigantic slates.

140a

140b

140a Added attic above cornice. Cracked angle of walling below, supported by raking shores.

140b Deep vertical cracking behind added tiles at angles of the house.

140c Preparing cracked corners of the house for reinforced stitching.

140c

140d

Deep vertical cracks near the outer angles of the house, caused by the iron spikes, were probably exacerbated by the added and unequal loading of this attic floor and possibly by lateral thermal movement of the thin outer skin. With the advice of the trustees' structural engineers, we embarked upon a method of stitching the cracked corners by an interesting technique of reinforcement. Using the principle of underpinning, alternate series of holes were cut into the brickwork and permanent steel 'stools' were set into these to support the walling above. Then the next series of holes was cut. The result was the gradual replacement of an entire bank of walling at floor level in each angle by a line of these 'stools', each provided with legs

140d,e Inserted 'stools' in holes alternately cut away, and providing for horizontal reinforcement.

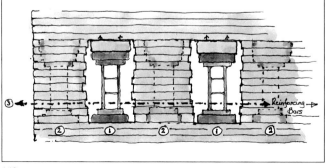

140e

140

between which lateral reinforcing bars would be thrust, the whole being then encased in concrete. Vertical reinforcement was at the same time set into the corners of the house to unite these stitches, and to form a homogeneous system of beams lacing the cracks, all within the thickness of the wall.

Two major issues were meanwhile discussed: how to reface the badly damaged surface of the walls, and what to do about the added box-like attic. What might it cost to remove and replace it with a sloping hipped roof, while refacing the walls with brick? Or should these be simply rendered or harled? We investigated all the alternatives and discussed the possibilities with the planning authorities, the Historic Buildings Council and the trustees. It would, we felt, benefit the house to lose the added attics, which were now a structural embarrassment and were no longer required for actual accommodation. There was no reliable evidence of the exact form of the original roof: would the later pavilions now overmaster the main block without its top addition? Should its added lateral projections too come off? The options were all examined, and in discussion with the trustees we came gradually to a recommendation. We felt that whatever might be the theoretical merits of any proposals to remove the

additions and to return to the early 17th-century design, it was the Stanhope concept of the building that should be honoured. So the attics could go, and the rest should stay.

Meanwhile experiments with the outside of the walls were pursued. Might the original bricks, if enough could be extracted, be reversed so as to present their undamaged inner ends? We tried it; but they were mostly cracked beyond recall. Might there be a good local brick that, suitably bonded (to avoid a rather mechanical effect that we had recently noted at a re-faced Downing Street) and laid in a carefully chosen mortar, could echo the original and even complement the later brick of the two pavilions? Luckily there was, though we had to select the most suitable of them at the brickyard. We had also to find and order a softer brick for the radiating window arches, and a stone for the sills, as well as to devise a way of bonding the new work back into the old walls.

Another problem was how to reinstate not the original but the present forward line of the wall face, including the lime and the tiling, because the added stone pilasters and dressings and even the elaborate wooden cornice had all been set forward to match it.

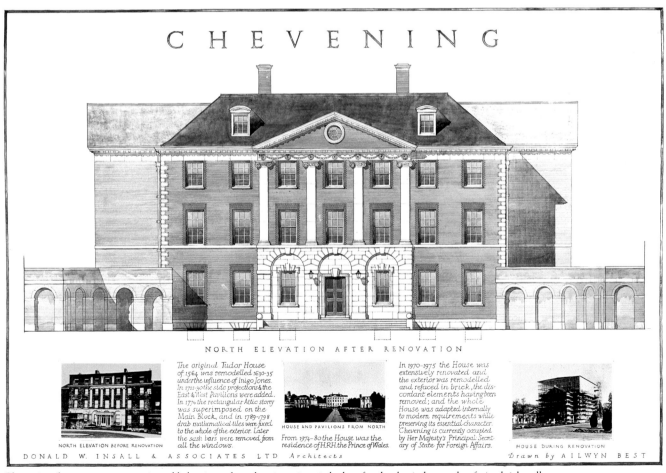

CHEVENING

NORTH ELEVATION AFTER RENOVATION

The original Tudor House of 1564 was remodelled 1630-35 under the influence of Inigo Jones. In 1721-30 the side projections & the East & West Pavilions were added. In 1776 the rectangular Attic storey was superimposed on the Main Block, and in 1789-1798 drab mathematical tiles were fixed to the whole of the exterior. Later the sash bars were removed from all the windows.

NORTH ELEVATION BEFORE RENOVATION

HOUSE AND PAVILIONS FROM NORTH

From 1974-80 the House was the residence of H.R.H. the Prince of Wales.

In 1970-1975 the House was extensively renovated and the exterior was remodelled and refaced in brick, the discordant elements having been removed; and the whole House was adapted internally to modern requirements while preserving its essential character. Chevening is currently occupied by Her Majesty's Principal Secretary of State for Foreign Affairs.

HOUSE DURING RENOVATION

DONALD W. INSALL & ASSOCIATES LTD Architects

Drawn by AILWYN BEST

Chevening: front entrance, removing added attics and porch, reinstating pitched roof and sash windows and re-facing brick walls.

142a

142a The house
    scaffolded and with
    a cover-roof during
    removal of attics.

142b Attics during
    demolition, taking
    up load of tie-bars
    to floor below.

142b

Eventually, the broken facings were trimmed away and two highly experienced bricklayers began to restore the integrity of the piebald walls with new handmade brick, built up ring-by-ring in courses around the building, securely bonded back and tied into the older work. The brickwork pointing was a particularly delicate exercise, carried out as the work proceeded, and set back just sufficiently to avoid smearing the face or losing the arrises. Every load of sand was tested for salt, to be sure that no efflorescence would disfigure the final result. Gradually the new facings rose to meet the cornice, and at last the walls looked healthy again.

Meanwhile, from an immense scaffolding and cover-roof, which incidentally seemed to have a short-lived architectural dignity and glamour all of its own, the unsightly added attic storey was removed. We almost immediately hit a problem. The retained upper floors below it, having evidently sagged, had been supported by vertical hanging tie-bars from the now-missing top addition. But since no one knew at this stage whether

143a

the house would ever be occupied again, it seemed unlikely that the new roof space would need to be habitable. So steel was inserted to pick up the vertical hanging-bars, the tops of which could then be trimmed away. Although we would have preferred a new hipped roof structure entirely in timber, steel was also used for the trusses, on economic grounds. We were constrained within a budget and did not wish to compromise the exterior.

To arrive at the most satisfactory alignment for the new dormer windows, we made a scale model and first experimented. Then they were framed up, boarded and covered in cast lead. New cast lead was used for the flat top of the roof and also for the rainwater downpipes – luckily here we could avoid compromising quality by savings elsewhere, for which we thanked our quantity surveyor. The imperial-sized bricks ran out, and we had to use the new metric sizes for the chimneys; but in practice, the difference is undetectable. We were alarmed when the contractors arrived on site with a vast crane to deliver the new stone chimney cappings, but that was their choice. The roof slopes were carefully finished with selected Burlington stone slates; and stage by stage the scaffolding could be taken away.

143b

143a   Chevening House: the completed entrance-front.

143b   Two skilled bricklayers painstakingly re-faced the entire exterior with local hand-made bricks.

The Prince of Wales converses with the bricklayer (1974).

To restore their proportions, the window sashes of the elevations below were re-subdivided with slim astragals; but we had to make do with the slightly crooked 18th-century frames, risking the criticism of future occupants. Glazing and painting continued, and the house gradually arose phoenix-like from its scaffolded state. We were thankfully able to confirm how the roof-form of the main block, now incorporating a pediment uniting its pilasters, related beautifully with that of the flanking pavilions. The whole group, again reading as one, would continue as a lasting tribute to successive generations of the Stanhope family, as the generous final donors of this great estate.

It was at about this time, after much contradictory rumour and press speculation, that we were gratified to learn that the refurbished house, made so much more habitable, was to become the country home of HRH the Prince of Wales.

The major architectural interiors were painstakingly redecorated to schemes by John Fowler and others; new bathrooms were added, using the newly installed internal plumbing; and the trustees fitted-out a new kitchen. At last the house began to come back to life. At many points it had been close to spoliation and loss, but now it seemed safe, although as yet Chevening's

royal incumbent could find relatively little time to enjoy life in Kent.

In 1980, after some five years' residence, the Prince decided to move to an estate further west in Gloucestershire. There was an interregnum while successive ministers took the mantle of the 'nominated person' provided for by Lord Stanhope's will. The house seemed for a while underutilised, but then in a fresh wave of vitality it was decided to devote it to a programme of international hospitality by the Foreign Office to visiting diplomats and others, and as the official residence of the Foreign Secretary. The privacy and quality of the house make it highly suited to such a function and gradually it is re-acquiring character in its new role as something of a 'resident ambassador' for Britain. We were proud to be associated with the work and of the results, thanks to an exceptional team of craftsmen, engaged under such special circumstances.

The architectural solution to this particular problem was a radical one. One might say that the house could not be 'put back', so instead it 'moved onwards'. It now stands again in its own right, serving a valuable use and providing a heart for a great estate, as well as a living memorial to its beneficent donor.

Chevening House façade detail on completion.

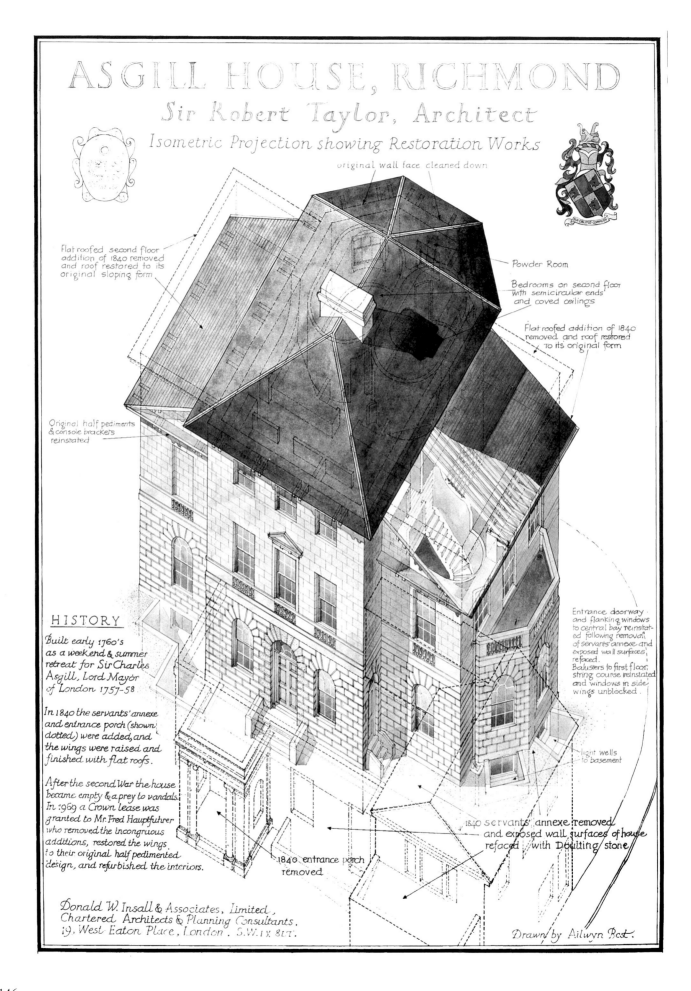

ASGILL HOUSE, RICHMOND

Sir Robert Taylor, Architect

Isometric Projection showing Restoration Works

original wall face cleaned down

Flat roofed second floor addition of 1840 removed and roof restored to its original sloping form

Powder Room

Bedrooms on second floor with semicircular ends and coved ceilings

Flat roofed addition of 1840 removed and roof restored to its original form

Original half pediments & console brackets reinstated

Entrance doorway and flanking windows to central bay reinstated following removal of servants annexe and exposed wall surfaces refaced. Balusters to first floor string course reinstated and windows in side wings unblocked.

light wells to basement

HISTORY

Built early 1760's as a weekend & summer retreat for Sir Charles Asgill, Lord Mayor of London 1757-58

In 1840 the servants' annexe and entrance porch (shown dotted) were added, and the wings were raised and finished with flat roofs.

After the second War the house became empty & a prey to vandals. In 1969 a Crown lease was granted to Mr. Fred Hauptfuhrer who removed the incongruous additions, restored the wings to their original half pedimented design, and refurbished the interiors.

1840 entrance porch removed

1840 servants' annexe removed and exposed wall surfaces of house refaced with Doulting stone

Donald W. Insall & Associates, Limited, Chartered Architects & Planning Consultants. 19, West Eaton Place, London. S.W.1X 8LT.

Drawn by Ailwyn Best.

146

6. Restoration and rebuilding

Asgill House

Our philosophy accepts the principle that time and change inevitably move forwards, and that only rarely can the clock with real grace be turned back. What we all commonly call 'restoration' is still new work, although it may be in the same form as the old. However, there are instances where missing buildings were so special, or so important to a larger whole, that their re-creation seems positively an obligation. This is even more the case with missing elements in a single architectural whole, which becomes relatively garbled or meaningless without them. When unity of concept and composition was a building's chief attraction and significance, rather than its sheer physical identity in terms of original bricks and mortar, there can be a strong case for simply renewing missing architectural elements, with the clear aim of redeeming that unity. In this sense, the word is correctly used.

Some buildings do cry out for restoration; our only caution would be to recall that the result is still of more than one date, the reinstated element being essentially of today, even if in the manner of yesterday. It need not assertively proclaim its newness; equally it cannot succeed in any pretence of age. It is also observably true, of course, that as more time passes, perspective will overtake and lessen any differences. Or equally, time sometimes makes them more interesting in their own right, and many earlier restorations already now have their own special quality and even significance. The excesses of our Victorian ancestors, and our own reactions to these, cannot outlaw architectural re-creation, whether of missing detail or of special elements which leave a major and damaging gap. The following examples illustrate this principle in practice.

Sir Charles Asgill, Lord Mayor of London from 1757 to 1758, conceived the idea of building this handsome stone villa at Richmond, subsequently in Crown Estate ownership. Alongside the Thames, it is accessible on formal occasions by river as well as by land from Westminster. He chose as his architect Robert Taylor (later to be knighted in 1782 when he became Sheriff of London) and the design is typical of his fine oeuvre of villas, some of which have now perished. This house at Richmond remains, and bears its patron's name.

147a

147a   Asgill House, Richmond: Taylor's original design.

147b   The house with later raised shoulders.

147b

In the course of history, there had been two main stages of subsequent change at Asgill House. Evidently, although this was by no means apparent to the casual observer, the two wings flanking the central section had been packed upwards with additional rooms on top of their original sloping shoulders. The work had been well executed in matching ashlar stonework, but it had destroyed the architectural proportions of the villa. Then and later, a series of rambling extensions had also been added to the back, masking the original stonework and handsome entrance. Our client, Mr Fred Hauptfuhrer, having acquired a lease from the Crown, was determined to set both defects to rights. Fortunately, old drawings survived and we were able to establish accurately what had been there originally, and to re-realise the Taylor design. This project also entailed some sympathetic alteration work within, creating a new kitchen at ground floor and an adequate first-floor bathroom. Then all the later extensions could be removed, to reveal the original architectural form. The house now stands externally as it was, rid of later extensions and additions and very much as this open-handed Lord Mayor of London must have left it.

148a

148a   Riverside façade during restoration.

148b   Overlooking the Thames: Asgill House, restored.

148b

149a

149c

149b

149a,b Entrance front and earlier additions, seen from garden.

149c   Restoration proposals.

149d   The restored entrance front.

149d

Kent House

Kent House[1] in Arlington Street, just off Piccadilly and behind the Ritz Hotel, was a fine and fashionable house of 1741–51, designed by architect William Kent for the Hon. Sir Henry Pelham. The original house had become totally lost among later alterations and in 1975, when a new office building was proposed on the street front, we were asked by architect colleagues (Stone and Toms) to research and advise upon the possibilities of accurately restoring the 18th-century courtyard façade of the original house behind it.

We discovered by careful research that an open arcade had extended along one flank of the front courtyard.

Following the evidence of the structure, we were able to secure the rebuilding of this arcade as a link between the newest and older buildings. We could then restore the missing front elevation of the house, whose original lower half had for such a long time been lost. We were also invited to create a new elevation for the existing extension building alongside it, crediting and respecting the restored front of the house, while not pretending to be of any earlier date than today. Our clients restored the interiors in lavish measure, to be used for entertainment and similar prestigious functions for which in turn Kent House has since been acquired by the adjoining Ritz Hotel.

[1] Earlier known as Wimborne House.

Proposal drawing: restored original elevation, and remodelling of earlier addition alongside.

150

151a

151b

151c

151a Overtaken by later neighbours, Kent House remained unseen behind the latest development proposals.

151b The front of the main house, after careful restoration.

151c The open entrance-arcade across the courtyard, now also restored.

Berrington Hall

Berrington Hall, in Herefordshire, was a distinguished architectural design by Henry Holland of 1778–81, and was a quintessential, sophisticated country house of its time. The handsome exterior echoes the classical longings of the period, reflecting the passion for historical correctness and symmetry, and taking a place in the line of development from Italian villas, only slightly adapted to our own colder climate. Its finely jointed pink sandstone comes from a local quarry. By the late 19th century, changing social and technical requirements had laid a heavy hand on Berrington. The need for running water called for supply-tanks at high level, and fully equipped bathrooms had become fashionable. To accommodate these, a tall tower, topped by a storage tank, was added onto the courtyard elevation. Romantically asymmetrical against the house, it was constructed in brick, covered with cement rendering and adorned with artificial stone. In time however, the roof finishes had worn and were admitting the weather. Plumbing leaks also conspired to soak softwood timbers within the tower, which became a hotbed of dry rot.

It now proved perfectly possible to provide sufficient neater bathrooms for modern requirements within the walls of the original structure. Once this had been done, the offending tower could be removed, thus revealing the original fine stonework of the main front of the Hall. Moreover, in restoring the cornice stonework, it became evident that the elevation had originally carried a central pediment. So here, surely, was a case for restoration – especially as the remaining detail was sufficient to re-establish with accuracy the original form (in the event, later confirmed by documentary discoveries).

There remains today only one anomaly. The present entrance doorway is set off-centre, the original central doorway having earlier been moved when the rear hall was converted as a sitting room. This had become the principal living room of Lady Cawley, an indomitable lady by this time in her 90s. In order to avoid wantonly disturbing her quarters, we agreed that the possibility of centralising the entrance should be deferred. So where the added tower once stood, there remains a bridge to the entrance door in its existing non-original position, one bay off-centre. Perhaps some future age may consider repositioning the entrance, but at present it is felt that the late Lady Cawley's sitting room has now an historical value of its own.

The partial restoration of the façade, on the removal of the old bathroom tower, and re-completion of its original pedimented architectural design, has enormously improved the presence and proportions of the Hall and its entrance courtyard. This was an almost straightforward case of restoring just what had once been there.

152a   Berrington Hall (1778): the south front.

152b   Courtyard front, before the removal of its added tower.

152c   Relieved of its ugly tower, the original façade can be restored.

152d   Berrington after restoration.

152b

152a

152c

152d

153a

The Inigo Jones Gateways, Covent Garden

In his design for the architectural layout of Covent Garden, Inigo Jones had flanked his porticoed façade of St Paul's Church (proclaimed as the 'handsomest barn in England') with a pair of symmetrically disposed arched gateways, each nearly 6 metres in height.

The church, commandingly set overlooking Bedford Square, was completed in 1633. Its magnificent stone portico was intended as the entrance to the church, while the two gateways were executed in rendered brickwork enclosing wooden doors, the latter and the adjoining brick walls being replaced respectively in 1714 and 1715 by iron gates and railings. In 1788, both gateways were partly refaced in stone; but in 1877 they were demolished and underground public lavatories were installed to the south of the church.

In the 1980s the Covent Garden area became the subject of an imaginative restoration programme by the Greater London Council, which planned the reinstatement of the two gateways and established funding for the exercise. On its disbandment in 1986, the project was taken up jointly by the Parochial Church Council and English Heritage, at first involving only the northern gate but subsequently, and with added financial support, undertaking the rebuilding also of the southern gate.

Following thorough research of the records, including an engraving of 1717 by Colen Campbell in *Vitruvius Britannicus*, the gateways were again constructed in rendered brickwork and set with reinstated wooden doors. Trial pits were dug, but operations were interrupted by the discovery of human bones – these were respectfully re-interred, and after obtaining competitive tenders, the work commenced. An enclosed seating terrace set with a fountain feature was incorporated on the south, and at the level of the Square.

The result was the recovery of the architectural character of this important metropolitan space, reinforcing the commanding presence of the great church and re-integrating it with the popular Square it overlooks to such effect, and thus re-completing the intentions of its celebrated architect and creator.

153b

Eardisley Park

A fine and much-loved Queen Anne house at Eardisley Park in Herefordshire was almost totally destroyed by fire in 1999 during the absence of its owners. Of its brick-built fabric on a stone plinth, all was lost except for fragments of walls and chimney stacks; alas, no trace remained of its pretty, panelled interiors. Its owners had loved the old house, and were determined it should be rebuilt.

Highly desirable and beautifully sited, Eardisley had however for two centuries been marred by the late 18th-century addition of an attic storey, which was masked by brickwork that had in turn been rendered over and later covered in spar roughcast. Other alterations had been less damaging. They included the 19th-century addition of a south-facing bow window answering to the magnificent view, and another two-storeyed bow window at the western entrance. Originally perfectly square on plan, the house still enjoyed that particular asset of its kind – double-aspect windows to the rooms at every corner, together with interiors thus daylit without any pools of indoor shadow.

It was decided to take this opportunity to lose the added attic storey, reverting to the main shape of the earlier house, and to reinstate its white-painted cornice and stone-tiled roof-slopes, set with their dormers, all again rising towards the central chimney stacks. Despite the alternative possibility of accurately reinstating the initial architectural design, it was also decided to reinstate, and perhaps to improve upon, the bow-windowed additions, which by now had become such a practical and settled architectural feature and asset.

Much of the quality of the house rested in its sympathetic materials. Rather than using newly supplied bricks, those surviving from the fire were carefully rescued and cleaned for reuse. Fortunately they had all been set in lime mortar, without any harmful repointing in cement. The brickwork repeated the English bond identified in salvaged walling left by the fire, and also the chequer pattern on the east front, with its penny-struck pointing, so the resultant texture is very much as it was. The rebuilt bow on the entrance front was constructed in header-bond brickwork, on the inspiration of a similar late 18th-century alteration to a somewhat comparable house not far away. Sash windows were set to the outer wall-face as before; since authentic crown-glass is no longer made, its texture was given the closest attainable match by using cylinder-blown glass, presenting comparable and interesting qualities of light reflection. Above the new cornice, the gently sprocketed lines of the reconstructed roofs were covered in second-hand slates still available from Cornwall.[1]

154a   The original house, but with its proportions marred by an added attic storey, and its brickwork rendered-over.

154b   After the disastrous fire (entrance front).

[1] All of these details required painstaking attention. For efficiency, the work was carried out in cooperation with Herefordshire architect Nicholas Keeble, enabling a close supervision on site.

154a   154b

155a

155b

155a   Post-fire rebuilding at Eardisley. Earlier alterations were reversed and the house restored, re-using all available materials.

155b   The rebuilt drawing room and bow-window, with a hand-printed 'Chinese' silk wallpaper.

155c   The oak-panelled study with a book-lined jib door to the drawing room.

155c

Eardisley is therefore not intended to be a totally accurate re-creation of the original. Its interiors now incorporate modern planning improvements such as a ground-floor (rather than previously basement) kitchen, some very adequate cloakrooms and upper bathrooms.

Only one fully panelled room has been recreated – the library, finished in oak and connecting by a book-lined jib door with the drawing room. The latter is decorated with a handpainted 'Chinese' silk wallpaper; elsewhere lighter-coloured variants of historic designs have been adopted.

Outside, links with the gardens include a pretty fountain-pool, aligned upon the front entrance and a new window over it, and a little formal canal tumbling away into the valley. In all these ways, the great merits of the house have been strongly followed. Its materials and textures breathe the same air as its predecessor, whose fate has generated a particularly lovely and liveable home, reinstated in its fine landscape setting.

Within the available range of degrees-of-change, Eardisley represents neither full restoration nor a clone, but a renewal of what was best of its inspiration, and an echo of its architectural parent.

Eardisley from the south (watercolour by the author, exhibited at the R.A. Summer Exhibition in 2002).

These four examples have involved, literally, the restoration of what was once there. Asgill House has regained and maintained its original domestic function, updated to meet modern requirements. Berrington Hall is nowadays a National Trust experience for visitors. Kent House serves again and in an ideal way, for corporate entertainment, which may not be too far from the message of its heyday. And Eardisley is once again a lovable domestic country house.

The house rebuilt: west front and landscaped garden.

Chimney stacks reformed in connection with reinstated fireplaces throughout the building

19th century slate roof renewed on part new roof structure (replacing parts lost by fire)

16th century oak framed walls & gables to central courtyard repaired with new seasoned & unseasoned oak sections scarf jointed to the existing: New leaded light windows & frames incorporated.

18th century panelled rooms with part raised & fielded panels & bolection mouldings repaired & missing sections reinstated. corner fireplace reformed.

Pair of 15th century cruck frames repaired & part missing section reinstated for display.

Brick facade rebuilt in lime mortar to early nineteenth century form with traditional shop front & shutters & street stalls

Former caged newel stair and balustrade, partly destroyed by fire, reinstated to earlier form.

17th century jettied timber framed gable repaired & brick infill panels reinstated.

Vault cleaned out & repaired for display.

Timber frame to 16th & 17th Century warehouse wing repaired & infill panels restored.

16th & 17th Century timber framed wall with brick/wattle & daub infill panels consolidated & left as in situ display with new viewing gallery.

19th Century cast iron fireplace/oven range by Needham of Stockport repaired

COURTYARD
Reformed by removal of 19th century infill structures

New three storey visitor building with lift providing level access throughout - with Education/Seminar Room/Shop & Cloakrooms. Balconied French Windows overlook the Market Square.

MARKET HALL

STOCKPORT MARKET
(Charter granted 1260)

For long forgotten and abused, Staircase House has emerged from the major restoration, outlined here, as a unique survival - its importance revealed by the investigations of the Manchester University Archaeological Unit, and through the vision of Stockport Council, assisted by English Heritage and with financial support from the Heritage Lottery Fund. Contractor: Linford Bridgeman.

STAIRCASE HOUSE

Donald Insall Associates
Architects + Historic Building Consultants.

Drawn by Michael Shippobottom

7. Rehabilitation

Staircase House, Stockport

Staircase House, in the northwestern industrial town of Stockport, was rescued and rehabilitated by the local authority as an exemplary exercise in urban regeneration and refurbishment. This remarkable medieval house-complex displays in turn every layer of its social and construction history since 1460. Faced with its seriously derelict and indeed collapsing condition, a perceptive local authority decided in 1994 to rehabilitate the house as a public museum and teaching resource, and at the same time as a catalyst for the wider regeneration of the town's historic core.

159a

The first task undertaken was to prepare a thorough study and understanding of the building's long history.[1] Grouped behind its brick face along the principal market place, it was identified as a town house of the 15th century, together with service and staircase wings and an extension of later date, all gathered around a central courtyard. The original gable-fronted structure had contained a cruck-framed open hall of three bays. In subsequent centuries this had evidently been expanded and developed, firstly converting the hall into a two-storey post-and-truss layout, then adding another oak-framed and jettied building at the rear, together with a stone-built storage wing. Meanwhile, its interiors were lined with panelling and fitted out with the very handsome 17th-century staircase that gives the building its present name, and which reflected the increasing success and status of its occupants. Further extensions were made through the 18th and 19th centuries, both upwards in new storeys and backwards about a characteristic access passageway. The site was then divided into two tenancies to realise its full commercial potential. In a subsequent economic downturn, the whole group had become neglected, steadily deteriorating in condition until it was now seriously at risk.

159b

159a   The brick street façade, containing a building of many dates.

159b   The handsome 17th-century staircase that gives the house its name.

[1] Undertaken by the architects in conjunction with the Greater Manchester Archaeological Unit, within Manchester University.

Staircase House from the south: a new modern wing echoes its older counterpart.

To realise and credit the significance of Staircase House, with its intriguing vernacular construction and social history, a decision was taken for its comprehensive refurbishment and conservation, making it in effect an interpretative display of itself. It was hoped this might serve as a focus for heritage and tourist activities in the town, and as a token and exemplar of urban regeneration. Presenting clear evidence of more than 500 years of occupancy, the project was linked with a current relocation on the site next door of the town's public museum, where a sympathetic new building could be added. This could provide the complex with additional stairs and a lift, a shop, education room, staff rooms and modern toilet facilities, all helping to free the historic structure of these extra pressures.

The conservation principles adopted by the design team involved minimal intervention, reinstating the damaged complex and revealing and displaying its evocative form and historic finishes. The courtyard was cleared of unworthy and collapsed infillings. Timber framing was repaired on a like-for-like basis, strengthening local weaknesses by splinting and flitching, to retain a maximum of original material. Masonry walling was knitted together, employing a system of embedded structural ties. In the courtyard, new balconies and ramps were added to facilitate safe access; these were of lightweight construction, avoiding any imitation, and designed in an honest and contemporary manner.

The new visitors' accommodation alongside the ancient structure is designed as a modern background building, externally respecting the materials and scale of its neighbour and urban setting. Complementary materials and finishes were selected, with oak joinery, stonework and matching limewashed brickwork. A new lift and access galleries give direct access to all the lower floors, while a steel and glass staircase with oak stair treads runs up through all four floors as well as providing a protected emergency fire-escape route.

The exposed west wall of the warehouse was found to display fascinating constructional examples of fragile wattle, daub and plaster. It contained infilled windows of several dates, set within fragile timber frames. Restoring this as a solid wall would have involved excessive rebuilding, so steel columns were installed alongside to take up the loads, allowing it to remain more nearly as found, while a viewing balcony would provide for its detailed examination by visitors.

While derelict, the house had suffered arson damage. To protect against fire, it was now compartmented to contain any outbreak. Historic doors were carefully upgraded for increased resistance and fitted with automatic fire-release devices. Detection systems were also discreetly installed throughout. Heating and plumbing and electrical services were entirely removed, planning for environmental conservation temperatures and as far as possible using existing chimney flues and ducts. New lighting was installed, employing advanced fibre-optic fittings. As in all such work, it was considered important to select equipment unlikely to be quickly superseded, and to give thorough consideration to future maintenance and servicing.

Ceiling, wall and floor surfaces received similar sympathetic attention, including the retention of some very decayed but visually interesting historic examples, displayed as evidence of every finish found in the building. Internal panelling and the handsome staircase were carefully pieced in, but retaining selected evidence of the fire damage – the charred remains were consolidated by specialist conservators. Based upon careful and detailed paint analysis, rooms were each decorated to represent specific periods in the history of the building, while on the exteriors, new timber framing was left exposed to weather naturally.

This example of positive refurbishment, involving a fairly extensive degree of intervention, has enabled the uncovering of an architectural complex revealing and displaying many layers of rich history. Above all, it has proved to be a catalyst in the active regeneration of an entire town centre.

161a

161a   Interiors, refurnished as a museum display.

161b   Repaired external west wall, with exposed oak framing and brick infill.

161b

Georgian terraced housing, Camden

The Camden area to the east of Bloomsbury, once on the fringe of London, was developed after the Great Fire and from the late 17th century onwards by a new breed of metropolitan building speculators. Land was acquired; money changed hands. Handsome new terraces of tall brick houses began to arrive, their mannerly exteriors presenting a new urban unity, while the interiors were left to be finished and fitted out in detail by individual lessees.

Of the currently surviving groups of houses at the eastern end of Great Ormond Street, a number date from the 1720s. These were originally meant for single-family occupation, with top-floor accommodation for servants. Those on the northern side, originally with open country at the rear, were especially grand and have main ground and first floor reception rooms lined with raised and fielded panelling, bold plaster ceiling cornices and rich classical detailing, while their staircases rejoice in features such as carved and turned balusters, handsome newel-posts and decorative tread-ends.

But as the wealthier merchants began to move to newer suburbs, there was a gradual shift in the social status of the area. Less money was available so the old houses began to receive less care. Increasingly they were subdivided into smaller units, often carrying much heavier use and structural loading than they were designed to receive. Reducing rents and increasing neglect took their toll; this was augmented by damage in two World Wars, when many buildings were badly shaken. Regular maintenance was deferred and repairs became too expensive to carry out. Increasingly stringent requirements of modern legislation, such as adequate means of escape in the event of fire, made it understandable that the owners of this particular estate, who were Rugby School trustees, had begun to find the properties an expensive and growing worry. And local residents were desperately campaigning for help.

162c

162a

162a   Fine panelling.

162b   Turned staircase balusters (although one of them is upside-down).

162c   Unsightly surface-mounted services.

162d   Bathroom: wash-basin conceals an old corner fireplace.

162b

162d

163a

163a,b 18th- and 19th-century
houses on the Rugby Estate,
in Camden.

LONDON BOROUGH
OF CAMDEN
RUGBY ESTATE
AERIAL VIEW

Donald W. Insall & Associates

19 West Eaton Place, S.W.1
drawn by Ailwyn Best.

163b

164a

164b

164c

164a   Local residents were campaigning for help.

164b   An urgent start: solid Victorian terraces for conversion in Orde Hall Street.

164c   Analysis plans: Great Ormond Street.

After two formal planning inquiries, the proposals for demolition or change of use to offices were rejected. In 1975 and following protracted negotiations, 42 houses were successfully transferred to the Borough of Camden, against an undertaking to spend the purchase-monies[1] on renovating the properties retained. This was an admirable arrangement, for public money could then in effect reap a double harvest. But to convert the houses for future use as local authority housing stock, while also retaining their historical integrity, proved extraordinarily complex. To make them all suitable for continued residential use involved almost every degree of architectural and structural intervention.

It was first necessary to assess all the assets and detractions of this new purchase, and to devise a match or compromise between all the varied claims of architectural merit, structural emergency and official housing standards. The project would at the same time have to attract public funding and be achievable within cost and programme.

Our brief required that former tenants be re-housed in appropriate accommodation. We were as far as possible to meet a stipulated local authority housing-mix with units for two-person (50 percent), four-person (20 percent), four- to six-person (18 percent) and six- to seven-person (12 percent) accommodation. A proportionate allocation was also set between bed-sitting rooms and one-, two- and three-bedroom

units. Incidentally, the alternative of clearance and redevelopment would simply not have been possible within the permitted densities of 130 persons per acre, which technically would allow only a single room depth from the street. So conversions had to take into account these requirements, while also respecting historic architectural elements.

Original fabric of value was to be respected and preserved, and disfiguring changes or additions removed. This task was complicated by inadequacies such as flimsy construction, with weak partitions consisting only of panelling exposed on both sides and in some instances actually supporting staircases. Since multi-occupation had never originally been intended, fire resistance between neighbouring units now became a major safety consideration, together with an escape requirement for smoke-check lobbies. The room layouts of the period had typically run ensuite, major room uses extending into features such as the projecting rear closets. Ready bathroom access needed considering, as well as an economical and non-invasive plumbing and service layout. Avoiding noise at night was a further concern, with possibilities of disturbance from an underground railway tunnel. Daylighting and public health standards included room-sizes and uses matched to their window areas and orientation; this variously meant reducing some rooms with least daylight by

---

[1] The condition of the major buildings was reflected very fairly in a 'nil valuation', which could well even have been a negative figure.

enclosing inner storage areas. A good deal of renegotiation of standards was in practice necessary.

On site, an urgent start was made with the group of houses considered architecturally least significant. These were the latest in date – solid Victorian terraces of the 1870s with repetitive paired plans, quite well built but lacking in amenities, and without regard for possible multiple use. Following a careful analysis, flats were provided in laterally combined units across major floors. The first completed conversions were made available within one year of acquisition, thus providing useful units for social continuity in the phased regeneration of the neighbourhood.

Next began the more costly work of rehabilitating the more valuable and highly graded houses of the 18th century, by now in poorer repair, but featuring panelled rooms on the main floors and some good staircases. Again the accommodation was analysed, the historical features identified and plotted, detractions were noted and positive opportunities recognised.

The very best interiors were if possible to be kept complete, and representative of single-family units of their period. To achieve this without dividing historic staircases, two main options were adopted. The first was to use the stairs for joint access to individual units on each floor. In the second option, the best stairs were retained within units planned as private from the ground floor upwards, formed by laterally combining the basements and attics below and above. Where access to rear closets made subdivision of rooms

165a,b Diagrammatic section and plans of proposed conversions: No. 3 with shared staircase to individual flats; No. 5 with private staircase in an eight-person house.

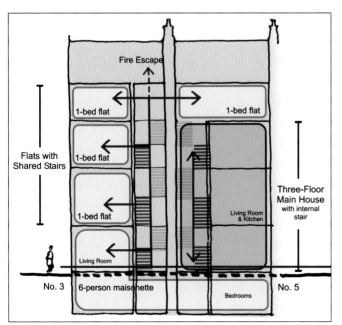

165a

165b

166a

166b

166c

unavoidable, partitioning was made removable in any changing future circumstances. Kitchen and bathroom layouts were designed for minimum disturbance of panelling, and all plumbing routed on the same principle.

The houses were built on soft and marshy ground in an inherently flexible construction of brickwork in lime mortar; they followed the London principle of constructing raised streets, leaving the back gardens at natural ground level. Their fronts, with their deep and railinged basement areas, thus appear one storey less tall than they are – it is a surprise to see elevational

drawings showing their full height, with thin piers of brickwork between five tiers of three (in one instance, four) long sash-windows running up through five storeys.

It also comes as a shock to examine their construction, and to realise their inherent weakness. Party walls are rarely bonded to the façades, while the heavily loaded front-to-back floor beams in many cases bring their

166a   Tall façades with thin piers between large windows. This house (No. 12) was built (1716) by a glazier!

166b,c   Some very comparable structural problems in Bruges, Belgium.

loads eccentrically on to the slender front piers. From here they span back onto internal cross-walls parallel with the street, which in many cases have since been subjected to some very weakening alterations. These central walls were initially provided with alternative structural openings, to allow for purchasers' choice of internal doorway and room arrangements. In practice, many of them have since been further perforated with more openings, and in some rooms even actually removed, leaving the remaining heavy cross-wall above, with all the beams it carries, to bear upon slips of wood intended only as shallow buried wallplates. An early 19th-century practice of forming openings between front and back rooms (which local residents have described as 'victory arches', celebrating the Battle of Waterloo) was particularly unfortunate in the structural weakening it had so often caused.

Structural work needed here included rebuilding shattered and overloaded brick piers between the windows, and relieving beams of their overloading by flanking them with steel channels. To restore strength to

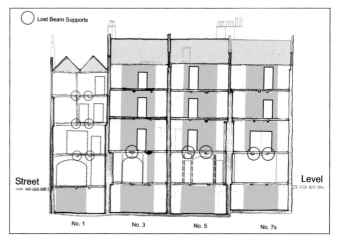

167a

167a   Weakened structure: the spine wall already had alternative doorway positions, but extra ones had been formed.

167b   A 'victory arch' has cut away the substance of the wall.

167c   Remedying structural weaknesses, where original spine-walls had been removed and beams left unsupported.

167b

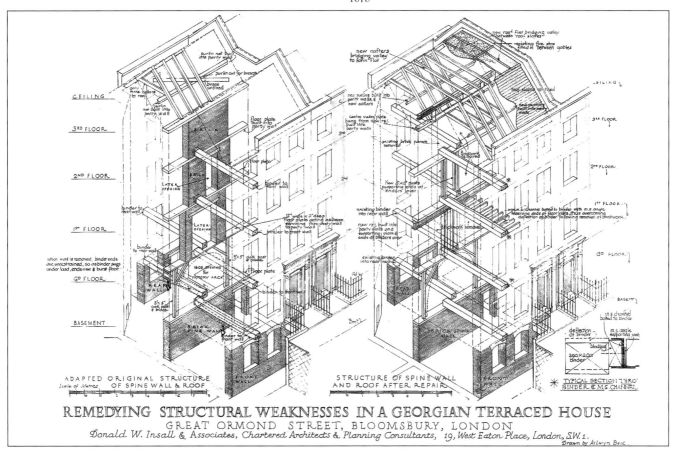

167c

168a

168b

the weakened spine-walls, while avoiding any intrusive new structure in the historic panelled rooms, an ad hoc approach was adopted. In some instances it was possible to re-support the weakened walls from below. In other cases they were removed altogether, the floors and stud walls being hung by tie-rods from new steel beams introduced above. Spanning access between the brick party walls, these could then be concealed within less important partitions or in roof spaces.

Finally, in terms of architectural intervention, a more radical approach was needed in dealing with the most dilapidated and largely lost houses on the south side of the street (numbers 9–15). In 1974 these houses had suffered the ultimate indignity – a precautionary dismantling exercise, deemed necessary by the District Surveyor. The upper floors had then been progressively removed, in turn exposing lower floors one-by-one to weather and successive demolition, until very little remained but fragments of front wall, a collection of railings and some handsome wooden front doorcases.

A more complete reconstruction of these listed buildings here became inevitable, and we had to take a

168a   Old photographs show poor state of back walls, many no longer standing.

168b   Rear of houses overlooking gardens.

168c   The restored street elevations.

168c

number of basic decisions. Should their street façades be reconstructed as they were originally? And as far as we knew? Or as they were when destroyed? After much discussion, it was decided that it was their variety, life and continuity, as well as unity, which had lent to this street so much of its attraction and that we should re-create each façade just as our own generation had received it.[1] The irregular alignment of frontages was maintained and the brickwork coursing and pointing were correctly varied from house to house. The new windows repeat the variety of those lost, some having retained their glazing bars, others having been renewed in the 19th century without them. The original railings were repaired and reinstated. As an admitted variant to meet interior daylighting requirements, the front basement windows were slightly enlarged, but were kept in sympathy with those above – otherwise all was as before.

At the back overlooking the gardens, on the other hand, housing standards and costings had to be applied; and numbers 9–15 were rebuilt in materials selected to harmonise with the 18th-century buildings alongside, but without historical echo. Indoors, the unit basis between party walls was fully maintained, with ceiling heights as before; finishes and detailing are plain and simple, to meet with official housing requirements.

This was, as will be seen, not merely an exercise of repair but a huge and complex equation to be met and solved. And the resultant costs, in their turn, would have to be balanced and held within limit, or the exercise would founder. Above all,

the programme was seen by Camden as a vital social regeneration exercise. An on-site exhibition was held in one house, and was widely attended and reported. A joint consultative committee was at the same time set up, to help to air and resolve tenancy problems, and to coordinate public participation in rebuilding the social unity of the neighbourhood. Some 370 people were in this way re-housed; for each returning tenant, a booklet on 'Your New Home' gave useful guidance on day-to-day maintenance.

The entire programme of work was completed in 1980. These Camden houses demonstrate graphically the wide range of degrees of intervention applicable in any building conservation project, except perhaps that of an absolute 'monument'.

[1] Interestingly, drawings circulating in 1968 designated those façades described as 'historically incorrect' – a significant difference in approach from that of today.

Door surrounds, railings and historic details reinstated.

The second barn, mounted on a cradle and wheels, was towed by a steam-tractor to its new location.

Two relocated barns at Knebworth

One further possibility sometimes occurs when rehabilitating old buildings. In special circumstances it may be perfectly justifiable to relocate a major feature – or even occasionally an entire building – from one site to another, but remembering that in some measure, its integrity will then be unalterably jeopardised, or at least, translated. Relocation is less drastic than total loss; but it disengages a structure from the intimate surroundings that helped to generate it. Even moving a building a few metres can ring false notes, as in the case of an Orangery at Kedleston, once re-erected by Lord Curzon very near to its original site, but which is now north-facing and hence horticulturally useless.

Without any exaggerated sense of puritanism, it is easy to see how a new site can immediately alter meaning. Some buildings have more 'contextual' content and as it were, more relationships than others. Georgian terraced housing, even if not always exemplary in relation to its surroundings, would still immediately feel 'lost' if transplanted today to areas where no self-respecting Georgian would ever have built. But other buildings were prefabricated anyway, and always intended for re-erection in new circumstances, as in the case of an agricultural barn, or the Crystal Palace, or indeed the machine-made units produced in Britain's post-war rehousing programme.

To meet public demand in many countries, very successful open-air museums of entire buildings have been created. Here dismantled structures from widely disparate areas find themselves collected together and rebuilt, and can be visited and studied in close juxtaposition. In this way they preserve a valuable knowledge of ways of building, although there will always be something about them of the self-consciously displayed specimen animals in a zoo.

Much the same sensation arises when a house in its original location, which has fallen empty, has been retrospectively refurbished with new furnishings, intendedly 'in period'. This will still feel different from another that has remained continuously occupied – even if its furniture is no longer original. A 'museum' house, re-bedecked with selected pictures but without its old dining table, can be curiously unsatisfying, and may have something about itself of the reheated meal. The point to remember is that a re-creation of the past may stand entirely justified on its own intellectual merits, but it will still 'read' as an interesting academic exercise.

Ideally, therefore, a site and its building and their furniture are all one within the vagaries of passing time: but a very few can be successfully transposed, especially for new purposes. An example of this was a

171a

171b

171c

171d

171e

171a–d   Knebworth: one barn was dismantled and re-erected nearby.

171e   Linked together, they were then converted as a Country Park restaurant.

pair of 17th-century agricultural barns, by now in poor repair and disused on the extensive estates (today a lively country park) at Knebworth. One of these was dismantled and newly re-erected near to its original site. The other, less accessible, was jacked up on large wheels, and then to great public delight towed bodily by a steam tractor for more than a kilometre to join it in a new location. The two barns were then linked by a new kitchen and facilities, and have become a busy restaurant. Even buildings can retire and take up new employment.

Winchester High Street: new buildings.

8. Reincorporating existing buildings

Winchester High Street

In the context of an historic area or town, or of any environment of special quality, new fabric must make for itself an accepted place. A whole range of relationships becomes possible, and they are likely to vary from the sometimes excessively modest near-replica to the often over-rash and blatantly aggressive contrast, and an infinite number of degrees between the two.

Further, the relationship (and every juxtaposition means that there must be one, whether consciously or not) varies not only between like and unlike, but within different modes and elements of architectural expression. For example, there may be either similarity or contrast in skyline, or in façade alignment, or in architectural scale. These may voice themselves in building materials, or in colour, or in degree of solidarity, or even of craftsmanship. And buildings can be alike in one respect, but totally unlike in another. The key to the success of a new relationship between architectural neighbours is not necessarily the degree of similarity, but the design skills that have gone into creating it.

One can happily accept the success of many new buildings that contrast strongly with their neighbours. There is a place for contrast, just as there is another place for harmony, a place for boldness and a place for reticence. But both call for a real appreciation and analysis of their context, from which comes a consciously established new relationship.

We were first commissioned jointly by the City and Hampshire County Councils to prepare a planning study of the Westgate area of Winchester, where recently arrived new buildings included substantial new law courts (1972). Elsewhere in the neighbourhood there had been unease about the hurtful and overpowering effect of other new building. Undoubtedly there were still opportunities here for redevelopment, and indeed a real need for it. What, we were asked, was the special character of the area and the buildings within it? Given the changing requirements, which of its elements could or should go, and which should remain? And what might be some alternative principles for the redevelopment of property to provide new offices in the High Street, on land owned by Hampshire County and set in the heart of the city? We were asked to suggest the effect, and jointly with Chesterton, as estate and property agents, to assess in outline the financial merits (in terms of cost and benefit), of three possible alternative architectural treatments: adaptation, part-renewal or building replacement.

Winchester – King Alfred's capital: the old High Street in the 1960s.

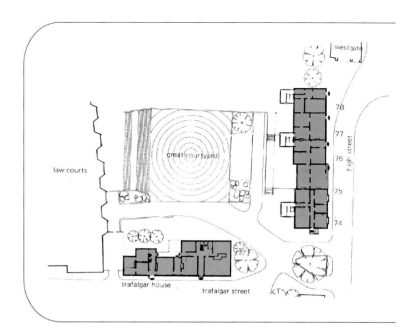

We analysed the character elements, identified the main merits and demerits of the area and made positive recommendations about them. We examined in outline the potential development projects that would merit further study, making models and sketches to illustrate these.

For the contentious High Street site and in accordance with our brief, we reviewed the alternative possibilities in three outline proposals. Scheme 1 would enable a maximum retention of existing buildings, refurbishing them internally around three new staircases to rationalise their circulation. The rear elevations to the new courtyard could then be tidied and re-cast, even if less satisfactorily than by replacing them. The scheme would provide in total some 11,750 square feet of usable offices.

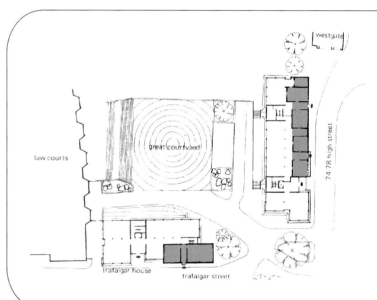

Scheme 2 offered an intermediate course of action. One listed building (Trafalgar House) and three unlisted, but characteristic, buildings in the High Street would be retained but extensively adapted. At their rear this would entail new staircase towers and a reorganised elevation, stepped with the slope to the existing floor levels, and providing some 18,750 square feet of office space at greater initial cost.

To meet the third alternative – this time, an entirely new High Street building – we recommended an articulated design with internal staircases and again a stepped design to the rear courtyard. Presenting a more acceptable architectural presence towards the law courts, it could contain four floors of useable office space (23,500 square feet). The annual cost would be comparable.

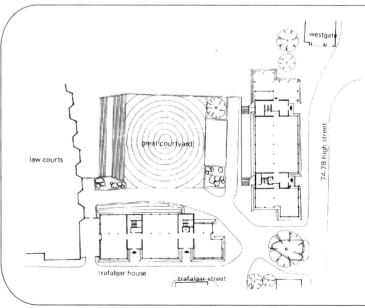

Alternative schemes

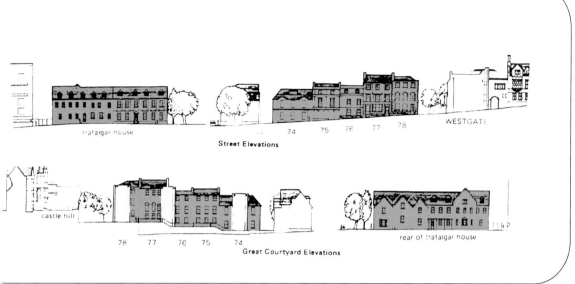

trafalgar house

Street Elevations

74   75   76   77   78   WESTGATE

castle hill

78   77   76   75   74

Great Courtyard Elevations

rear of trafalgar house

Scheme 1

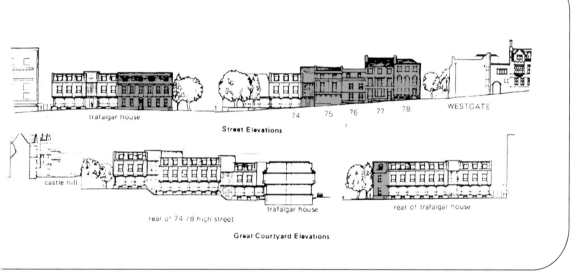

trafalgar house

Street Elevations

74   75   76   77   78   WESTGATE

castle hill

rear of 74-78 high street

trafalgar house

Great Courtyard Elevations

rear of trafalgar house

Scheme 2

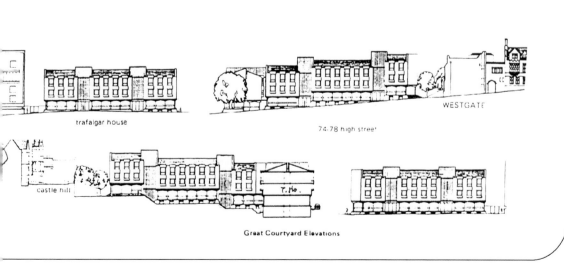

trafalgar house

74-78 high street

WESTGATE

castle hill

T. Ho.

Great Courtyard Elevations

Scheme 3

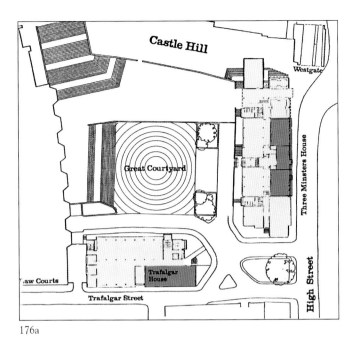

176a

176a The adopted scheme: combined redevelopment with accommodation much increased but incorporating existing buildings.

176b The unlisted but characteristic buildings on the High Street site.

176c In construction: three existing buildings adapted and included.

176b

176c

177a,b Elevations to the High
Street and Great
Courtyard. Existing
buildings saved for their
scale and reincorporated.

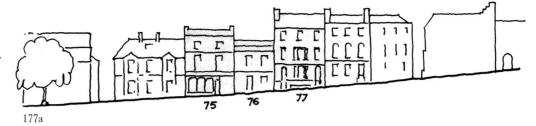

177a

177b

In our summary we recommended a compromise
solution, retaining Trafalgar House and suitably
redeveloping the High Street site, which would call
for a high standard of design but offer the best value.

The two authorities discussed the alternative proposals
and asked the architects to develop a design including
much more accommodation – perhaps in an extra floor
– with lift access between its now multiple levels in a
'combined redevelopment of both sites, but retaining if
possible some element of existing building'.

The riddle did not prove easy to solve. But after many
experiments, we clung to the concept of retaining and
adapting for the sake of their scale, the three existing
buildings that gave such character and interest to the
High Street, then flanking them by new buildings,
wrapped around their rear to overlook the Great
Courtyard. For the adjoining Trafalgar House, we
proposed a similar and related solution.

On detailed inspection, we found that at least the party
walls and front rooms could be kept and incorporated.
In particular, number 77 contained a grand first-floor
room with handsome plasterwork finishes, well worth
saving. Around these, the design could then be
generated about a pair of perpendicular axes. One ran
through the central building, given a more generous
entrance in place of its shop-front, towards the round-
table motif in the new courtyard behind; the other was
parallel with the High Street and stepped with its slope.

Extra accommodation could be provided in five floors,
with the lowest set into the ground and daylit from its
shoulders within a plinth, then rising through a ground
floor and three upper levels. A pair of lifts was set at
the crossing of the axes, well back from the elevations.

Three vertical stairway projections articulated the
stepped courtyard elevation. To avoid the error of over-
dominance evidenced in other new buildings locally,

178a   Our model illustrating the proposals.

178b   The rear elevations of the High Street new building, facing over the Great Courtyard.

the massing was broken up, with recessed top floors in the mansard-roofed ethos of its date. Concrete framed, the building was given courtyard elevations of local Hampshire brick, blended around into stuccoed façades and taking up the cue of the neighbouring buildings and their vertical window groupings.

Construction work started with reduction and demolition; the front room with its plasterwork was virtually parcelled up, and protected throughout the exercise. Its inclusion determined some adjustments in floor levels, but these give added interest to the interiors. They were also colour-coded to add to clarity of location.

The completed High Street building and its relation to Westgate.

On the High Street side, a way through the building at its upper end was signalled by a projecting feature to catch and deflect the eye. At the lower corner a magnificent ilex tree (later replaced by smaller trees) would act as a 'stop' to the building, masking the vehicle entry to the law courts and their concealed parking under the upper courtyard.

The interiors were designed as open-plan, although subject to any changing policies and users who might wish to subdivide them. Because the main building was located on an exceptionally noisy street with uphill traffic, as well as being deep in plan, it was mechanically ventilated and air conditioned. Around the corner in Trafalgar Street, the accompanying new building embracing the retained Trafalgar House was on a quieter and shallower site, and could be naturally ventilated.

Completed in 1976, the building was soon occupied by the County Architect and his staff, who have contributed their own personal stamp of furnishings and internal arrangement.

The Winchester buildings represent the result of incorporating unlisted but attractive elements of the existing High Street scale, then designing outwards from these and the accommodation requirements, all in answer to a new architectural environment. The demand for more accommodation has generated a considerably bigger building than initially proposed by the architects, but the result has been happily absorbed into the sensitive townscape of a major historic city. It well illustrates the approach laid upon us in designing within an urban context and without copying, but acknowledging and relating to its special site.

Cambridge: new, in context (p. 190).

9. New buildings in context

A sense of neighbourhood: residential developments in Durham

The next degree of intervention is the design of entirely new buildings, set in relation to an existing built environment.

An increasing concern during the 1960s was how to regain our sense of neighbourhood and of community. House building is one thing – the creation of a neighbourly grouping of homes is another. A few enlightened developers (one of the best known being SPAN in the southeast) were beginning to realise the inherent potential and value to be gained in designing houses not only related to their place, but grouped to reinforce their mutual sense of community.

Shincliffe Village

The Dean and Chapter of Durham owned land in the village of Shincliffe, just outside the city; they decided in 1959 to take up the challenge for the northeast, when making this site available for residential development. Taking their cue from garden-city thinking, with its sense of responsibility about land ownership, they commissioned a village study to see how a backland site, enclosed between an L-shaped village and its bypass, could best be brought within the village community.

Here, there had been the remains of two fields, separated by a line of trees and sloping up to the village church with its focal spire. Having analysed the possibilities and local architectural character in detail, and also with regard for current market requirements, we recommended the idea of a layout in two interrelated groups of houses. The upper cluster with its green could, we suggested, be strongly linked into a curved terrace rising towards and anchored on the spire, while the lower group would be set in pairs about a second green. Related single-storey dwellings would be sited overlooking the best available entry point, already known as 'Low Green'.

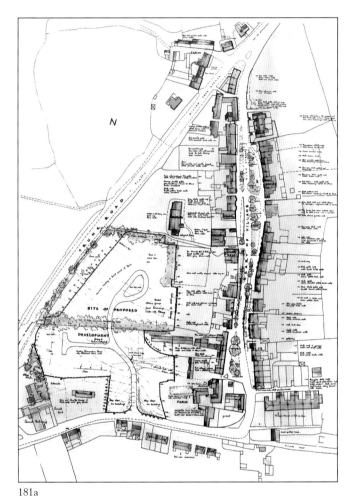
181a

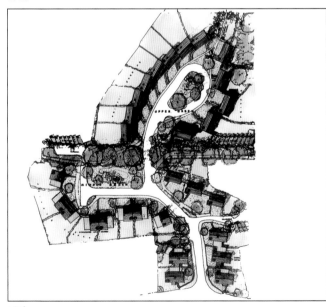
181b

181a Shincliffe: a village analysis explores possibilities of well-integrated residential development.

181b The layout around two enclosed front greens.

The upper crescent of houses were stepped up in pairs towards the church, each pair being also stepped back on plan and so combined within a united front roof slope. To reduce the visual impact of parking, garages were set back between them. The 'Middle Green' house type was designed with its upper floor set across the lower and jettied forward for interest and variety. At the entry to the site, garages were grouped away out of sight, the houses being canted in layout to look across the open space.

In this way, the forecourts of each group could be combined as a single green, maintained by the community (at one point, a focal stone 'igloo' feature was also erected for children, but it did not survive, although the children did). To reflect the strong local vernacular, white-painted woodwork was concentrated at the façades, contrasting with dark brick flanks, emphasising their form even in grey weather, and giving a kind of anthropomorphic smile of greeting to each house, together with a sense of direction and unity to the whole group. Local materials were reflected in selected brick and in roofs of large concrete tiles, answering to the stone tradition of the locality. Gap-sites in the main village street were at the same time infilled in similar spirit. The intention of the whole exercise was to complete and strengthen the social and architectural unity of the village.

182a

182b

182c

182a Middle Green and retained trees.

182b Upper group of paired houses, overlooking a combined front green …

182c … and leading up to the village church.

Hill Meadows

A comparable but different opportunity occurred in 1960 in a layout for 41 houses on an exposed nearby hilltop site outside the village, rising above a busy traffic approach but accessible near the top, and with fine outward views back towards the distant cathedral.

Here again the particular site was analysed, to assess and reveal its own merits. To encourage a sense of community, the central space carrying a single access road and turning point was again retained and gardened in combined ownership. Near the entry, two combined and screened garage areas served a majority of the houses.

At the inner end of the site, a protective arm of houses were arranged end-on and with linked arms, overlooking and enclosing a sheltered small green, and backed by additional trees to plant out noise from traffic below.

At the more exposed outward viewpoint, the neighbouring new houses were spaced with their outlooks unbroken towards the key distant view, some being split-level in plan and set just over the shoulder of the land so as to avoid any undue hilltop dominance from beyond. Here are also situated a children's play-area and viewing-platform; a footpath winds up the hill from the school and main road below.

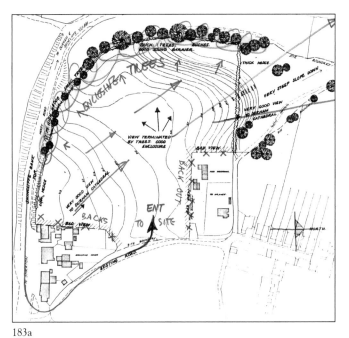

183a

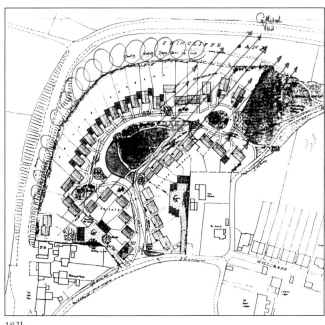

183b

183c

183a   Hill Meadows: analysis of site assets and detractions.

183b   Layout designed to maximise feeling of community, and to retain outward views.

183c   An informal model enables proposals to be checked.

183d   Perspective sketch of the completed layout.

183d

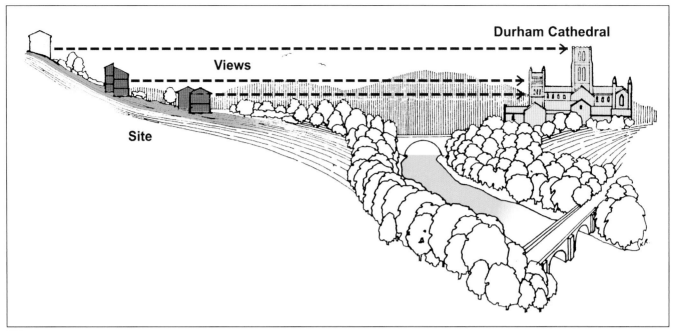

Briardene, Durham

A third project carried out for the Dean and Chapter was designed to take best advantage of some steeply sloping derelict land, this time within the city and surrounded by earlier terraced housing, but here with magnificent eastward views across the river towards the cathedral. It had evidently once served as two large gardens, but these had been gradually surrounded by stepped terraces of Victorian slate-roofed housing. After a period of use as allotments, the land was now vacant. The planning authority had accordingly given an outline consent for new housing of good quality, which would have ready access both by road and on foot to the centre of Durham.

Following an analysis of the site and its merits, the design principle adopted was firstly to relate the development to the surrounding terraces, and then to take the fullest benefit of the eastward prospect. Above the shoulder of the site, other houses already enjoyed these views and it was decided if possible to avoid interrupting their benefit. Other features included an existing footpath leading down across the site towards the shopping centre. In addition, there were some very good trees, of which a careful survey was prepared, with a view to saving and reinforcing with new planting.

The main entry point was planned at the centre-point of the lower boundary, to allow maximum visibility to traffic in both directions and for safety. A narrow road

DURHAM:
BRIARDENE.

For the Dean and Chapter of Durham

Donald W. Insall & Assocs.
Architects.

184a   A steeply sloping site with superb outward prospects.

184b   Briardene houses, on a site across the river from Durham Cathedral.

already climbed up one flanking boundary and continued along the top, to serve existing housing beyond the site, looking away over its own long views in the other direction. At that point it became possible to plan our new houses backing them, and set higher up the slope. Here, they were designed with three storeys, with their entrance from behind at a middle floor level. In this way, the entire view-side of the houses would also overlook a large communal green space between them and the lower terrace.

To maintain local character and identity, and despite a lingering local prejudice, the new housing was planned in terraced form. The upper terrace was set a little way down the slope, to retain its neighbours' existing outlook, and a second terrace was in turn set just sufficiently below to avoid interrupting the view-line of the first. The terraces are staggered in plan, to give interest and form to their layout, and especially to express the sloping nature of the site.

To take advantage of the particular merits of each part of the site, there are five house types. The upper terrace on the south has three storeys, is entered from the front and has integral garages. The two residential floors above can thus enjoy the prospect to the full. A development of this house type is also used for the

lower terrace on the north, but with protected garage access from the rear. In the southern half, the lower terrace has been kept down by restricting it to two floors in height, and is thus of a wider layout with integral garages.

All new buildings are simply a natural product of user requirements, expressed in relation to their locality, site and setting. Even if materials are less specifically local than they used to be, there is still a satisfaction in 'belonging'; an architecture that ignores its neighbours is itself the loser.

Architecturally, the houses were given long windows echoing the vertical sashes of earlier buildings in the area, but with the upper half top-hung and with undivided glazing. These were set in brickwork of a selected dark local brick, with matching pointing in colour characteristic of Durham. The low-pitched roofs, covered in large grey concrete tiles, were stepped at the ridge to give lighting and ventilation to internal spaces and stairs. The middle-entry houses have also tile-hung walls jettied forwards to express the main living rooms. Apart from coloured doors for individuality, hardwood joinery throughout is otherwise unpainted and stained.

Terraces spaced to share the outward views across the river. Combined front spaces and private rear gardens.

All 34 houses in the group are terraced, with green landscaped communal areas between their private gardens. A major consideration in all these layouts was the then-current influence of Radburn-type siting with grouped garages and communal gardens (also visited by the architects and seen at Reston, in the USA). But in the Durham examples, only the front spaces became community gardens, retaining separate back gardens to the houses, which (perhaps on the anthropomorphic model) were felt to be in this way psychologically more self-protective and private.

For the Shincliffe village projects, the contract and legal arrangements were provided by means of a building lease to a family firm of local contractors (Bell and Ridley), whose principals took a personal interest in the development. In Durham, the architects were responsible to the Dean and Chapter for design drawings until the stage of planning approval, and were thereafter nominated for retention by the developers (Shepherds of York) in a regular consultant capacity, but without undertaking formal direction and cost control. In all these cases provision was then made for a continuing ground-rent to the sponsors, while setting up a residents' association to ensure the maintenance and care of the combined landscaping.

The houses sold very successfully on long leasehold and continue to be very popular. Their mounting market values in subsequent changes of ownership reflect the continued desirability of the residential schemes initiated in this way by the Dean and Chapter.

Briardene: main living rooms set high for maximum benefit of outlook.

New mews houses at Bowland Yard, Belgravia

The problem of introducing new development with an existing neighbourhood of special character (specifically designated as a conservation area) arose in London's elite residential area of Belgravia, dating mostly from the 19th century and still today in carefully managed Grosvenor ownership. Here, in the 1980s, and by an accident of history, a surviving but intrusive industrial use had run its course, releasing valuable but inaccessible back land for redevelopment 'in context'.

Belgravia presents an engaging blend of grand fronting terraces, grouped into handsome squares, crescents and terraces, and backed in turn by much smaller mews properties. The mews originally provided service tenancies, stabling and coachhouses. But with increasing urban pressures, the main terraces have often been divided into flats, while the lesser back streets have become immensely sought after as individual small town-houses, sometimes linked as a series of enclosed mews courts.

The actual site available was extremely restricted, measuring only 33 by 14 metres, and it was approached only through a single narrow entrance way and archway between existing houses. The older warehouse building had almost entirely covered the land and overshadowed the neighbouring houses. Proposals were now openly discussed with the residents. As grouped garaging had already been provided locally, pedestrian circulation could be improved by linking the brick-paved courtyards, and careful thought was given to reduce any overlooking and avoid any restriction of daylight to adjoining dwellings. To prevent any sense of constriction in this tight site, windows were planned to take advantage of all available outward views.

In terms of design and materials, the tightly interlinked houses are small in scale, providing a mix of eight

A constricted urban site in Belgravia, previously occupied by an industrial warehouse.

separate units – houses, maisonettes and flats. Their larger rooms are mainly at first floor and each has its own private terrace or town patio. All are simply detailed in traditional stock brickwork with roofs of Welsh slate, colourwashed rendering and hardwood joinery.

These modern mews houses have immediately found an exceptionally ready market. At the same time, they add to the environmental quality and property values in a highly attractive London conservation area. They again illustrate the principle of carefully integrating the new with an existing neighbourhood.

188a   Bowland Yard: a sketch to explain the proposals.

188b   Ground floor plans with main entry from street archway at the right.

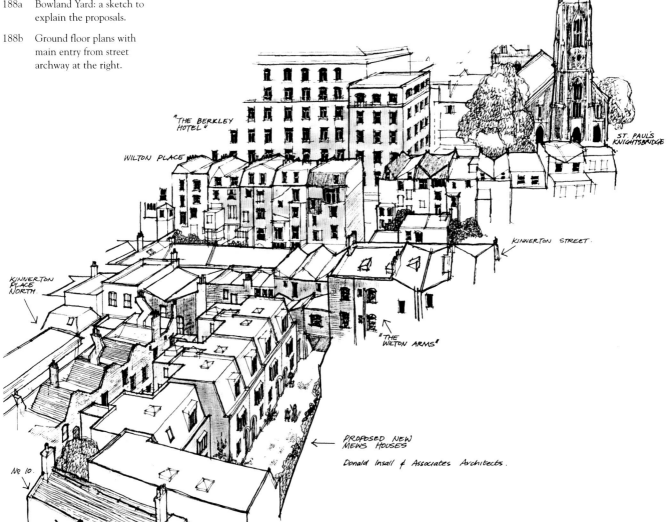

188a

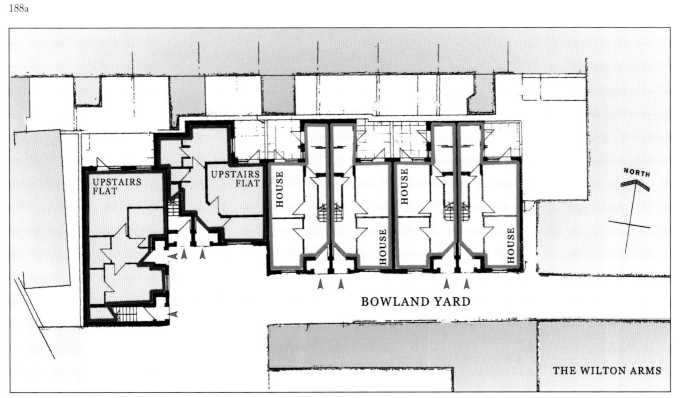

188b

The new mews houses were instantly occupied (1982).

The Stephen Hawking Building: Gonville and Caius College, Cambridge

Surrounded by other and already famous modern buildings in Cambridge, including the well-known Faculty of History Library by James Stirling, Foster and Partners' Law Library and Harvey Court (Leslie Martin and Colin St J. Wilson) was the site of an Edwardian villa (once the home of Professor Stephen Hawking), still carrying a number of fine specimen trees. These had brought difficulties in negotiating planning consent for an urgently needed new building, to provide student rooms, sets for Fellows and teaching rooms, together with new conference and student recreation facilities.

Following an analysis of the site and its potentialities, a new building was designed with an unusually sinuous footprint, avoiding and embracing the existing trees and answering to and complementing the surrounding

190a   Top floor, set back behind an open gallery.

190b   The new building, 'tuned' to respect its neighbours and existing planting.

190a

190b

191b

191a

191a,b   One of the new building's two
        elliptical staircases.

architecture. Faced in Ancaster Hard White stone above an Ancaster Weatherbed plinth, this echoes the vertical articulation of adjoining Harvey Court, whose parapet line it follows, with a set back roof balcony and curtain-walled upper floor.

Internally, finishes were designed for longevity, with floors of stone and hardwood, and with high-quality carpeting specifically designed for the building. Special attention was given to enabling all maintenance to be carried out without disturbing occupied rooms; services are throughout accessible from lift-off panels in the

main circulation corridors. Energy conservation has also received special care. Fresh air is drawn into the building through earth-tubes beneath the underground car park, exploiting the temperature difference between subterranean and exposed surfaces: heat-exchangers also recover some 80 percent of otherwise wasted heat from exhaust air in winter.

Much-needed accommodation has here been provided in a new building that makes a very positive new contribution to its challenging landscape and architectural context, on such a key site in Cambridge.

193a

192, 193a,b,c Importantly sited in Cambridge, the new building has been sensitively designed in relation to its immediate setting, its serpentine form adapting to the existing landscape.

193b

193c

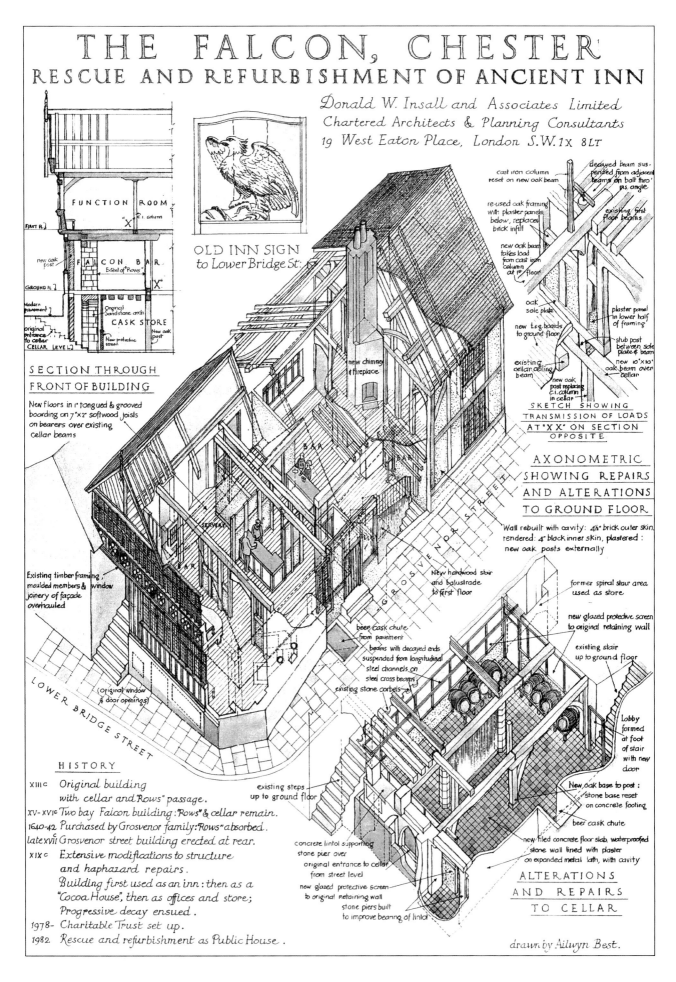

THE FALCON, CHESTER
RESCUE AND REFURBISHMENT OF ANCIENT INN

10. Conservation in a changing historic area

Chester

Finally in this range of degrees of intervention, let us consider some techniques and lessons of conservation on a larger canvas, as exemplified in the historic city of Chester.

Conservation in historic towns presents its own problems, not only in the scale of the work but in the administrative complexity of the task, and in influencing a multi-owned and multi-occupied collection of buildings, all of widely varying dates and uses. Of necessity, the concept becomes altogether broader and very much wider than the 'preservation' exercise applicable when

dealing with a single, specific monument. For cities are alive and changing. Their energies are powerful and difficult to guide. Yet given determination and a specific and imaginative policy applied with energy over sufficient time, we can do much to conserve and enhance their special essence and identity.

In 1966 the Government decided to commission four pioneer pilot studies of historic towns. One of these, which we were invited to undertake, was for the historic city of Chester. We were set a very open brief, which was to 'study and report on the implications of a

Chester: Bridgegate from the air.

196a

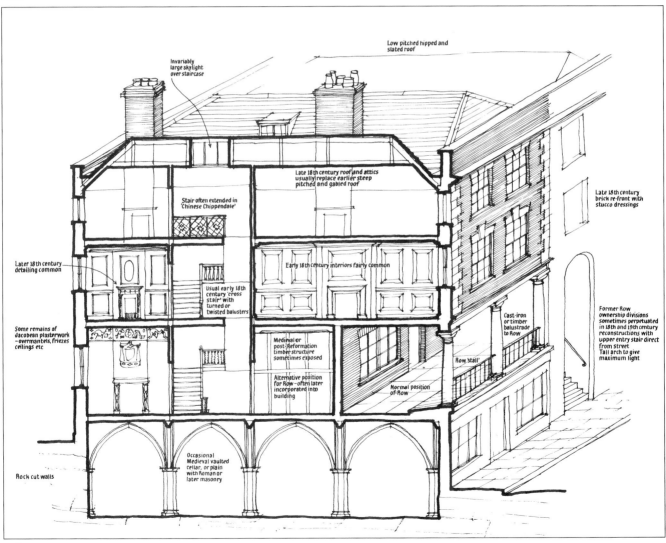

Low pitched hipped and slated roof

Invariably large skylight over staircase

Late 18th century roof and attics usually replace earlier steep pitched and gabled roof

Late 18th century brick re-front with stucco dressings

Stair often extended in 'Chinese Chippendale'

Later 18th century detailing common

Early 18th century interiors fairly common

Usual early 18th century 'cross stair' with turned or twisted balusters

Cast-iron or timber balustrade to Row

Former Row ownership divisions sometimes perpetuated in 18th and 19th century reconstructions with upper entry stair direct from street Tall arch to give maximum light

Some remains of Jacobean plasterwork – overmantels, friezes cellings etc

Medieval or post-Reformation timber structure sometimes exposed

Alternative position for Row – often later incorporated into building

Row stall

Normal position of Row

Occasional Medieval vaulted cellar, or plain with Roman or later masonry

Rock cut walls

196b

196a   Chester: the River Dee, bridge and city wall.

196b   Ancient cellars, and a covered shopping row: an illustration reproduced in our report.

conservation policy', designed 'to preserve, promote and enhance the architectural and historical quality of the area', and 'to maintain its life and economic buoyancy'.

We spent six busy months on this survey, and another six in producing our report. Following earlier experiences elsewhere, we visited as a team and we followed our guiding principle of working from whole to part. We examined first the regional setting, its pressures and implications. In the time dimension, we explored the historical continuity within which the city had grown and is alive today. We set out to analyse the specific character of the place, and to identify its key features and elements. We identified these as the river bridge-point and city walls, the unique two-level shopping area (Chester's 'Rows') at the city centre, and the remarkably persistent black-and-white architecture of its buildings. We recognised the strong dynamic pressures and forces acting upon the city, including social change, movement patterns and shifting economic demand.

Next, we gave more detailed study to specific smaller areas, selected for their neighbourhood identity. The method we developed in each area was to appraise first the townscape, then the architectural quality of its buildings and spaces, and finally their individual ownership, use and condition. We inspected more than 400 buildings, both outside and inside, from roofspace to basement and recorded and plotted their positive possibilities, advancing for each sub-area a series of specific proposals for its physical conservation and enhancement.

197a

197b

197a   'The Rows': two-level shopping in the city centre.

197b   Chester's characteristic black-and-white buildings …

197c   … persistent through the centuries.

197c

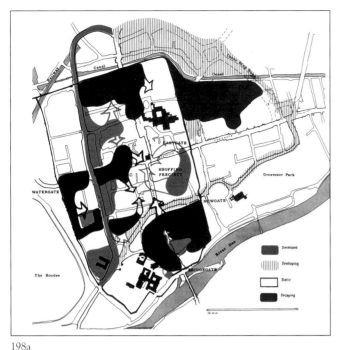

198a

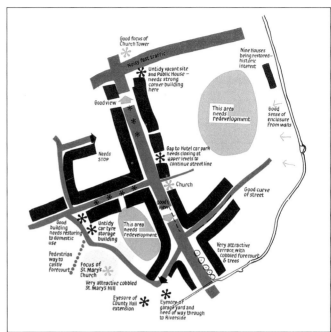

198b

198c

We drew up our recommendations in the form of a phased and costed conservation programme. This proposed firstly the designation of a conservation area, evaluating and mapping its historic buildings in detail and advancing a firm but imaginative policy of control. Recognising that change and redevelopment in any city are continuous, we suggested undertaking pilot schemes in deteriorating areas and we identified some possible agencies who could help in achieving them. These included the city itself (as owner, or in consortium with developers), private owners and also semi-public bodies such as local housing associations/societies. In some instances encouragement might also be sought from national resources. In this way, identifying the major ways and means, we set up a tabulated programme

for the reconditioning of historic buildings, phased respectively over one year, five years and 15 years, and preceded in specific cases by urgent first-aid action.

Following our brief in broader terms, and in wide consultation with many national organisations, including every major planning authority, we carried out an analysis of current legal powers and set out recommendations for nation-wide action. These included a financial involvement in continuing conservation

198a   Commercial and economic trends and pressures: a dynamic diagram.

198b   Comments and suggestions in a sub-area identified for detailed study.

198c   Individual city-centre properties: uses surveyed and categorised by merit and opportunity.

Lower Bridge St. East

Lower Bridge St. West

Lower Bridge St. West

199a

projects such as this, and even the idea, if necessary, of setting up an historic towns corporation with the appropriate powers. We further advanced specific proposals for improved and more positive procedures in local planning, in allocating grant aid, and in securing better encouragement and efficiency in day-to-day conservation practices nation-wide. This section of the report was submitted urgently in advance, for central government consideration in then-current revisions to the planning legislation.

Meanwhile, the report was carefully considered by Chester's city council. After what seemed a nerve-racking silence (ideas do need time to take root), the council came to a fundamental and important decision – it would indeed adopt and support a declared policy of conservation in Chester. Further, and as the first city in the country to do so, it decided in December 1969 to back this policy by making a definitive financial allocation in each year from the general rate fund, to help in setting up and pursuing a conservation programme. As we had suggested, this proved to attract valuable matching support from government sources. In 1971 we were invited to take up a new role as the city's conservation consultants, and from April of that year the council also acted upon a further idea we had suggested by appointing, within the planning office, a specific Conservation Officer (the first of his kind), to

199b

be given the task of encouraging and organising activities 'on the ground'. In their various ways these decisions, and Chester's energy in following them, have been basic to the remarkable success of the ensuing conservation programme. The appointment of a Conservation Officer has become widely accepted and adopted in local government planning offices, leading to the establishment, in fact, of a new profession.

199a   Strip-elevations of major streets, identifying currently empty property.

199b   A regular 'heartbeat' of meetings helps to review and promote action.

A regular pattern of quarterly meetings and productive consultations emerged, at which suitably senior officers – the Director of Technical Services, with his appointed Conservation Officer, the Planning Officer, Treasurer and Conservation Consultant and also a visiting representative of the relevant government department, could all gather to discuss, decide and promote action on current cases. To set the example, token public improvements were activated, including the cleaning of the stonework of the Town Hall.

The next idea adopted was to initiate an exemplary pilot scheme. For this we selected an area of noticeably advancing decay, which we called the Bridgegate Area. Taking advantage of the available resources of two visiting students, a bird's-eye view and table-top model of the area were quickly put in hand, as useful tools in considering architectural and redevelopment proposals. Using a periscope enabled us to check in three dimensions and in miniature, their effect upon the skyline from different viewpoints. We carried out a more detailed survey of 77 individual properties, and prepared a further report recommending further immediate action. This included the acquisition by the city at low cost of available and unimproved key buildings. At the time the area was beset by uncertainty and implied threats of redevelopment; we set out a financial strategy, including an application for central government support. At the same time, negotiations were opened in London. We stressed the point that a policy agreement between the city and county councils, suitably publicised, would greatly help the sense of security in the area and re-encourage prudent property investment. Environmental

200a

200a,b   To set an example: cleaning Chester's
         town hall.

200b

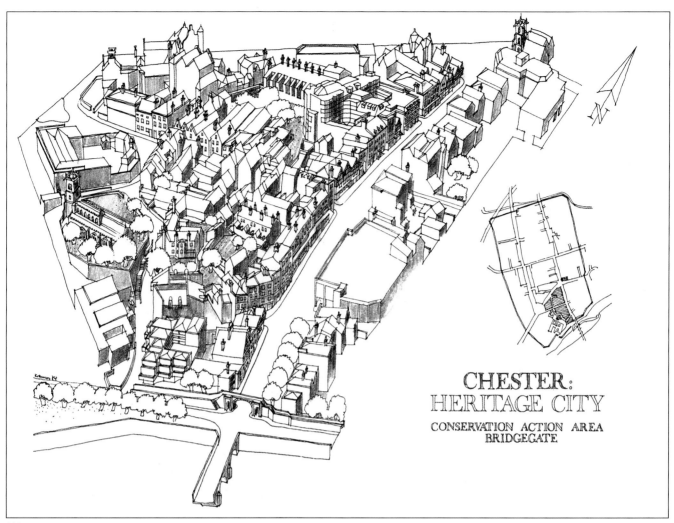

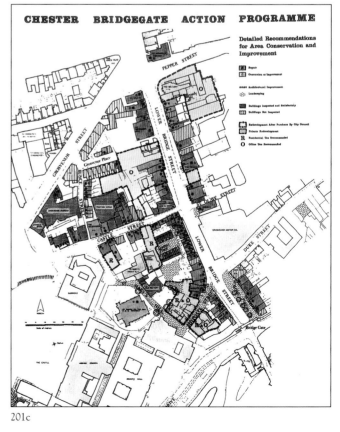

201a   The Bridgegate conservation action area.

201b   A tabletop model, to enable assessment of any proposals in three
       dimensions, checking street-level views with a periscope.

201c   The pilot action programme (1982) to promote attention to a run-
       down city area.

improvements were proposed and a framework suggested, within which the owners of a series of the worst-affected properties could be offered financial aid and advice. To assist, we set up a weekly 'clinic' in a disused local shop. In a burst of activity and initiative, the city celebrated European Architectural Heritage Year (1975) and purchased the redundant St Michael's church for conversion as a city heritage centre. Incorporating audiovisual displays and exhibition space, this was again the first such enterprise in the country, if less elaborately fitted-out than its almost-contemporary cousin in York.

In the longer time-scale and following the first decade of action and progress, a conservation review study was set up in 1976 and carried out jointly by the consultants with the Director of Technical Services. Its aim was to identify all continuing building conservation problems, each according to its priority. Three categories of urgency were established, related back to those in the original study; and an analysis was made of likely sources of finance, whether owner, city or nation – applied in turn to each of the priority buildings still needing attention.

Chester's Conservation Programme

1. Assumptions: National and regional.
    City plan
    City accommodation demands

2. Chester Conservation Area:
    Designation
    Maps and plans
    Control

3. Redevelopment of deteriorating areas: Pilot schemes
    City corporation
    Private owners as developers
    Redevelopment by a Housing Society
    Local redevelopment by national resources
    Local and national investment

4. Reconditioning historic buildings: a phased programme –
    Ways and means –
    Year 1: a first-aid programme
    Year 1: 'early warning' care for building groups
    Years 1–5: an initial repair programme
    Years 5–15: a continued repair programme

    Approximate costs:
    Public facilities and environmental improvements
    Pilot redevelopment schemes
    'First-aid' protection
    First phase: reconditioning
    Second phase: reconditioning

202a

202a   Principal headings of the Chester Conservation Programme.

202b   Decay and neglect in Lower Bridge Street: Gamul House.

202c   A corner-site in Bridgegate: properties purchased by the City ...

202d   ... and made available for restoration by private enterprise.

202b

202c

202d

203a

203b

203a,b   Gamul Terrace and Gamul House in 1968, and restored to use in 1986.

203c   'A Review of Progress in Bridgegate' (progress report of 1982).

The review, recognising the problems of wider areas and groups, proposed additional studies and action areas, noting specific design opportunities and acknowledging the existence of any specific but surmountable local problems. Particular recommendations were made for additional protection by listing buildings and by designating extra conservation areas, all within a pattern of continuing progress reviews. The HMSO agreed to publish a report for us entitled *Conservation in Action* (1983), setting out in detail all the initiatives by which the Bridgegate area had now been brought so visibly back to life. Despite inevitable losses, the general decline of the area and its previously decaying properties has been not only arrested but quite dramatically reversed.

The main message that emerges from the Bridgegate experience has been the positive power of commitment, allied with a refusal to give up, and coordinating every possible resource into concerted action. City initiative, aided by central government support, has led in turn to company and private investment, sometimes backed by housing association, county and other funds, to the extent that an entirely new financial buoyancy has been created. In the city centre nearby, the same has been true for once-neglected areas like King Street, now busy and prospering again.

Renewal and replacement constantly take place in the patchwork of any city, and architects are not always adept at integrating new buildings with old ones. Individual replacements are in many cases easier to design appropriately, rather than entire cleared streets or building groups, so the City has suffered less than some others, and has a strong

203c

policy of design guidance and some interesting new architecture.

What has been the result of all this concerted activity, both for Chester and for the conservation movement at large?

204a

204b

204c

204a–d A discovery. At successive floors in a shop in Pepper Street were found the bases (204a), then the capitals of some columns (204b) and finally the apex of a pediment (204c). All these were revealed and the full façade exposed as a condition of planning permission in new redevelopment (204d).

204e A little-used backland site bought by the City for redevelopment …

204f … enabling the construction of new houses for city-centre living.

204d

204e

204f

There is no doubt that the city itself has prospered in extraordinary measure. Despite changing national fortunes and the competition of other towns, trade and tourism here are at a high level and Chester's physical appearance and presence have benefited immensely. To judge from old photographs, the general condition of its buildings has perhaps never been better. Change has continued, but under firm guidance. Despite changing shopping habits, the Rows still present a lively variety. Pedestrian priority has been greatly

205a

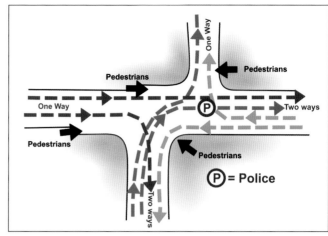

205b

205c

205d

improved, stage-by-stage, until the central streets of the
Rows area echo once more to the sound of human
conversation and human feet. It is already difficult to
believe the strictures of the 1968 report about the
then-current degree of traffic nuisance and noise
(p. 72). Thanks to the initiative of the Chester Civic
Trust, it has been possible to reinstate the old High
Cross, re-set in 1975 in its original position where 10
years before the buses used to turn and tangle. There
could perhaps be no more permanent and persuasive
anti-traffic bollard. The Trust has also now taken the
initiative in issuing an excellent visitors' guide and has
designated the popular 'Millennium Trail' in Chester.

Chester was awarded the Europa Prize for the Preservation
of Monuments in 1982, and soon afterwards the Europa
Nostra Medal for 'Conservation Activity and Example'
in the Bridgegate area; many international visitors come

205e

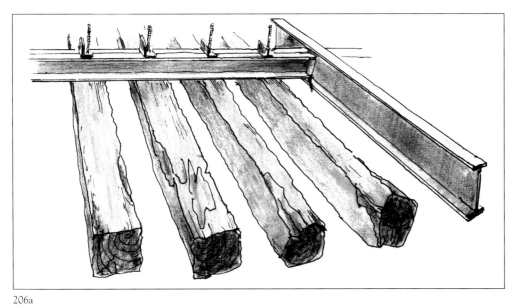

206a

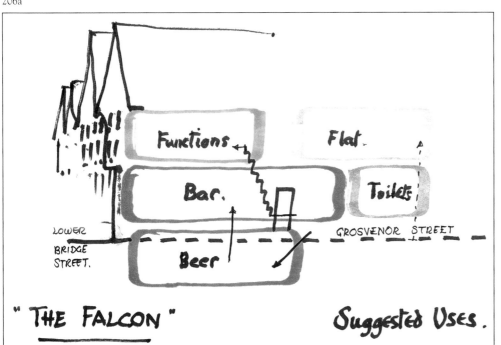

206b

206c

206a The Falcon. Massive 13th-century floor beams, hung from new supporting steelwork.

206b 1970 proposals: diagram of suggested uses.

206c The Rows in Eastgate Street: a strip elevation from our report.

to study and enjoy the project. The fact that it has never been necessary to set up the national body envisaged as a possibility in the pilot report reflects the strength of impetus generated purely at local level. Chester must always be grateful for the willing support firstly of the Historic Buildings Council and then by its successor, English Heritage, as well as taking pride in the devotion of elected representatives and officers and of the public whose efforts have made all this possible. The keynote of the conservation exercise has been the success of its positive and remarkable teamwork.

Conservation and enhancement at this end of the graded scale are closely linked. They can and must accommodate continuing change, but this can only be achieved by first recognising and underlining existing merits, and then by an energetic performance of constant and consistent daily management.

Urban conservation is a dynamic and a continuing exercise, and cannot be achieved overnight. Decades later the conservation programme is still alive and active in Chester, meeting ever-new changes and challenges. It has sufficient vital momentum to carry it forward long beyond present lifetimes.

207a   Chester's Falcon in 1968.

207b   The Falcon in 1975.

207a

207b

Degrees of intervention: a review

To summarise the lesson of these examples (pages 98–207) and to recapitulate:

It has been illuminating to remind ourselves how many **differing degrees of intervention** are available, remembering that in practice the whole range of these varied degrees may occur alongside one another.

1.

Regular daily care must always take pride of place. To prevent decay is more sensible than to delay and then attempt to remedy it.

Pages 98–105

2.

Programmed maintenance becomes possible for a group of buildings in single care, and again brings high dividends.

Pages 106–115

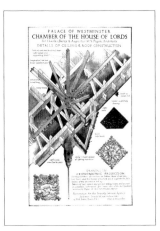

3.

Major but conservative repairs may still be made without significant architectural alteration, for example, when structural emergencies and functional changes overtake prudent advance planning.

Pages 116–125

4.

Repairs incorporating changes may have to be combined, when even essential repairs and adaptations accumulate, delayed by the disturbance they bring, or by raising funds.

Pages 126–135

5.

More radical interventions and alteration are sometimes essential to secure a building's continuing life.

Pages 136–145

6.

Restoration to a building's original or previous form calls for yet more replacement and renewal. Actual physical identity of its fabric may then yield place to accurate replication.

Pages 146–157

7.

A rehabilitation programme involves higher degrees of intervention and change. Its aim is to retain character and features, but within extensive adaptation to new purposes.

Pages 158–171

8.

Renewal incorporating existing buildings or elements, whose continuity is for one reason or another adjudged as being of value, brings yet more change.

Pages 172–179

9.

Completely new buildings gain hugely by considering their context, crediting and complementing existing neighbours, and even if themselves totally new.

Pages 180–193

10.

Urban change, involving property in multi-ownership, brings strong challenges and yet a vibrant opportunity for proactive and dynamic management.

Pages 194–207

Finally, let us now examine one quintessential dilemma where at a single and complex historical monument, a sudden major emergency demanded **every degree of intervention** – from continuing care, through major repair and improvement, to restoration and sympathetic but total renewal: the post-fire restoration at Windsor Castle.

The disastrous fire at Windsor in November 1992.

Intervention: in practice

Post-fire restoration at Windsor Castle

This whole range of degrees of intervention was exemplified at Windsor Castle, in the restoration work following the disastrous fire of 1992. At first, there was an overpowering sense of national loss, but surprisingly soon a more positive and constructive spirit began to emerge.

The Royal Household prepared a considered and careful assessment and review of the situation, with all its complex alternatives, exploring the relevant principles and some likely comparative costs. The philosophical aspects of reconstruction work at the Castle demanded the closest and most balanced consideration. What guiding principles should its conservators adopt? The possibilities were wide open, and of high significance. Should this superb national treasure, the outcome and symbol of centuries of royal history, be restored exactly as it was before the fire? Or should the calamity be seen as an opportunity for new and modern designs, materials and constructional techniques, stitched into the ancient fabric but speaking entirely of today, and independent of the past? Detailed decisions would also need to be taken about degrees of restoration and whether, for example, any decorative architectural finishes recreated might now be backed on a modern construction, or whether the infrastructure and its craft techniques should themselves literally and exactly repeat their predecessors. The conclusion eventually reached was that modern constructional techniques and materials would not be outlawed, but that the new architectural finishes must then be historically and decoratively perfect.

On site, urgent protection and rescue work were put in hand, recording and collecting what could be saved and initiating a drying-out exercise to deal with more than a million gallons of water used in combating the fire. Expert committees were set up and a team of technical advisers selected and appointed to help in directing the work.

The first task was to reach a true understanding of the life and growth of the Castle through its long history, and the relative significance of its physical features

today. Research into all available written records was supplemented by observation on site, for example by the useful device of preparing successive dated plans as transparent overlays. The story of all its buildings could in this way be studied, observed and appreciated, in all their living complexity.

Restoration of the Castle Staterooms

The fire had largely destroyed a major part of the superb interiors, created in the late 1820s by interior designers Morel and Seddon, within a structure largely then being recast for George IV by his architect, Jeffrey Wyatville. Their contribution to Windsor had in its time taken up and extended the varied architectural

211a   Lost upper floors above the destroyed staterooms.

211b   The Crimson Drawing Room, soon after the fire.

211a

211b

212a

212b

212c

212d

history and flavours of a constantly changing programme of rebuilding, carried out in waves over eight past centuries. Wyatville's handling reflected both the lavish taste of his royal client and that of his period, in what he saw as a revival of what was essentially a commanding Gothic castle, defensive, grand and comfortable, albeit permitting new classical symmetries of layout and detail. He united the previous hall and chapel, previously situated end-to-end, and joined them into a single and immensely long hall for great royal functions. To this he gave a strongly Gothic character with its flattish arched ceiling of plaster reflecting earlier oak construction, all strongly decorated with heraldic devices, and inspired by traditions of St George and the Knights of the Garter. Very nearly all of this had perished in the fire.

The adjoining continuous sequence of staterooms had received from its 19th-century interior designers a luxurious overall treatment, ranging in style from Classical Revival to Rococo; each was elaborately finished and furnished. They culminated in the Grand Reception Room, lined with re-used and adapted French panelling, mirrors and tapestries, and crowned with an elaborate plasterwork ceiling. This too, the fire had largely consumed. With two exceptions (the Green and White Drawing Rooms), this range of staterooms had now alas, been lost.

Two limited architectural competitions were launched. The first of these was promoted to inspire any alternative ideas for the two dining rooms, which had suffered the most damage. Some remarkable submissions were received, and all were considered in detail by the design committee. But none were felt, in the last analysis, to be better or more apposite than the Morel

213a

213b

213c

and Seddon work destroyed by the fire. In addition, most of the furnishing and contents had been safely away in store at the time of the fire, leaving a high proportion intact and still available, thanks to the bravery and skill of the firefighters. So after much debate, it was agreed that the soundest principle to adopt would be to reinstate this handsome set of staterooms as a sequence. The two dining rooms would therefore be recreated to their 19th-century form, although rectifying any minor mischiefs they might

213a In the State Dining Room, ancient features long-concealed behind later panelling, now again made accessible by the fire.

213b Surviving plaster fragments reincorporated in new work. The ceilings are completed by hand.

213c The restored Crimson Drawing Room.

214a

214b

since have suffered. The remaining succession of staterooms could also be accurately recreated, relying upon traditional materials and methods for their substructure but correctly reproducing their historic interiors. This would demand a great deal of straightforward and careful restoration.

Precise copies of the plasterwork ceilings were assembled, cast from salvaged fragments and reproduced on an expanded steel backing. In the State Dining Room, although all the original wooden ceiling pendants had perished, good photographs were fortunately available, allowing them to be re-created. The work was entrusted to expert carvers, maintaining a just-sufficient design supervision to ensure that the copies were as lively and spirited as their forebears. Where in that room some great stone wall arches had been revealed by the fire, these were made accessible for display behind great jib doors now formed in the fastidiously copied replacement panelling. Every opportunity was taken to retain original features, even if those had not been readily visible immediately before the fire.

Reincorporating historical features in the Royal Kitchen

In continuous practical use since at least 1350, this remarkable kitchen had been largely destroyed. Its ruins presented some particularly lively questions about degrees of feasible conservation. The wooden trusses of the plaster-coved roof, together with its long crowning lantern, were plainly in the style of Wyatville. But when the timbers were being decharred, to determine whether enough strength might remain to rely upon them, it was suddenly apparent that evidently an original ancient oak roof, mostly of the 14th and 15th centuries, had been merely encased and dressed in Gothic fashion – in fact, in 19th-century softwood. The surviving original structure, although weakened and much wounded, was clearly of sufficient importance to justify retention, if at all possible. So a decision was taken: it could be saved. Its hardwood members were given fresh courage by traditional methods of scarfing-in new oak, backed where necessary by invisible steel strengthening. Surviving

214a   Inspecting charred roof timbers of the destroyed Royal Kitchen.

214b   New oak, scarf-jointed and bolted to the damaged roof trusses.

214c   The kitchen roof-lantern under reconstruction.

214c

215a

215b

215c

original hardwood timbers were pieced-in with new oak and all retained; finally, any missing softwood casings by Wyatville were recreated in matching deal. The cast-ironwork of the windows, undamaged by the fire, was rescued from the floor below and simply reinstated.

Meanwhile some practical necessities had again to be accommodated. It was realised that the great open roof-lantern, which Wyatville had glazed with cusped sub-lights, was itself of more than one early date, and had already been extended at both ends. A location had to be found for the air-handling equipment so essential in a modern kitchen. So the extended form was retained complete, while its added end bays were used to hide away this heavy machinery. To carry it, cranked steel trusses were incorporated invisibly within the deeply coved kitchen ceiling.

Other discoveries were also made. The kitchen had been built hard against the inside of the Castle's protective curtain wall, itself unperforated by original windows. Curiously however, some blind openings had later been cut in this outside face, evidently for the sake of an

215a   The Royal Kitchen: restoration almost completed.

215b   Section drawing: Kitchen inside the Castle's curtain wall(*). China corridor added outside (at left). St George's Hall (at right), above extended earlier vaulting and the added Larderie Corridor.

215c   A discovery: window now internal, between kitchen and later extensions.

architectural match with 18th-century windows in the walling at one point alongside. When, in the ensuing century, Wyatville had added a linking passage along outside the old curtain wall, these recesses were adapted as indoor china cupboards, so this had become known as the China Corridor. In one of these cupboards, at a

216a

216b

216a   Discoveries: a trompe-l'oeil
window in the Castle wall
below the China Corridor
(* in section).

216b   An ancient well, opened up
for inspection.

216c   Rebuilt kitchen extension,
set away from the original
external wall with its
revealed windows.

216c

which indoor views over the Royal Kitchen can now be enjoyed. They are today re-glazed in fire-resistant glass. What was originally external stonework in the new indoor corridor has not only been left unplastered, but is further emphasised by setting back the new floor construction, and by incorporating a continuous strip of roof-lights, from which daylight spills down to reveal and delineate its textured detailing. So again the revealed historical detail is credited and amplified, taking every opportunity for its future display and appreciation.

Other surviving features of historical value here included three long semicircular-headed windows in an outer wall within the courtyard: they were at the same time reincorporated in the new design. But the old walling was weak, so the new service building was constructed upon a light steel framing, its alignment and foundations carefully planned to avoid disturbing underground features. At this point and excitingly, the Castle's original deep well was now discovered, already filled but long forgotten. The well has been made accessible again for inspection. The aim, once again, has been to accept and release every evidence of history.

storey below, a careful trompe-l'oeil treatment was found, exactly duplicating the effect of the ferramenta and leaded glazing of the earlier windows, even complete with cast shadows. No trace remains of the openings which had inspired this detail, so this has now become one more fascinating feature in the display of the Castle's history.

In the wall of the kitchen facing over the old courtyard, traces of much earlier 14th-century windows were found. These were carefully explored and re-opened. For practical reasons it was essential to rebuild later extensions into the previous kitchen courtyard, incorporating essential working space. But their planning was reorganised to bring the internal corridors directly against these old reopened windows, through

217a

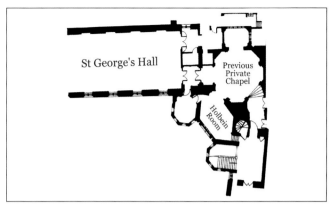

217b

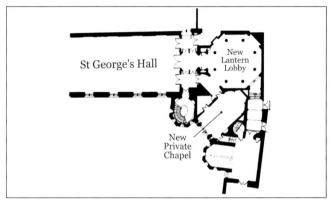

217c

The stone-vaulted undercrofts below St George's Hall had been untouched by fire, but were much damaged by water. The opportunity was taken to remove unsightly later partitions and additions, and to reveal their original scale and grandeur. At the same time, it was possible to restore the circulation pattern and practical workability of this extensively used royal building, revealing and displaying historical features such as earlier windows and doorways, complete even with newly discovered details including the original portcullis grooves, and celebrating the continuity of the Castle's long history.

217a Discovered and revealed: portcullis groove (at left) and 'pintle' for the original kitchen gate.

217b Plan before the fire, which had spread from the impractical 19th-century chapel.

217c A new lantern-lobby on axis with the hall; the private chapel is relocated off the circulation route.

217d Ancillary improvements: previous rooms beneath St George's Hall, reunited as a single vaulted space.

217d

New design in historical context: St George's Hall

The severely damaged area of the previous Chapel – itself the seat of the fire – and especially the adjoining St George's Hall, along whose roof-space it had so greedily spread, lay outside the sequence of the destroyed stateroom interiors by Morel and Seddon. A protective outer steel roof had been urgently installed within the exact ridge-line of its predecessor; but might a more radical design-intervention within it now be acceptable? The question of improvements again arose. The practical layout of this zone had been very unsatisfactory and the previous chapel had in reality become something of a draughty access corridor. Indeed, perhaps this was why its heavy curtains had concealed the incipient fire. Might it now be possible to relocate this chapel, and so to create a more satisfactory grand circulation route between the Castle's royal quarters and St George's Hall?

An architectural competition was again held and some very interesting schemes were received. The winner was a design by Giles Downes of Sidell Gibson Partners; this was further developed in close discussion with the design committee chaired by Prince Charles. The main axis of the Hall would culminate in a top-lit octagonal lantern lobby, possibly with an upper gallery and crowned by laminated timber vaulting. The new Chapel could then be relocated alongside it, where it might take advantage of a traceried window occurring very nearly centrally in its rear wall. Giles Downes devised an extremely attractive vaulting pattern for this room; it was executed in laminated timber and was very much in the Gothic spirit, but new. The window now contains memorial glazing designed in close discussion with Prince Philip, Duke of Edinburgh, and features the fire, together with Wyatville, the firemen and St George – not to forget the dragon.

Meanwhile the immense length of St George's Hall, within its newly constructed outer roof, offered a similarly demanding design opportunity. The winning design has a long ceiling – something of an echo of its forebear – but with powerful improvements. The shoulders of its Gothic-inspired inner roof were dropped a little lower, increasing its apparent pitch, and the trusses are this time executed in real English oak, linked in a series of longitudinal arches to emphasise the length and proportions of the Hall. The new rhythm has more life than the previous roof and reincorporates all its decorative armorial shields and heraldic devices. St George, on horseback, remains in station at the far end, while at the other, grand double doors link axially under a balcony into the new octagonal Lantern Lobby.

Vaulting of the new Chapel.

These three new rooms – the Lantern Lobby, the Chapel and St George's Hall – are thus of strong modern design, adopting the powerfully Gothic spirit of the Castle, but without reproducing any actual previous forms. They are executed in fine craftsmanship, right down to details such as beautiful joinery and door furniture, honouring the earlier work and the careful restorations alongside, but in a blend of old and new, all attuned within the special image of the place.

The challenge of restoring Windsor Castle after the fire demonstrates what an extraordinarily wide range of solutions may be appropriate, involving many degrees of intervention within the same monument. In a way, it is a classic example of the long chain of sensitive choices and evaluations that have to be so responsibly made in every responsible task of architectural conservation.

219a   St George victorious, in a renewed chapel window.

219b   The new oak ceiling under construction.

219a

219b

Windsor's history is continued: the new St George's Hall, almost completed.

Intervention and change

As we have repeatedly seen, the degree of intervention appropriate in any project is in most instances complex, rather than clear-cut. Significant parts of a historic building may well be best left alone or repaired, while others are accurately restored, and others again improved or indeed totally redesigned. These varying degrees of conservation may find themselves exemplified within the same building or architectural group.

Our first task is always a careful and thorough analysis of each town or building, its current and future requirements and the pressures upon it. We may ask: what is most significant about it? Is it a prime architectural example of a style, a period, or a famous architect? Is it the product of some unsung genius, or quintessential of some lost social group? Does its importance lie in the individuality of the craftsmanship – in carved ornament or sculptural decoration? All these are 'original' features, some of whose appeal speaks to one viewer, and some to another. All may justify and even demand respect, admiration and enjoyment.

Evaluation comes before understanding, and assessment before action. Sometimes it is the changing pattern of a building's continuing history that holds its greatest value and fascination. Its significance may have originally been its connection with an important historical person – a birthplace, the house where a first concert was given or a treaty signed, or the home of a dastardly plot. But the pattern of its ensuing change and development can equally have its own or even greater validity. A venerable and weathered quality may speak of long exposure and age, the agents of John Piper's 'picturesque decay'. On occasions, history even includes an accepted literary fancy (like the legendary home of Sherlock Holmes in Baker Street). To different viewers, it is not only the bricks and mortar that speak their message of value.

In their turn, some constructional materials will themselves have aged more than others. Some will have greater intrinsic merit or interest; others may now be unobtainable, or may yield place to more effective replacements. Human requirements change amazingly, and what was once accepted may now be irrelevant. Or past changes may even themselves have become of new interest, specifically as social history.

We must simply open ourselves to every element of each building, to be receptive to whatever it has to give, and without preconceptions. We must let it speak to us before we address it. When we know what attracts us, or what is seen to have special value (now or someday in the future), we will be best placed to guide. Then we can help to cultivate and 'garden' it like a plant towards its continuing best. There are no universal or objective rules, such as 'go back to the original', or 'to the best period'. That was a mistake too often made in the 19th century. We can only ask ourselves 'what is most significant, of what we now have?' and 'how can this best be guided onwards and enjoyed in the future?'.

Architectural conservation starts with recognition and evaluation, stimulates active attention and continues into care. Eyes, minds and hands each take their successive part.

Even a monument such as a venerable memorial, innocent of any daily 'use', is still vulnerable to self-ageing and change, and cannot escape the influence of time. For without exception, **'Buildings are Alive'**.

APPENDIX

Living buildings: Great Gate, Trinity College, Cambridge.

A young apprentice mason in the 1940s.

TRENDS AND ISSUES

An anniversary postscript

When a retired archbishop looked up from his gardening in a Dorset village in 1967, he noticed me with a sketch pad and a clipboard, evidently involved in survey. 'Are you', he asked, 'one of Mr Insall's young men?'

In those halcyon earlier days of our practice, we were seen as puzzling and unrepentant reactionaries – a shock to the Establishment system. These rather surprising architects were surely out of step? We had repeatedly to explain and to justify our puzzling preferences, and the principles and practices for which we stood. Now and surprisingly soon, all is different: the concept of conservation takes root in architects more readily than it used to do. Meanwhile too, the new profession we launched (almost by accident) in Chester days – that of the Conservation Officer, as an architecturally aware variant of the planner – has proliferated and has found its feet. Thus do ideas and social movements prosper and grow, and perhaps they always happen in waves. Yet it still feels strange to have straddled between the depressing deprivations of the 1940s and the affluent extravagances of a new century, and it is disquieting to witness other incipient and gathering clouds, over uncertain futures yet to come.

The world is a less self-sure place than our forebears knew. But we still stand firmly witness to the basic philosophy distilled into my family motto – the spirit of 'Bring Forth the Best'. This is the unchanging principle that guides our continuing message and our method. But what have been the major changes and trends, during these first five decades of our practice's lifetime? And, where may they next lead?

Social and economic changes in our building environment

Britain is increasingly a nation of skilled service providers; our declining manufacturing industry and lower military priorities have released a flood of older buildings for conversion and reuse. Increasingly too, we are a multi-racial, multi-cultural and multi-faith society. Although we still have 42 cathedrals and a multitude of ancient churches, many religious buildings have now become redundant. So have many older dockland and barrack buildings. Adapting them, if

assessed in terms of wasted energy and materials, is more economic than new building. Already too, some areas of postwar rehousing – especially those in unneighbourly tall blocks, which dominate by their sense of overlooking – are being redeveloped. Meanwhile commercial and especially the architectural 'icon' buildings take over their place and dominate the urban skyline.

A second tendency has been to gather activities such as shopping, medical care and education into larger, more widely located units. The corner shop, local surgery and school are losing out to supermarkets, super-hospitals and colleges. Town centre vitality finds itself exported to the urban fringe, where these are generally located.

The unspoken assumption has been our acceptance of more and more travel, principally by private car for consumers and also in servicing by heavy road transport. More space is taken up by new roads and car parks – the urban fabric is dispersed, while town living is seen as less attractive. We forget that fossil fuels are not endless but decrease in availability and increase in cost, and that the likely future counter-trend is a return to living in towns.

In the countryside, agricultural methods have been revolutionised by mechanisation. The country house of yesterday, with its internal community and mutually dependent staff, has survived in an altered form. Whether in family or in institutional use, it is seen much more as a visitable heritage asset.

Political attitudes and provisions

Conservation in the UK has been stimulated by public awareness, and by a remarkable number of private amenity societies, whose multiplicity and effectiveness surprises every visitor. Despite their limited financial resources, they combine and focus the energies of local people and influence government to marked effect.

The task and opportunity of guiding change and development are most effective when coordinated within the legal and control network of our town and country planning system. This is where they belong, at the point of maximum awareness and practical influence. Alongside thus, the arrival of English

Heritage has provided an invaluable focus of technical knowledge and influence and centre of excellence, although its financing is vulnerable to political swings of emphasis. Other semi-public bodies responsible for assets such as the royal palaces, the royal parks and national parks are similarly susceptible. The real danger is the short-term political awareness of those entrusted with long-term values.

Our suggestion in the 1960s of a national historic towns corporation, reflecting the postwar activities of the New Towns Commission, proved unnecessary at that time. It might still prove a valuable reserve concept in any change of balance or energy between central and local government and the responsible public agencies. But in dealing with the pressures of a multi-owned existing town or city, the mechanisms of local democracy remain surprisingly strong.

Technical developments

Building techniques continue to evolve rapidly. Local materials no longer have such a key influence; short-term construction costs and a shorter projected building life justify lower investment and produce less demand for quality. A new town hall, once a social symbol, becomes today an expendable urban facility. A new office block may be short-lived, and something to surpass next time.

Information technology meanwhile makes huge advances, comparable perhaps with even the invention of printing. Data storage and interpretation and comparison are immensely easier; our problem is now in selecting and limiting what we record. Paper, once expected to vanish from office life, increases daily. Computerisation aids the day-to-day monitoring of valued buildings and can greatly facilitate their proper management and care.

Town planning methods and techniques continue to evolve. Earlier solutions such as use-zoning, street widening and devices such as frontaging lines have served their time and gone. There is still insufficient acceptance of the principle of 'capacity planning' and of managing places within their own optimum size and potential. Design control over individual building projects is often seen as an unimaginative, if valuable restraint. One missing element is the more conscious detailed design of large buildings for their interest at street and human access level.

The listing of buildings and the designation of special conservation areas has mostly proved workable and positive. Conservation and management plans, by whatever name, are valuable in stimulating interest and awareness – in helping people to look, and to care for

their surroundings. They call attention to local distinctiveness and quality, and should always lead on to positive proposals. We need more proactive and imaginative studies, simple to set in motion if given the political will and adequate resources. The aim must be to recognise and encourage opportunities, with more attention to improvement and enhancement. For planning and building care are no more than good asset management.

In the daily practice and guidance of building conservation, an unexpected trend has been a growing interest in the surviving evidence of past change itself, whether for better or for worse. This can become an obsession, resulting in not only an appreciation of the past, but of resistance to all change, forgetting that today is also tomorrow's history. There is sometimes even the added danger when 'interpreting' a building, of inventing what its viewer may wish to see. The ultimate danger is then the theme park, complete with costume and background music – all of it delightful in an exhibition or display, but a stranger to real life.

Craftsmanship

Only at our peril do we forget the most vital factor in securing successful building conservation – the continuity of traditional craft expertise. The dangers are as natural as they are real. Just as mechanisation and mass-production have overturned an economy based upon human and animal muscle-power, so in turn do our manufacturing industries now find themselves priced out in an international market. So employment opportunities for brain-work exceed those for manual skills; this is reflected in our education systems. Apprenticeship has been largely overtaken by academic training, but the educated head cannot on its own replace the skill of trained hands. We need both.

It is true that we get what we deserve. Only a demand and respect for good workmanship can ensure its adequate reward, and hence its continued availability. Quantity can be measured; quality is more difficult to define, yet it is at least equally to be valued. In maintaining and caring for our past, the continuity and encouragement of an able building workforce, complete with its specialist skills, is increasingly a primary need.

The broader issues: human behaviour and climate change

During the writing of this book, our consciousness of new dangers has deepened. We may only now in effect have fully realised the fact, but there seems to be no doubt that climate change is accelerating and threatening our human welfare – perhaps, in time, even humankind's ultimate survival.

An appreciable factor in this progressive and potential suicide is our excessive travel, and the atmospheric damage this entails. We have become increasingly world-conscious, with new perspectives of distance, time and movement. And in addition, human numbers increase in geometrical progression with every second. Our scientific and technical skills and abilities progress at a huge rate, and are unstoppable.

Although we are beginning to realise all this, there seems little likelihood of correcting such a headlong trend. Our inward-looking human natures will not readily allow us to modify our own lives for unborn future generations.

The increasing upper-atmosphere pollution by carbon products will almost certainly continue for as long as fossil fuels remain unconsumed. Travel in the air feels effortless, and is direct and friction free, compared with laborious movement on land, and makes it amazingly economic. Flying costs and cheap airfares carry little burden of surface engineering and maintenance, as (whether paid for or not) do railway, roadway and water systems. Having achieved air travel, science is unlikely to find any means of surface travel to compete with it. Consequently government action in all countries will continue to be aimed at expanding airports. Having learned to fly, man will fly.

Our ambitions to travel cannot realistically be muzzled, or our technical abilities strangled. Whether or not they are an 'advance', these are explosive trends, and cannot

be reversed. Our five-minutes-to-midnight recognition of our impending future, even if still generations away, is too weak to arrest history. Behavioural patterns change irreversibly. The only real remedy may be that population expansion will somehow stabilise itself, and that technical advance will turn urgently to offsetting the harm and damage we continue to cause, by some means of cancelling them out – of somersaulting the effects of atmospheric pollution and controlling solar gain, even perhaps turning it to benefit.

This may eventually be the only means of human survival. Have we realised it too late?

The plight of Venice is a quintessential example. We know we are on a crash-course with the damage we have caused, and already entering new and uncertain waters. As in every other art and science, the whole demands, grammar and vocabulary of environmental conservation are certain to change. We begin to see that coastlines will change, plant life will change, whole populations will relocate. Our behaviour-patterns are only beginning to adapt to all this. The principles by which we can hope to guide and manage our lives and surroundings will hold soundly enough, but within a very new frame of environmental pressures, challenges and opportunities.

Our crystal ball is cloudy, and has disturbing gaps, like those we have made in our atmosphere. We can but trust that everything we have learned may now stand the future in good stead.

227a The one asset we cannot afford to destroy – our atmosphere.

227b But industrial pollution grows over Venice.

Living wood: a timber from the author's home at Kew Green, recently identified by dendrochronology at the Department of Archaeology, the University of Sheffield, as being of Scandinavian origin and probably felled in the winter of AD 1699/1700.

Living Buildings: the architect's role

For the architect who has the good fortune to be able to work with old buildings and their owners, there are scores of ways in which his advice may be useful. Each brings its own problems, requiring their own response. Each will entail much of the same basic sequence: first to look and understand, then to analyse and recommend, and then to assist in carrying out whatever work is needed. The following are some examples of the ways in which the conservation-oriented architect's special skills and experience can help.

Casebook examples

- Access and safety, fire prevention and escape
- Advisory services
- Churches: inspections, care and re-ordering
- Conservation and management plans
- Converting and adapting buildings
- Emergencies: defects and problems
- Environmental improvements
- Funding: obtaining and monitoring grant aid
- Historical research and analysis
- Interiors: replanning, redecoration and refurnishing
- Maintenance and care
- Memorials, garden and park features
- New design: sensitive sites
- Refurbishment and repair
- Service installations and lighting design
- Structural remedy

Access and safety, fire prevention and escape

Key improvements needed may include providing better public access, reducing bottlenecks, compartmenting structures against fire-spread and providing special toilet arrangements. Much wasteful disuse can be overcome by analysing and replanning circulation routes, and by providing adequate means of emergency escape. Increasingly, owners are obliged to review their premises from a standpoint of health and safety requirements.

230a

Health and safety

Safe visitor access is a paramount requirement and not always easy to provide in old buildings.

Fire protection

A three-person government inquiry, with Donald Insall as architect member, was set up in 1990 after the major fire at **Hampton Court** to investigate the problems of fire protection for the royal palaces. The advisory report published by HMSO is a primary guide for action in responsible anti-fire management.

Fire protection measures for the Royal Palaces

A report by
Sir Alan Bailey KCB
Donald Insall OBE
Philip Kilshaw OBE

230b

231a

231b

Restoration to full use

To facilitate greater public use of **Liverpool Town Hall** (architect: John Wood the Elder, 1754; restored in 1802 by James Wyatt), an access-audit now enables the city to overcome the major handicaps that were previously preventing any full use of the building. By attention to these key problems and requirements, it can again be used for the purposes for which it was designed.

LIVERPOOL TOWN HALL

OFFICE

MEETING ROOM

ENTRANCE HALL

GRAND STAIRCASE

WAR MEMORIAL HALL

COUNCIL CHAMBER

MAJOR'S PARLOUR

OFFICE

KEY

○ Doors upgraded
--- Escape Routes
〜 New Fire Doors
▬ New Fire Partitions

FIRE ESCAPE ROUTES: ground floor

Public access

A planning study commissioned in 1998 investigated the possibilities of greater access to **Somerset House**. To enable the opening of the courtyard to the main building and its interiors, newly converted to art galleries, special provisions are made for disabled visitors. One such feature is an inclined access bridge, linking this repaved space across deep perimeter light-areas with the restored interiors.

231c

231d

Advisory services

In varied permutations and degrees of service, the architect's aim is to provide whatever skilled help an owner will find most useful, devoting his best talents to the special needs of the moment. Once a brief has been agreed and met, there may be no need for any extended involvement or responsibility; and a ready flexibility in this respect can be helpful to many owners.

For example, in helping anyone already engaged in the building industry, this may only entail preparing analyses of existing structures and sites, developing design drawings and negotiating statutory approvals and consents.

Thereafter only a more limited service of regular visits may then be required, to advise upon building works supervised and executed in-house.

Not infrequently, for reasons of geography or availability or to make available special architectural skills and experience, one architect may be called upon to advise another. Sometimes too, an owner or his estate may already retain its own building skills. In all these instances, a simple advisory service can be helpful and expedient.

232a

Advice on traditional construction
Specialist advice about traditional construction informed subsequent repairs to **Thaxted Guildhall, Essex** carried out under contract management by Essex County staff.

232b

232c After repairs

232d

Technical advice
Advisory services have enabled comprehensive stonework cleaning and repairs of the **All Hallows Church Tower, Staining, London**.

Design advice
At **Rycote, Oxfordshire**, architectural designs and details prepared in close discussion with the owner are carried out by his own directly managed labour force.

233a

Specialist advice on historic interiors

For new lessees at **Chandos House, London**, specialist advice has guided the restoration of features such as Adam interiors and decorations and the creation of historically appropriate carpets and furnishings, while the freeholders' executive architects carried out general design and direction of conversion works.

At London's **Mansion House**, carpets were specially woven from archived 19th-century designs.

233b

233c

233d

Historical analysis and condition assessment

For the **Witley Court ruins in Worcestershire**, advice has promoted subsequent repairs, interpretation and display, planned and completed by English Heritage.

233e

Churches: inspections, care and reordering

Places of worship of all traditions and persuasions (some 14,500 of these in England are listed buildings) need periodical improvement and updating to meet changing user requirements, and with due respect for historic fabric. The excellent Church of England system requires regular maintenance inspections, identifying priorities for attention. This calls for sympathetic understanding of an ecclesiastical building and its users.

234a

Repairs to stonework

St Luke, Chelsea, a handsome London church of 1824. During programmed restoration, discoloured and damaged masonry has been cleaned and repaired.

234b

Redecoration schemes

Enhancing **St Paul's, Knightsbridge, London**. New lighting and decorative schemes reveal adornments previously almost lost.

Accommodation

Replanning has created a new social area, and (by the insertion of a new floor) an additional meeting room in the medieval tower: **St Mary's Woodnesborough, Kent**.

Ecclesiastical furnishings

New houselling benches designed and made at **St Nicholas Chapel, King's Lynn, Norfolk**.

234c

234d

235a

Ironwork

Missing churchyard railings reinstated on a prominent site at
St Mary-le-Strand, London.

St Mary le Strand

RENOVATION OF CHURCH RAILINGS

Eight panels of 19th Century cast iron railings have been repaired and re-erected on new Portland stone plinth walls, two matching panels incorporating notice boards and the new gates and piers create a centralised composition.

DONALD W. INSALL & ASSOCIATES · ARCHITECTS · 19 WEST EATON PLACE SW1

235b

235c

Leadwork of a spire renewed

Improved constructional details are incorporated in a major restoration of the spire at **Guilden Morden, Cambridgeshire**.

235d

235e

Conservation and management plans

Following the techniques long advocated and pioneered in studying and analysing significant historical and architectural sites, conservation plans are now increasingly a formal requirement by national, local and grant-giving bodies, to ensure that care and development proposals are made in their appropriate context.

236a

236b

Conservation plans

Conservation plans may equally be needed for widely varying subjects such as the major national hospitals (St Thomas' Hospital, London, 1866–71, inspired by Florence Nightingale), for intensely busy working monuments such as the Palace of Westminster (prepared for the Director of Estates) and for rapidly changing city-centre commercial sites, such as London's Regent Street, for the Crown Commissioners.

Industrial archaeology sites

Sites such as **Chatterley Whitfield, in Cheshire,** may call for new policies once they have been abandoned.

236c

237a

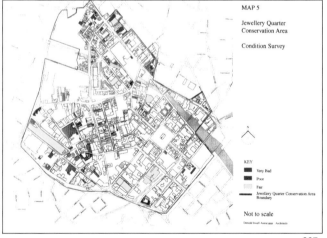

237c

Old industrial areas

Birmingham's Jewellery Quarter called for special study (in association with English Heritage and Birmingham City Council). This distinctive area has a huge number of characteristic small workshops, whose future is uncertain. A survey and analysis led to a conservation plan, used as a guide in the City's continuing planning control.

237b

237d

Converting and adapting buildings

Times change, and bring new requirements. Often these cannot be met without considerable alterations. Where historic buildings are concerned, alterations and adaptations must be carried out with due sensitivity.

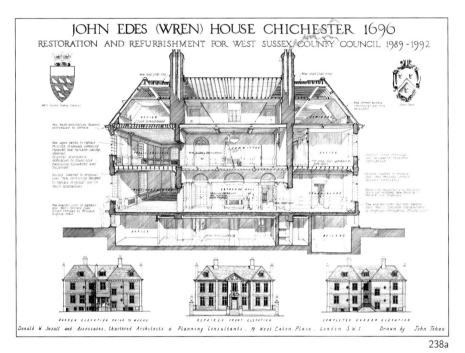

238a

238c

238d (after conversion)

Administrative headquarters

Wren House in Chichester (1696) now forms a distinguished 'front parlour' for the adjoining headquarters of West Sussex County Council. The exterior was comprehensively refurbished in 1989–92. The converted interior includes a lift, an escape stair and new services, and provides generous space for public events.

238b

238e

Visitors and display

Conversion for English Heritage as a museum of a great man's life and work, together with associated education and staff premises: **Down House in Kent**, once the home of Charles Darwin.

239a

239b (after conversion)

239c

Public occasions and entertainment

Exterior repairs and interior conversions at **Cardiff Castle** allow greater use of the building, in turn providing income for its continuing care and maintenance.

239d

Adaptation

The ancient **Tide-Mill at Woodbridge, Suffolk**, is now converted for visitors and display. Rescue by a local charitable trust enabled installation of access and escape arrangements. Its mechanism and equipment are in order, with explanatory drawings prepared for education and interpretation purposes.

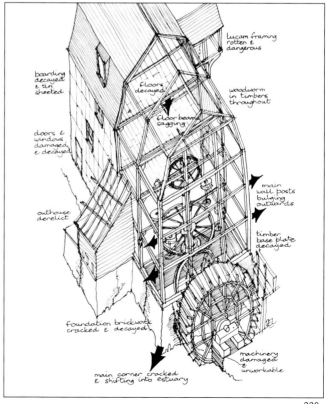

lucam framing rotten & dangerous

boarding decayed & tin sheeted

floors decayed

woodworm in timbers throughout

doors & windows damaged & decayed

floor beams sagging

main wall posts bulging outwards

outhouse derelict

timber base plate decayed

foundation brickwork cracked & decayed

machinery damaged & unworkable

main corner cracked & shifting into estuary

239e

Emergencies: defects and problems

Architectural services are often needed in identifying particular troubles (for example, structural failure, dry-rot outbreaks, flooding or fire damage), recommending upon and executing their correction and cure.

240a

240c

240b

Rebuilding after fire

A serious fire occurred in 1992 at **Athelhampton in Dorset**, a fine historic house of the 15th century onwards. Following negotiations and agreement with insurers, the destroyed interior of the east wing is now painstakingly restored and reopened for its family and visitors.

Leaking roof feature

Old Public Record Office, Chancery Lane, London. An auxiliary glazed lantern is installed above the previously leaking dome of the reading room, with automatic smoke-release in the event of fire.

240d

240e

241a

Structural problems

Located near London's Bank of England, **St Margaret's Church Lothbury** has suffered severe damage after the construction of large new neighbouring buildings. Each had involved deep excavations, providing support from new foundations to carry the east and west ends of the church. But an underground river below (the Walbrook) has since dried and shrunk, and the church has sagged between them. While the problem awaited further funding, the emergency was met by a reinforced concrete beam within the walls.

241b

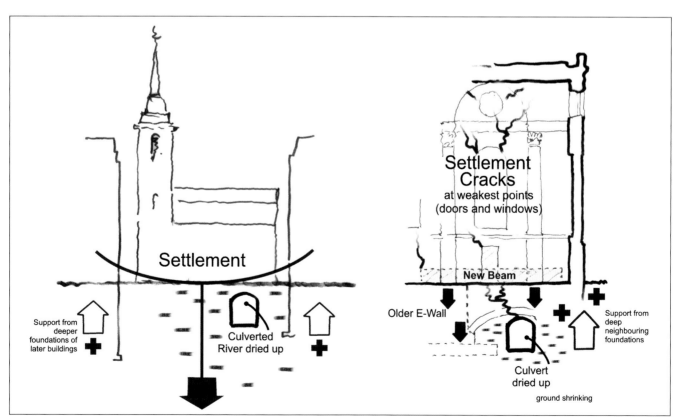

Settlement

Support from deeper foundations of later buildings +

Culverted River dried up +

Settlement Cracks at weakest points (doors and windows)

New Beam

Older E-Wall

Support from deep neighbouring foundations +

Culvert dried up

ground shrinking

241c

Environmental improvements

Public spaces are an invaluable asset, but less useful when their surfacing and street-furnishing are worn out and neglected. They deserve good design treatment and considered detailing.

242a

242b

Street furniture

At **Old Palace Yard,** street lamps alongside the Palace of Westminster copy the original Barry pattern. Railings and barriers are simplified and reorganised for maximum public safety, all within a rationalised scheme of pedestrian paving and vehicle parking.

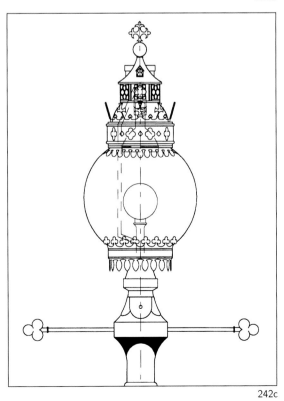

242c

243a

Repaving, fountains

The great courtyard at **Somerset House, in the Strand**, was for many years wasted in use as a car park. The Somerset House Trust, in rehabilitating and converting the building, has made this valuable space available for public gatherings and events. It is now equipped with associated underground toilet and service facilities, and supplied with 44 decorative fountains with special lighting. Historic railings and lamps are reinstated in the Strand. The courtyard, which accommodates a winter ice-skating installation, has become a highly popular public and tourist venue.

243b

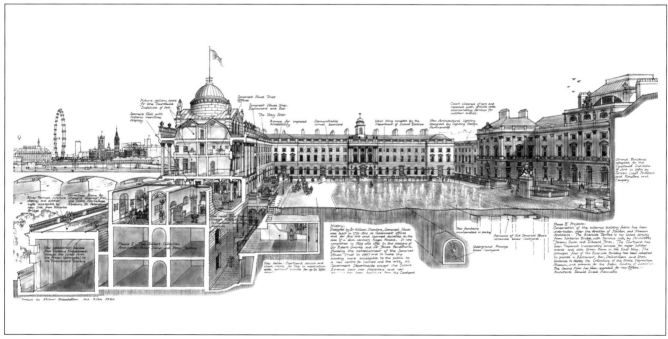

243c

Owners often require help with fund-raising, or with the preparation of proposals for grants from bodies such as the UK Heritage Lottery Fund, charitable foundations, or the European Commission.

Conversely, funding organisations themselves may also need expert services in selecting from the submissions they receive, and subsequently in monitoring the expenditure of grants they have given. Among others we have assisted are the committees of the Getty Grants Programme, the Council of Europe, the European Commission and the World Monuments Fund, in their work of encouraging good building and conservation by grant-aid, sometimes on a world-wide basis.

244a

244b

Funding

The Getty Grants Program has carried out studies to promote restoration at **St George's Hall in Liverpool**. This research included the provenance and history of major features such as the original gas lighting and ventilation systems (the Hall was in effect, a very fascinating early example of air-conditioning), together with major sculptures, art objects and quintessentially period materials such as encaustic floor tiles, all of which could then be appropriately addressed in any continuing restoration works.

The main Hall floor was for long concealed by a protective timber decking, but has survived underneath in repairable condition.

244c

244d

Multiple funding

Garrick's Temple, Richmond. Restoration work was resourced jointly by as many as 24 national, local and charitable organisations, all coordinated by the Temple Trust.

245a

245b

245c

245d

Local authority financial initiatives

The City of Chester purchased houses in **King's Buildings**, severely cracked by foundation settlement, for sale to developers who have inserted a new basement beam and rebuilt the brick façade to the street, restoring a distinguished terrace for continuing occupation.

Historical research and analysis

Accurate historical restoration frequently entails painstaking preparatory research into the life-story of buildings, and research from all available records.

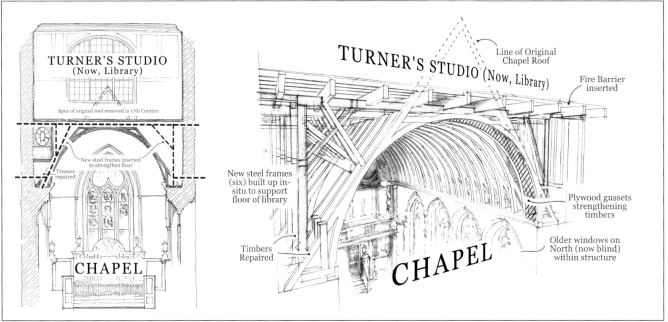

TURNER'S STUDIO
(Now, Library)

Apex of original roof removed in 17th Century

New steel frames inserted
to strengthen floor

Trusses repaired

CHAPEL

Line of Original
Chapel Roof

TURNER'S STUDIO (Now, Library)

Fire Barrier
inserted

New steel frames
(six) built up in-
situ to support
floor of library

Plywood gussets
strengthening
timbers

Older windows on
North (now blind)
within structure

Timbers
Repaired

CHAPEL

246a

246b

Discoveries

Immediately above the private 13th- and 17th-century chapel at **Petworth House in Sussex** is a room that became the studio of the great artist, JMW Turner RA. We found that the apex of the chapel roof had been severed to make this room possible. Structural work accommodates the vicissitudes of history and the results of hidden beetle attack.

Research

The **Chinese Pagoda at Kew** was completed by Sir William Chambers in 1760 as one of a series of architectural landscape features, not all of which survived for long. The tower still incorporates considerable changes from quite early in its life. One missing feature, of which any surviving evidence is still sought, was the series of 80 carved dragons that decorated its tiers of roofs. Where did they go? The degree of earlier alterations makes it impossible to reconstruct history in all its detail, but adequate research informs accurate repair.

Kew

Kew Pagoda

Left: Chambers drawing of 1760
Right: Drawing by a student of Sir John Soane
in 1820

246c

247a

Accurate restoration

Careful historical research has enabled accurate restoration of the historic auditorium and public circulation spaces at the **Royal Albert Hall** in London (1872). During a comprehensive refurbishment and overhaul programme by the Trustees, the opportunity arose to correct damaging earlier alterations and to introduce full modern services.

247b

247c

Aiding rescue

Wotton House, in Buckinghamshire (1704–14), rescued from destruction just in time. Historical research for its purchaser, Mrs Elaine Brunner, established the major involvement of Sir John Soane, who had been called in to renovate the house after a fire in 1820, and who extensively recast its design.

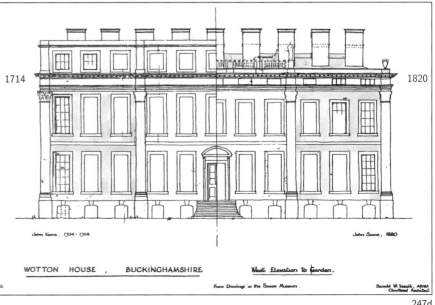

1714   1820

John Keene. 1704 - 1714.   John Soane, 1820

WOTTON HOUSE, BUCKINGHAMSHIRE   West Elevation to Garden.

From Drawings in the Soane Museum.

Donald W. Insall, ARIBA
Chartered Architect

247d

Interiors: replanning, redecoration and refurnishing

Architecturally significant interiors deserve special attention. Sometimes they have slipped into neglect, or are simply unappreciated. This may call for historical research, and is an important opportunity for imaginative decorations, fabrics and furnishings.

248a

248b

248c (after refurbishment)

Refurbishment

Magnificent historic interiors at **Raby Castle**, accurately restored. In the Octagon Room are re-woven silk finishes and fine fittings by Burn (1848), cleaned and re-embellished for the owner, Lord Barnard and his family. Elsewhere the requirements of everyday living are met by including modern furniture, carefully selected to tune with historic interiors.

249a

Interior replanning

At **London's Mansion House** (architect: George Dance the Elder, 1752), evacuated for repairs in 1991–93, the opportunity arose to replan and enhance the interiors and their accommodation, taking full account both of historical merits and of the practicalities, improving the circulation and providing for escape and servicing. Here too, particular attention is given to furnishing principal apartments, and to the display of a magnificent recent acquisition of paintings.

249b

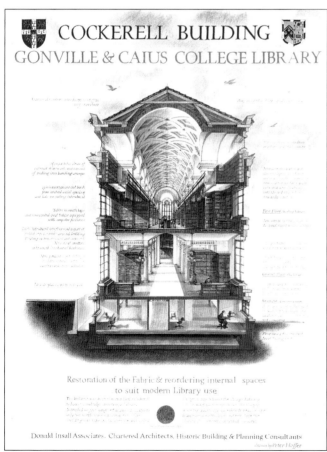

COCKERELL BUILDING
GONVILLE & CAIUS COLLEGE LIBRARY

Restoration of the Fabric & reordering internal spaces
to suit modern Library use

Donald Insall Associates, Chartered Architects, Historic Building & Planning Consultants

249c

249d

Replanning, repairs and refitting

The Cockerell Building in Cambridge has been completely repaired and restored as a library for Gonville and Caius College.

Maintenance and care

Well-informed and regular maintenance means forestalling problems, as well as curing them. By timely attention, continuing deterioration and costs can be conscientiously avoided and controlled. This calls for foresight and planning, and an awareness of their structural and functional requirements, materials and lifecycles.

250a

Corporate owners

The National Trust keeps a careful eye upon its properties, enabling it to protect their integrity and enhance their life-span. **Speke Hall** dates mainly from the early 16th and 17th centuries onwards, and represents a fine example of regional construction in oak. Timber-framed structures tend to fail at joints, or where over-stressed or exposed, but when given due attention, they are remarkably tenacious.

250b

250c

250d

251a

Private owners

Kedleston Hall in Derbyshire, when still in family ownership, was under our care as maintenance architects for some 30 years. Owners value the benefit of continuity, experience and understanding. Each building has its own strengths and weaknesses, and each owner too has his own special concerns and circumstances. Building elements such as old roofs with inherent design problems all demand regular monitoring and attention.

251c

251b

251d

Memorials, garden and park features

Celebratory civic furnishings add immensely to urban character. But they must be well-designed for their site. Especially where fountains and water are introduced, they must work well and be reliably maintained.

252a

252b

Restoration

A delightful sculptured fountain in the courtyard of **St Bartholomew's Hospital**, restored to its highly decorative use in 1990.

Public sculpture

Architectural advice may be valued in siting and design, negotiating consents and executing the work in association with selected specialist sculptors. Set squarely before the entrance, in the grounds of the **Royal Hospital at Chelsea**, is this statue of *The In-Pensioner*, by sculptor Philip Jackson, giving point and emphasis to Wren's celebrated masterpiece.

Garden feature

This little shell-grotto in the grounds of **Hampton Court House in Surrey** became desperately neglected, despite its obvious charm. External repairs have enabled a painstaking restoration of its interior features.

252c

253a

Memorials

In 2005, a suitable site on **London's Victoria Embankment** was found for a memorial celebrating the Battle of Britain. In this location stood a disused bulwark of masonry (earlier intended as a ventilating chimney for the underground railway below, when steam trains were in service). By cutting a diagonal path through this, its flanks are now available for the display of new bas-relief sculptures of air heroes together with a lively background of civilians, all beautifully realised and cast in bronze by sculptor Paul Day.

Stonework repairs and lighting

In Oxford, the celebrated **Martyrs' Memorial** has required stonework repairs and cleaning, and is now lit at night from concealed sources.

253b

New design: sensitive sites

New buildings may be proposed for significant or highly attractive sites, or as neighbours for others protected by listing or in important conservation areas. An historic building may outgrow its use, calling for internal or external additions and extensions. This demands high skill in design, and sometimes sympathetic negotiation; these are abilities that a responsible architect must possess.

254a

New building on a difficult site

Alongside the celebrated **Wren Library in Cambridge**, extra storage accommodation has been provided for 250,000 books. To respect its famous neighbour, the new building is constructed largely underground, despite the immediate presence of the adjoining river Cam. An interesting problem is the necessity of ensuring that an excavated basement does not rise like a boat during construction work.

254b

255a

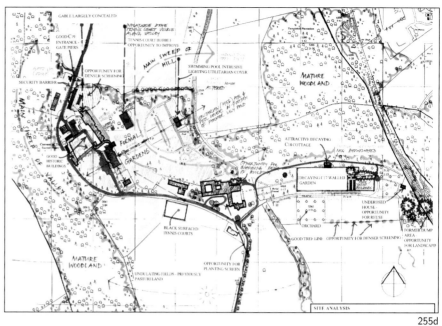

255d

255b

255e

255c

Schools constantly change and develop

At **Woldingham School**, situated in an attractive valley landscape in Surrey, new teaching provisions had been promised to school parents. A full conservation and development plan set proposals in their longer-term perspective for negotiation with the authorities. Next, a new sixth-form centre was designed and completed in 1972. As part of the continuing development programme, a new arts centre and an assembly hall, designed and fitted to the highest technical standards, now stand close to the main existing and listed buildings.

Refurbishment and repair

As well as being of great architectural merit and significance, and even apart from their importance as heritage assets, historic buildings incorporate vast investments in materials and constructional energy. Their responsible restoration enables them to earn their keep, and solves huge problems of economic sustainability.

256a

256c

Structural repair

Kew Palace was built in 1631 as the home of a wealthy London merchant and later became a much-loved royal palace. It was eventually abandoned in favour of Windsor. The ancient brickwork of many dates, combined under limewash, was in a dangerously cracked and deteriorating state. Following a programme of extensive roof repairs, the distorted brick walls were examined and plotted in extreme detail for Historic Royal Palaces. The building then repaired and made safe, ready for its subsequent conversion and public opening to visitors.

256b

256d

257a

257b

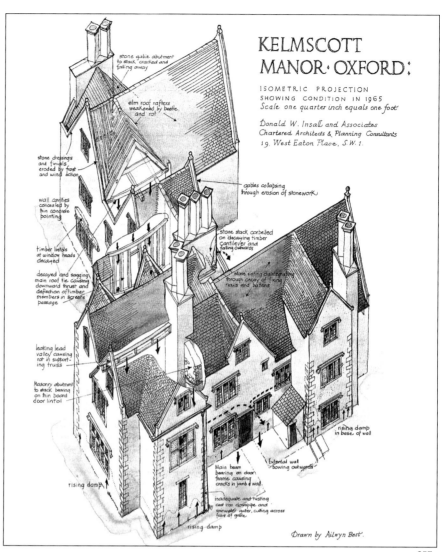

KELMSCOTT
MANOR · OXFORD :

ISOMETRIC PROJECTION
SHOWING CONDITION IN 1965
Scale one quarter inch equals one foot

Donald W. Insall and Associates
Chartered Architects & Planning Consultants
19. West Eaton Place, S.W. 1.

stone gable abutment
to stack cracked and
falling away

elm roof rafters
weakened by beetle
and rot

stone dressings
and finials
eroded by frost
and wind action

gables collapsing
through erosion of stonework

wall cavities
concealed by
thin concrete
pointing

stone stack corbelled
on decaying timber
cantilever and
falling outwards

timber lintels
at window heads
decayed

stone slating disintegrating
through decay of fixing
nails and battens

decayed and sagging
main roof tie causing
downward thrust and
deflection of timber
members in screens
passage

leaking lead
valley causing
rot in support-
ing truss

Masonry abutment
to stack, bearing
on thin board
door lintel

rising damp
in base of wall

rising damp

Main beam
bearing on door
frame causing
cracks in jamb & wall

External wall
bowing outwards

inadequate and rusting
cast iron downpipe and
spragrapefe gutter, cutting across
front of gable

rising damp

rising damp

Drawn by Ailwyn Best.

257c

Refurbishment

Kelmscott Manor dates from 1570 and was enlarged a century later. It was the country home of William Morris from 1871 to 1896. Under the terms of his daughter May's will, the house was left on her death (1938) to the University of Oxford, but with the strictest provisions against all alteration or even any improvement, making it virtually unusable. In 1962 the Society of Antiquaries negotiated possession, enabling much-needed repairs and the addition of essential facilities such as new bathrooms. The house has been reorganised (including the provision of a new side entrance and an added attic stair) to permit its use partly for visitors and partly as accommodation for a curator. A key clue to decisions was 'what would Morris himself, if he lived today, have wished to do?' Now, by prior arrangement, the house receives more than 10,000 visitors each year.

257d

257e After refurbishment

Service installations and lighting design

Compared with historic structures, modern services enjoy a short lifetime. Technical developments are continuous and most of them (if not quite all) offer real improvements. Deteriorating older service installations have often become unsightly, bringing risks of accident, flooding and fire.

258a

258c

Lighting for safety

At **Goldsmiths' Hall**, lighting gives opportunities for careful attention to detail; here, lighting maximises safety with the treads illuminated and the risers in shadow.

Lighting improvements

Lighting transforms the interior of the **Chapel of Pembroke College, Cambridge.**

258b

Public lighting

Chester's famous Rows are an important night-time asset to the city and their lighting has called for urgent improvement. Their daytime appearance also now benefits from the neatly concealed wiring and specially designed fittings, all located for maximum effect. A working collaboration between architects and lighting consultants (here, Graham Phoenix Lighting Design) can bring helpful results.

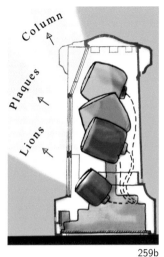

259a

259b

259d

New services

During a major repaving of **Trafalgar Square** in 1988–89, to deal with increasing damage by irresponsible use and traffic, new drainage, services and street furniture were incorporated. At the foot of Nelson's Column, lighting fittings are now concealed inconspicuously within new iron bollards, while Nelson himself is spotlit from surrounding rooftops. The work was executed in planned phases, closely programmed for minimum disruption to public access (especially during Christmas).

259e

259c

Refitting

Redecoration of the **Codrington Library at All Souls College, Oxford**, is extremely conservative, maintaining the subtle, but powerful, attractions of a great interior. Adjacent new staff facilities and stack rooms now make the library easier to maintain and run and new lighting enhances its use by students and staff.

Structural remedy

Structural movement (indeed sometimes, eventual collapse) is mostly an outcome of uneven ground support or structural loading, or of unresolved structural weaknesses. Sometimes this has been further compounded by unconsidered solutions, such as mistaken underpinning or buttressing. Experienced advice from architects and structural engineers can ensure the most acceptable and efficient remedies and costs.

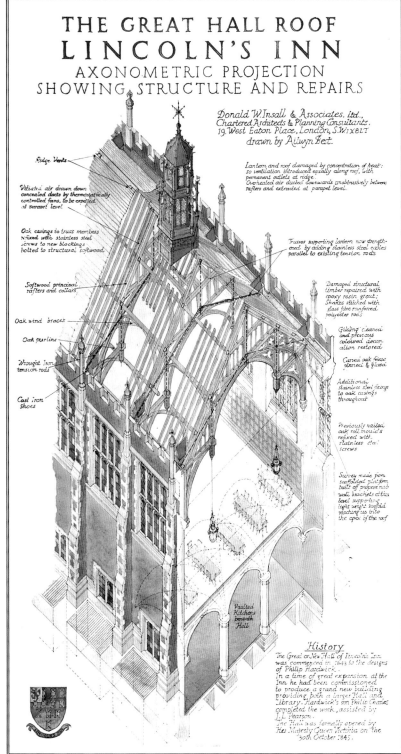

260a

260b

260c

Structural strengthening

Lincoln's Inn Hall was built by Philip Hardwick in 1843–45 but the great timber roof is not entirely what it seems, and relies much upon unseen ironwork. Damage, particularly caused by overheating, has been corrected by a new ventilation system. Defective timbers are now reinforced by polyester rods and epoxy resin, together with additional stainless-steel cables and fixings.

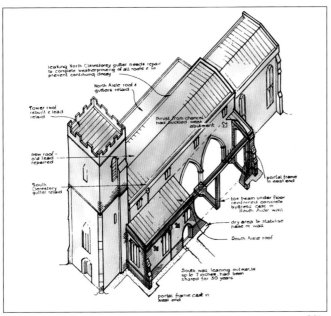

261a

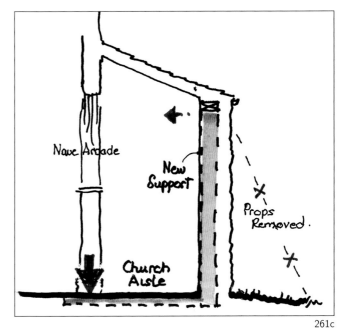

261c

Restraining and correcting movement

The leaning south aisle of a handsome country church at **Marston St Lawrence** in Nottinghamshire was for many decades propped and shored up. The remedy has been to install substantial L-shaped internal buttresses supporting the walls from under the floor, with their heels tucked under the pillars of the nave arcade and their upstands within the walls.

261d

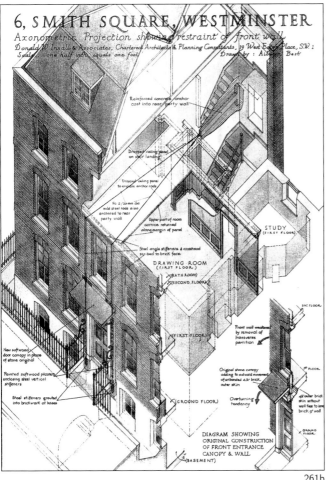

261b

Strengthening

This fine Queen Anne house at **Smith Square**, in London's 'Division bell' sector of **Westminster**, had long been weakened by the removal of internal cross-walls. It has been given fresh heart by introducing tie-rods to re-anchor the façade to solid brickwork at the rear.

261e

Eastgate, Chester.

D.W! Apl. 2000

Awards to Projects

International Awards

Association for Preservation Technology International: the Harley J McKee Award
Donald Insall CBE (1999)

Europa Nostra Awards, Medals and Commendations
Chester Conservation Project: Medals of Honour 1983 and 1989
Bowland Yard, Belgravia: 'Sensitive Residential Development in a Typical London Mews' (1989)
Trinity College, Cambridge: 'Major Restoration Project to the Highest Standards' (1991)
Speke Hall, Liverpool: Restoration of Hall and Recreation of Garden (1993)
The Bath Spas: Repair and reinstatement of missing original features (1993)
The Mansion House, London: Restoration, repair and alteration (1994)
Cockerell Building, Gonville & Caius College, Cambridge: Diploma (1997)
Windsor Castle: Medal for Post-fire Restoration Work (1999)
Donald Insall CBE: Medal of Honour (2000)
Somerset House, London, Phase II: Diploma (2001)
Royal Albert Hall: Diploma (2003)
Palace of Westminster Conservation Study: Medal (2007)

European Architectural Heritage Year Awards 1975
Chevening House, Kent: Restoration (Medal for Scheme of Exceptional Merit)
Gamul House, Chester: Restoration and Housing Rehabilitation
Blanchland, Northumberland: Village Conservation Programme
Wren Library, Trinity College, Cambridge: Restoration
Selbys Farm, Hildenborough, Kent: Historic Building Improvements
Stoke Park House, Buckinghamshire: Reconstruction of Cupola

European Prize (F.V.S. Foundation, Hamburg) for the Preservation of Historic Monuments
Chester Conservation Programme (1981)

Fondation Philippe Rotthier pour L'Architecture European Award
Windsor Castle Fire Restoration: Commendation (1998)

UK Awards

BURA Awards for Best Practice in Regeneration
Staircase House, Stockport (2006)

City Heritage Awards and Commendations
45 Cloth Fair, London: Conversion and refurbishment for Landmark Trust (1977)
St. Margaret's Church, Lothbury: Repair of Wren City Church (1978)
Clothworkers' Hall: Remodelling and Refurnishing Interiors for Livery Company (1987)
St. Bartholomew's Hospital: Restoration of Fountain in the Square (1990)
Mansion House, London: Refurbishment of the Residence of the Lord Mayor of London (1994)

Civic Trust Awards and Commendations
Shincliffe, Co. Durham: Residential Development for the Dean and Chapter of Durham (1962)
Lavenham, Suffolk: Town Enhancement Programme (1968)
St. Peter's Church, Thundersley, Essex: New Church, retaining medieval building (1968)
Blanchland, Northumberland: Village Conservation Scheme (1971)
Berrington Hall, Herefordshire: Restoration (1971)
Monmouth Market Hall: Reconstruction as Museum, Post Office, Restaurant and Shop (1973)
Asgill House, Richmond-upon-Thames: Restoration to Original Design (1973)
Thaxted Guildhall, Essex: Consultancy for Restoration (1978)
Victorian Society Headquarters, London: Environmental Improvements (1979)
Leeds Castle, Kent: New Kitchen, Fairfax Hall (1980)
Alton Towers Conservatory and Banqueting Hall (1982)
Hyde House and Barn: Archaeological Resources Centre for the City of Winchester (1982)
Grovelands, Enfield, London: Repair and extension of house by John Nash (1987)
Hampton Court House, Surrey: Renovation of 18th-century Grotto (1987)
St. Bartholomew's Hospital: Restoration and conversion of Henry VIII Gatehouse (1989)
St Luke's Church, Chelsea: Exterior Cleaning and Repair (1992)
Windsor Castle: Post-fire Restoration (1999)
Garrick's Temple, Richmond-upon-Thames: Restoration of Temple and Riverside setting (2000)
Raoul Wallenberg Memorial, Westminster (2000)
City of Chester Rows Lighting (2001)
Somerset House, London, Phase II (2002)
Martyrs' Memorial, Oxford (Mention 2005)
Battle of Britain Monument, Thames Embankment, London (2006)
Staircase House, Stockport (Access Award) 2006

Good Design in Housing Awards and Commendations (DOE)
Shincliffe, Co. Durham: Two Village Development Schemes for Dean and Chapter of Durham (1962)
St. Mary's Hill and Castle Street, Chester: New Town Houses in Conservation Action Area (1980)

Royal Fine Art Commission Trust Building of the Year – Public Space
Somerset House Courtyard (2001)

RIBA Awards for Architecture

Palace of Westminster: Restoration of the Ceiling of the House of Lords Chamber (Special Mention 1987)

Windsor Castle Fire Restoration (Award 1998)

Chandos House, London W1 (Conservation Commendation 2005)

The Stephen Hawking Building, Cambridge (RIBA East Spirit of Ingenuity Home Award, 2007)

The Cross Bath Restoration, Bath (RIBA South West Region Town and Country Conservation Award, 2007)

Royal Institution of Chartered Surveyors Conservation Awards and Commendations

Blanchland, Northumberland: Village Conservation (1972)

Berrington Hall, Herefordshire: Restoration (1972)

Knebworth House Estate, Hertfordshire: Conservation of Historic Barns (1972)

St. Lawrence Church, Blackmore, Essex: Conservation of Timber Framed Tower (1972)

Woburn Abbey, Bedfordshire: New Pavilion in Abbey Grounds (1972)

Gamul House, Chester: Restoration and Housing Rehabilitation (1976)

Woodbridge Tide Mill, Essex: Restoration (1978)

29 to 31 Farm Street, London: Reconstruction to create prestige offices (1982)

Trinity College, Cambridge: Library Extension (RICS Efficient Building Award, 1993)

Windsor Castle Fire Restoration: Conservation Award (1998)

Donald Insall CBE: People in Conservation Award (1999)

Staircase House, Stockport: North West Region Conservation Award (2006); and North West Region Building of the Year (2006)

Devonshire Royal Hospital, Buxton: Alteration & Refurbishment: East Midlands Region Conservation Award (2006); and East Midlands Region Building of the Year Award (2006)

Cardiff Castle: House and Clock Tower Exterior Conservation (Regional Conservation Award, Wales, 2007)

Nantclwyd House, Ruthin: Wales Regional Building Conservation Award (2008)

Royal Town Planning Institute Awards

Royal Town Planning Institute Awards for Planning Achievement (Silver Jubilee Cup): Chester Conservation Programme Highly Commended (with Chester City Council) (1985)

Staircase House, Shawcross Fold, Stockport: North West Planning Achievement Award (2007); and North West Award for Heritage and Urban Regeneration (2007)

Royal Victorian Order

Alan J Frost LVO as Team Leader, Windsor Castle Restoration

Royal Warrant Holders Association Plowden Medal

Donald Insall CBE (2001)

Design and Craftsmanship Awards

Architectural Ironmongery Specification Award
The Mansion House, London (1994/5); Windsor Castle Fire Restoration (Special Heritage Award 1998/9)

Brick Development Association Awards and Certificate of Merit
22 Arlington Street, London SW1 – Restoration of William Kent façade (1981)

Building Construction Industry Awards 1998 Special Commendation
Windsor Castle Fire Restoration

Chester Civic Architectural Design Awards
Grosvenor Estate Office (2005) and Eccleston Primary School, Chester (Commended 2005)

City of Westminster Design for Excellence Award
St Mary-le-Strand Church (1993)

Consortium of Local Authorities in Wales: Building of the Year Competition
Ty Coch Barns, Ruthin (Commended 2007)

Consultative Committee Award for Outstanding Craftsmanship (E. Midlands)
St. James' Church, Louth (1988)

Contract Flooring Installation of the Year
Royal Albert Hall, London (2003)

Cookson Award for Craftsmanship in Conservation and Restoration
St Mary-le-Strand, London (1993)

Copper Development Association John Smith Award for Craftsmanship
The Nicholson Institute, Leek (2001)

County Design Award for Conservation
Wren House, Chichester, West Sussex (1992/3)

Craftsmanship Awards of Cambridge Association of Architects
Trinity College, Cambridge – Leadwork on Whewell's Court (1984)
Trinity College, Cambridge – Restoration of Great Gate (1985)
Trinity College, Cambridge – Great Court South Range and Essex Building (1988)

David Urwin City Heritage Award
Repair and Conservation of Listed Garden Walls, Jesus College, Cambridge (1991); Bateman Auditorium, Gonville and Caius College, Cambridge (1997)

The Georgian Group
Architectural Award for Best Restoration of a Georgian Country House
  Eardisley Park, Herefordshire (2003)
  Restoration of a Georgian Building in an Urban Setting: Exchange House, Holywell (Commended 2005); The Cross Bath, Bath (2006); Benjamin Franklin House, London (Commended 2007)

Green Apple Award for Environmental Best Practice
  Molineux Hotel, Wolverhampton (2006) and Ty Coch Barns, Ruthin (2007) and Nantclwyd House, Ruthin (2008)

Hammersmith Society Award for Conservation
  St Andrew Bobola Polish Church (2008)

LABC Built in Quality Awards, East Anglia Region
  Best Housing/Residential Projects Award: The Stephen Hawking Building, Gonville & Caius College, Cambridge (2007)
  Best one-off House, Conservation or Extension Award: 12 Lansdowne Road Cambridge (2007)

Lighting Design Award
  Highly Commended in Community Lighting Category: Somerset House, London, Phase II (2002)
  Highly Commended in Special Projects Category: Battle of Britain Monument, London (2006)

Masons' Company Award for Excellence in Restoration and Repair
  Public Record Office, London (1986); and The Bank of England (1990)

NFPDC Painting and Decorating Trophy Awards Highly Commended Certificate
  The Mansion House, London (1994)

Natural Stone Awards Commendation
  The Gate of Honour, Gonville & Caius College, Cambridge (1993)

Natural Stone Awards (Slate Category)
  Stair at Windsor Castle (2000)

Oxford Preservation Trust Award
  The Martyrs' Memorial, Oxford (2003)
  Repair and Restoration of Nos 16–21 Pembroke Street, Oxford (2007)

Painting and Decorating Association Premier Trophy Award
  Kensington Palace Chapel (2003)

The Plaisterers' Trophy
  Windsor Castle Fire Restoration and Knebworth House, Herts (1988); Windsor Castle Fire Restoration (Special Regional Award, 1998)

Richmond-upon-Thames Conservation & Design Award (Highly Commended)
  6 Ormond Road, Richmond (1992)

Richmond-upon-Thames Sustainable Design Award
  73 Kew Green, Kew (2000)

The Richmond Society Awards
  Kew Palace external refurbishment (1998); Cropley Monument, St Mary Magdalene (Commendation 2005)

Royal Academy: AJ/Bovis Award for Best Architectural Drawing in Summer Exhibition
  Plumpton Place, Sussex (1989)

Royal Borough of Kensington & Chelsea's Environment Award
  St Luke's Church, Chelsea (1992)
  In-Pensioner Statue, The Royal Hospital Chelsea, SW3 (2001)

Shrewsbury Civic Society Award of Merit
  The Nag's Head, Wyle Cop (1996)

Shrewsbury & Atcham Borough Council Design Award
  The Nag's Head (1996)

Stone Federation Design Commendations for Natural Stone
  Magdalene College, Cambridge: Restoration of the Pepysian Library (1987)
  Trinity College, Cambridge: Great Court, South Range and Essex Building (1989)
  The Cross Bath and Old Royal Bath, Bath (1989)

Sussex Heritage Award
  Saltdean Barn, Saltdean (2005)

Wolverhampton Environmental Awards Commendation
  Wightwick Old Manor House Repair and Conversion (1996)

The Wood Awards
  Staircase House, Stockport (Highly Commended 2005)

The Worshipful Company of Carpenters
  Windsor Castle (Special Award 1999)

Living buildings: stone vaulting at the Henry VII Chapel, Westminster Abbey.

Illustration credits and copyrights

Except for the following list, and dependent upon date, illustrations and material are copyright Donald Insall or Donald W Insall & Associates, or Donald Insall Associates Ltd.

Any enquiries should be addressed to Donald Insall Associates Ltd, Architects & Historic Building Consultants, 19 West Eaton Place, London SW1X 8LT.

Every effort has been made to contact copyright holders of all material reproduced in this publication. Any omissions are inadvertent, and will gladly be corrected in future editions if notification of an amended credit is sent to the publisher in writing.

Copyrights and credits:

18a Chester Chronicle
21a, 21b NTPL/David Watson
23c Department of Culture, Media and Sport
50a, 191a, 231a Timothy Soar
54, 55c The Goldsmiths' Company, Photographer Crispin Boyle
72c AF Kersting
87a Wallwalkers Ltd
111a Parrish
128b Lynn News
133a Eastern Daily Press
151c, 151b, 169, 168b, 168c, 172, 179 ColinWestwood/RIBA Library Photographs Collection
153a, 153b Jonathan Law
154a, 154b,155b Nicholas Keeble
159a, 159b, 160, 161b Padraig Boyle Photography

182b, 182c Ward Philipson
186 Turners
187, 195 Blom Aerofilms
189 Martin Charles
192 Dan White
210 Rex Features
211a,b; 212a,b,c,d; 213a,b,c; 214a,b,c; 215a,b,c; 216a,b,c; 217a,d; 218; 219a,b; 220 Crown Copyright
231b, 231d Roderick Coyne
235a Caulfield-Dollard
237a English Heritage NMR
243b Peter Durant
248c, 249d Martin Charles
249a, 249b John Laing Photographic Services
253a Woodhouse
255c, 255e Crispin Boyle/RIBA Library Photographs Collection
257e *Country Life*
259d Matthew Antrobus

We are grateful to the many clients and friends who have so readily agreed to the use of illustrations and descriptions of work undertaken with them or on their behalf, and which it has been such a pleasure to recall in detail here.

Leuven

Donald Insall

Acknowledgments

This book began its life in response to a proposal from the RIBA, and to meet continuing demand for an update or successor to our book, *The Care of Old Buildings Today* (1972). It owes its main structure to long-ago discussions with its initially intended editor, Prof. Derek Lindstrum of York.

For the main ideas and spirit of the book, I owe unfailing gratitude to the encouragement and inspiration of the Society for the Protection of Ancient Buildings – to the late Monica Dance, Secretary, together with its Committee and co-workers with whom I have long served, to co-founders and their successors and professional staffs of English Heritage, and to the annual task for three decades of speaking and teaching at the international courses of the Catholic University of Leuven, as well as discussions with many an audience and group in Europe and the wider world. The field of architectural conservation is an amazingly international brotherhood; and we all learn, every day.

Above all, it is to our growing team of colleagues here and at home, in whose lives and work we have all shared, that this book owes its message and its contents today. In the earliest years of our Practice, I owed much to the support and help of my dear and generous late father. To my wife Libby, his successor as administrator and then as a founding Director, as well as at home, and to all our family, my gratitude for their wholly unfailing patience and support. To Nicholas Thompson as our Chairman and leader since 1998, my immense appreciation and thanks. To co-Directors, Associates and colleagues of yesterday and today is due the great credit for the many projects named, and for very many more. We all owe special honour to the memory of Ailwyn Best, creator for us for so many of the beautiful axonometric drawings illustrated, and whose skills in architectural draughtsmanship so few today can match.

In compiling this book, my grateful thanks are due to individual helpers and Secretaries, to my PA Sue Machin, to our graphics specialist Ann Humphrey, to Idil Sukan for diagrams and layout advice, to Asif Ali, our ICT specialist, and to all who have contributed so much. We have also been extremely fortunate in the unstinting sharing of her wide experience by our Reader, Bridget Cherry, former editor of the unique Architectural Guides initiated by Nikolaus Pevsner, whose influence and friendship I so keenly recall.

Over the years, our team has become a wide extended family in whom I take the greatest pride, and whom I most warmly thank. Our individual names may pass; but I believe our message will not, and we are thankful to have this opportunity of sharing it with the many readers and enthusiasts who simply love old buildings and take responsibility for their lives and care.

Beyond our team, I am grateful to Prof. Dennis Sharp for introducing me to The Images Publishing Group. To Images Directors Paul Latham and Alessina Brooks, Senior Editor Robyn Beaver and to Rod Gilbert and the graphic design team, I give the warmest of thanks.

We owe our great gratitude beyond our team, to our clients and friends and to the contractors and craftsmen alongside whom we have been engaged, from all of whom I have learnt so much. In our challenges at Windsor for example, to those in charge of the project: to Sir Michael Peat, Sir Hugh Roberts, Sir John Tiltman, and to Chris Watson and his colleagues at GTMS. In Chester, to two decades of teamwork with the City and its officers, led by Cyril Morris as their able and devoted Director of Technical Services. Each project has brought its own group of special talents and skills; it is hard to stop naming names, as I now regrettably must.

All of us hope that you as our readers may enjoy as much as we have, taking part in this review of half a century's opportunities in helping what we may so truly together honour as our 'Living Buildings'.

Index